Birds of Northern India

Princeton Field Guides

Rooted in field experience and scientific study, Princeton's guides to animals and plants are the authority for professional scientists and amateur naturalists alike. **Princeton Field Guides** present this information in a compact format carefully designed for easy use in the field. The guides illustrate every species in color and provide detailed information on identification, distribution, and biology.

Birds of Kenya and Northern Tanzania: Field Guide Edition, by Dale A. Zimmerman, Donald A. Turner, and David J. Pearson

Birds of India, Pakistan, Nepal, Bangladesh, Bhutan, Sri Lanka, and the Maldives, by Richard Grimmett, Carol Inskipp, and Tim Inskipp

Birds of Australia, by Ken Simpson and Nicolas Day

Birds of Europe, by Killian Mullarney, Lars Svensson, Dan Zetterström, and Peter J. Grant

Birds of Nepal, by Richard Grimmett, Carol Inskipp, and Tim Inskipp

Birds of the Seychelles, by Adrian Skerrett and Ian Bullock

Stars and Planets, by Ian Ridpath and Wil Tirion

Butterflies of Europe, by Tom Tolman and Richard Lewington

Mammals of Europe, by David W. Macdonald and Priscilla Barrett

Minerals of the World, by Ole Johnsen

Birds of Southern Africa, by Ian Sinclair, Phil Hockey, and Warwick Tarboton

Birds of Thailand, by Craig Robson

Mammals of North America, by Roland Kays and Don E. Wilson

Marine Mammals of the North Atlantic, by Carl Christian Kinze

Reptiles and Amphibians of Europe, by E. Nicholas Arnold and Denys W. Ovenden

Birds of Chile, by Alvaro Jaramillo

Birds of the West Indies, by Herbert Raffaele, James Wiley, Orlando Garrido, Allan Keith, and Janis Raffaele

Birds of Northern India, by Richard Grimmett and Tim Inskipp

Birds of
Northern India

Richard Grimmett
Tim Inskipp

**Illustrated by Clive Byers, Daniel Cole, John Cox,
Gerald Driessens, Carl D'Silva, Martin Elliott, Kim Franklin,
Alan Harris, Peter Hayman, Craig Robson,
Jan Wilczur, and Tim Worfolk**

Princeton University Press
Princeton and Oxford

THE COLOR PLATES
Clive Byers 91–98, 104, 105, 108–119
Daniel Cole   1–5, 23–27, 32, 33
John Cox 28, 29, 34
Gerald Driessens 22, 88, 89
Carl D'Silva 11–21, 30, 31, 60–73, 90, 106, 107
Martin Elliott 43–45
Kim Franklin 48, 49
Alan Harris 46, 50 (part), 51, 52, 57, 58, 74–84
Peter Hayman 35–42
Craig Robson 85–87, 99–103
Jan Wilczur 6–10, 59
Tim Worfolk 47, 50 (part), 53–56

Published in the United States, Canada, and the Philippine Islands by
Princeton University Press, 41 William Street, Princeton, New Jersey 08540

In the United Kingdom and European Union, published by Christopher Helm, an imprint
of A & C Black Publishers Ltd., 37 Soho Square, London W1D 3QZ

Photographs by Tim Loseby

ISBN 0-691-11738-1

Library of Congress Control Number 2003105342

This book has been composed in Garamond (main text); Photina MT (headings).

www.nathist.princeton.edu

Printed in Hong Kong

10 9 8 7 6 5 4 3 2 1

CONTENTS

FOREWORD

M. ZAFAR-UL ISLAM AND ASAD R. RAHMANI
BOMBAY NATURAL HISTORY SOCIETY, MUMBAI, INDIA

India comes in the top ten of the world's biodiversity-rich nations. Its immense biological diversity represents about 7 per cent of the world's flora and 6.5 per cent of the world's fauna. It embraces ten biogeographic zones and 26 biotic provinces (Rodgers and Panwar, 1988). There are more than 600 species of amphibians and reptiles, nearly 1300 species of birds and 350 species of mammals in India. Among the larger animals, 173 species of mammals and 78 species of birds (Islam and Rahmani, 2002) are considered
threatened with extinction.

Among all the groups of animals in the world, birds are most liked owing to their rich coloration, song, easy recognition and liveliness. Moreover, birds are present everywhere – from forests, grasslands and wetlands to crop fields and city gardens. With proper care, we can even attract birds to our balcony or veranda. Fortunately, our country is very rich in bird life. Of nearly 10,000 different kinds of birds in the world, 1300 species, or about 13 per cent of the world's birds, are found in the Indian subcontinent. They range from the majestic 2 m-tall Sarus Crane to the 8 cm Pale-billed Flowerpecker weighing just 8g. The Pale-billed Flowerpecker is only slightly bigger than the smallest bird in the world, the Bee Hummingbird *Mellisuga helenae*, weight 5–6g, of Cuba, whereas the Sarus Crane is the tallest flying bird in the world. The main reason for the very rich bird life in India is the presence of varied habitats, from the hot arid deserts of Rajasthan to the thick tropical rain forests of the Western Ghats and northeast India. We also have many types of grasslands, wetlands, mangrove forests and islands that support various species of birds and other animals.

Stories about birds are a part of our culture. *Ramayana*, *Mahabharata* and *Rigveda* are full of interesting tales about birds. In most parts of India, birds are given local names. The great naturalist, Mr Dharmakumarsinhji of Bhavnagar, documented Gujarati names for all of the 435 species that he found in Saurashtra. In Hindi, 503 different birds are identified, which again proves that Indians from ancient times had some knowledge of local birds and specifically identified many species. In Sanskrit, mother of all Indian languages, very good descriptions of bird behaviour and habits are given; some may not be scientifically correct, but they are still interesting to read.

The Mughal emperors, especially Babur and Jahangir, were greatly interested in flora and fauna. Babur, the founder of Moghul rule in India, was a keen observer of nature and he used to describe it in detail and wanted to know more about it. Babur, who came from Central Asia, recognised that four or five species of quail were new to him. Jahangir, who ruled from 1605 to 1627, had a special team of wildlife painters headed by Mansur. Jahangir's description of the mating behaviour of Sarus Crane and Rose-ringed Parakeet are remarkable for their accuracy. In addition, he knew that birds migrate over long distances.

Yet this remarkable bird life, which features so prominently in our history and culture, is under unprecedented pressure. The main environmental problems can be classified into two broad categories: (a) those arising as negative effects of the very process of development; and (b) those arising from conditions of poverty and underdevelopment. The first category relates to the impact of efforts to achieve rapid economic growth and development – poorly planned development projects are frequently environmentally destructive. The second category relates to the impact on the health and integrity of our natural resources – such as land, soil, water, forests and wildlife – as a result of widespread poverty.

India's population has risen from 370 million in 1947 to 1 billion in 2000, or 18 per cent of the world's population. India also has 15 per cent of the world's livestock. Increasing population, along with widespread poverty, has generated pressure on our natural resources and led to degradation of the environment. Of the 329 million ha of total land area in the country, it is estimated that about 174 million ha are degraded, comprising agricultural as well as non-agricultural lands and forests.

The forest resources are threatened owing to overgrazing and other forms of over-exploitation, both for commercial and household needs, and the expansion of agriculture and development activities. It is estimated that fuel-wood removal from the forests exceeds 235 million cubic metres per year, as against a sustainable level of production of only 48 million cubic metres. Over much of our forests, natural regeneration is inadequate owing to the grazing of livestock, the population of which is estimated to be 450 million. The over-exploitation and loss of habitat constitute a serious threat to the rich biological diversity in the country.

Increasing destruction and degradation of forests and woodlands, especially in the Himalayas and other hilly areas, contribute to the heavy erosion of top soil, erratic rainfall and recurring floods. It is causing an acute shortage of firewood and loss of productivity as the lands are eroded and degraded.

It is indeed very sad to know that habitat destruction, illegal shooting and trapping are putting many of our birds at risk of extinction. Pink-headed Duck and Himalayan Quail are probably already extinct, and some extremely beautiful birds – such as Indian Bustard, White-bellied Heron, White-winged Duck, Siberian Crane, Bengal Florican and Lesser Florican – are heading that way.

Northern India has a long history and tradition of bird keeping. Partridges, quails, pheasants and ducks are caught mainly for eating. During festivals, especially *Makar Shankaranti*, captive birds are released, particularly in Uttar Pradesh and Gujarat. It is not uncommon for religious-minded businessmen to release some birds before starting a business, or before opening their shop in the morning. Another reason that birds are caught, and one that is perhaps confined to the Indian subcontinent, is fortune telling. It is a common sight in every town to see a roadside fortune-teller with his pet Rose-ringed Parakeet and a bundle of horoscope cards. In addition, owls are caught for black magic and sorcery.

For many years, India was the major world exporter of birds and bird products (e.g. peafowl feathers and the neck feathers of male Grey Junglefowl), but since 1991 the trade in birds has been totally prohibited in India. However, thousands of birds are still available in domestic markets. You can help to stop this illegal business by not buying these birds and reporting to the nearest forest officer and police if you see someone selling birds. Birds are more happy free and wild. Our government has taken some measures to halt this trade, but it cannot be stopped unless we cease buying wild birds.

In order to protect wildlife, including birds, in 1972 a strong Wildlife (Protection) Act was enacted by the parliament. This was mainly at the initiative of the late Mrs Indira Gandhi, who was very interested in wildlife and forest protection. Despite her busy schedule, she was a keen birdwatcher and frequently carried Dr Salím Ali's books during her tours. Under the Wildlife (Protection) Act most bird species are totally or partially protected, and penalties are prescribed if these rules are broken. This act has four schedules, or lists, under which various species are protected. The 18 most endangered species and some other important species are listed in Schedule I, e.g. Black-necked Crane, Indian Bustard, Siberian Crane and Indian Peafowl (our national bird). Presently, almost all species of birds are protected under the Wildlife (Protection) Act and their hunting and trapping is not allowed, except under licence. Only the House (Common) Crow is listed under vermin (Schedule IV) and can be destroyed.

The main strategy for conservation of biodiversity is protection of habitats in representative ecosystems. In this region, we have nearly 186 sanctuaries and national parks where habitat destruction and hunting are not allowed. Most of these sanctuaries and national parks were established to protect large mammals, but 35 sanctuaries were established specifically for bird protection. The most famous is Keoladeo National Park in Rajasthan, world renowned for its large numbers of waterbirds, nesting colonies of storks, egrets, ibises, herons, darter and cormorants, and the only remaining site in India for the migratory Siberian Crane. Throughout the Gangetic plains there are many bird sanctuaries, not as famous as Keoladeo but unique in their own ways, which play an important role in protecting our birds. Saman, Lakh-Bahosi, Nawabganj, Patna, Sursagar and Sitadwar in Uttar Pradesh, and Sultanpur and Bhindawas in Haryana are some important waterbird habitats. The Bombay Natural History Society has identified 116 Important Bird Areas (IBAs) in North India, as part of BirdLife International's global IBA programme.

India therefore faces some massive challenges over the next century. Much greater progress is needed in the move towards sustainability in the use of our forests, especially the extraction of timber and firewood, and in our agricultural practices. Our protected areas need larger budget allocations and greater staffing, and ways need to be found to integrate park management with the needs of local communities. New conservation measures are needed for IBAs that are unprotected, and concerted effort is required to prevent the extinction of our threatened wildlife.

INTRODUCTION

Northern India is defined for the purposes of this book as comprising the states of Jammu & Kashmir, Himachal Pradesh, Uttaranchal, Uttar Pradesh, Madhya Pradesh, Haryana, Punjab, Rajasthan and Gujarat, and the Union Territory of Delhi, which is arguably the area best known in Indian ornithological terms. The avifaunas of the Union Territories of Chandigarh and Diu are poorly known and they are here treated with Punjab and Gujarat, respectively. The book does not cover the states of Bihar, Jharkhand, West Bengal and northeast India because their inclusion would substantially increase its size. The region is bounded by Pakistan and the Arabian Sea to the west, Tibet to the north, northeast India to the east and southern India to the south. There are 812 species that regularly occur in the area and a further 94 species have been recorded as vagrants.

HOW TO USE THIS BOOK

Taxonomy and Nomenclature

Taxonomy and nomenclature largely follow *An Annotated Checklist of the Birds of the Oriental Region* by Tim Inskipp, Nigel Lindsey and William Duckworth (1996). The sequence generally follows the same reference, although some species have been grouped out of this systematic order to enable useful comparisons to be made. In cases where differences in taxonomic opinion exist in the literature, the species' limits are fully discussed in that work, to which readers requiring further information should initially refer. The taxonomy differs in several respects based on recent published works that are considered to provide justification for the new treatments. Long-billed Vulture *Gyps indicus* has been split into two species: Indian Vulture *G. indicus* and Slender-billed Vulture *G. tenuirostris* (Rasmussen and Parry, 2001). The Indian Spotted Eagle *Aquila hastata* has been split from the Lesser Spotted Eagle *A. pomarina*, with the latter being extralimital (Parry *et al.*, 2002). The Large-billed Reed Warbler *Acrocephalus orinus*, which was considered to be referrable to Blyth's Reed Warbler *A. dumetorum*, is now considered to be a valid species, albeit known from only one specimen (Bensch and Pearson, 2002). Golden-spectacled Warbler *Seicercus burkii* is split into several species, two of which occur in the region: Golden-spectacled Warbler and Whistler's Warbler *S. whistleri* (Alström and Olsson, 1999). The Rufous-winged Bushlark *Mirafra assamica* is split into two species in the subcontinent, but only one of these, the Bengal Bushlark *M. assamica*, occurs in the region (Alström, 1998). The Yellow-legged Gull *Larus cachinnans* has been split into two species: the Yellow-legged Gull *L. michahellis* in Europe and the Caspian Gull *L. cachinnans* further east (Klein and Buchheim, 1997; Liebers *et al.*, 2001).

Colour Plates and Plate Captions

Species that occur regularly in northern India are illustrated in colour and described in the plate captions. Vagrants and very rare species are described in the Appendix, with reference to distinguishing features from other more regularly recorded species where appropriate. The illustrations show distinctive sexual and racial variation whenever possible, as well as immature plumages. Some distinctive races as well as immature plumages are also depicted. Where possible, species depicted on any one plate have been shown to approximately the same scale.

The captions identify the figures illustrated, very briefly summarise the species' distribution, status, altitudinal range and habitats, and provide information on the most important identification characters. Such characters include voice where this is an important

DESCRIPTIVE PARTS OF A BIRD

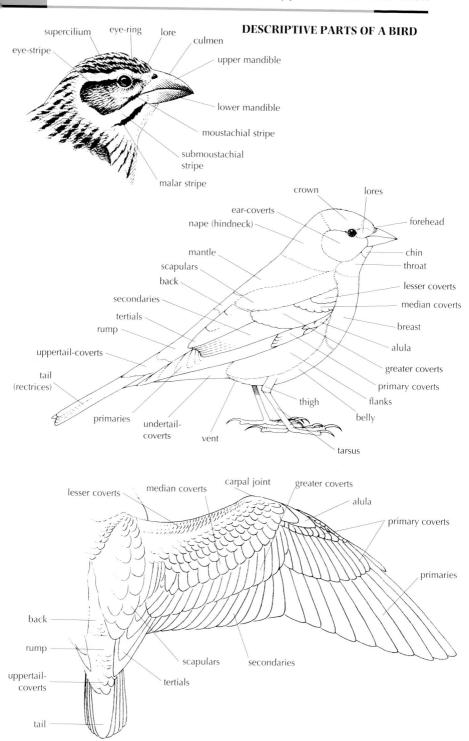

supercilium
eye-ring
lore
culmen
eye-stripe
upper mandible
lower mandible
moustachial stripe
submoustachial stripe
malar stripe

crown
lores
ear-coverts
forehead
nape (hindneck)
mantle
chin
scapulars
throat
back
lesser coverts
secondaries
median coverts
tertials
breast
rump
alula
uppertail-coverts
greater coverts
tail (rectrices)
primary coverts
thigh
flanks
belly
primaries
undertail-coverts
vent
tarsus

lesser coverts
median coverts
carpal joint
greater coverts
alula
primary coverts
primaries
back
rump
uppertail-coverts
scapulars
secondaries
tertials
tail

feature, and approximate body length of the species, including bill and tail, in centimetres. Length is expressed as a range when there is marked variation within the species (e.g. as a result of sexual dimorphism or racial differences).

The identification texts are based on R. Grimmett, C. Inskipp and T. Inskipp *Birds of the Indian Subcontinent* (1998). The vast majority of the illustrations have been taken from the same work and wherever possible the correct races for northern India have been depicted. A small number of additional illustrations of races occurring in northern India were executed for this book. The text and plates are based on extensive reference to museum specimens combined with considerable work in the field.

The status of each species is defined as one of the following: a resident, winter visitor, summer visitor, passage migrant or altitudinal migrant. Data on actual breeding records and non-breeding ranges are very few, so it has not been possible to give comprehensive details. In addition, space limitations have meant that the simple terms 'summers' and 'winters' are used to describe altitudinal ranges and habitats for many species. Note that many Himalayan species are recorded in summer over a wider altitudinal range than that in which they actually breed. Globally threatened species (species at risk of global extinction) are indicated as such, following the BirdLife International Red Data Book (BirdLife International, 2001), with the IUCN threat category given in parenthesis.

Key to Distribution and Status Information

DE = Delhi
GU = Gujarat
HA = Haryana
HP = Himachal Pradesh
JK = Jammu & Kashmir
MP = Madhya Pradesh
PU = Punjab
RA = Rajasthan
UP = Uttar Pradesh
UR = Uttaranchal

cp = common passage migrant
cr = common resident
cs = common summer visitor
cw = common winter visitor
cwp = common winter visitor and passage migrant
lcp = locally common passage migrant
lcr = locally common resident
lcs = locally common summer visitor
lcw = locally common winter visitor
np = not common passage migrant
nr = not common resident
ns = not common summer visitor
nw = not common winter visitor
nwp = not common winter visitor and passage migrant
v = vagrant
xr = extirpated resident
xp = extirpated passage migrant

Plumage Terminology

The figures on page 10 illustrate the main plumage tracts and bare-part features, and are based on Grant and Mullarney (1988–89). This terminology for bird topography has been used in the captions. Other terms have been used and are defined in the glossary. Juvenile plumage is the first plumage on fledging, and in many species it is looser, more fluffy, than subsequent plumages. In some families, juvenile plumage is retained only briefly after leaving the nest (e.g. pigeons), or hardly differs from adult plumage (e.g. many babblers), while in other groups it may be retained for the duration of long migrations or for many months (e.g. many waders). In some species (e.g. *Aquila* eagles), it may be several years before all juvenile feathers are finally moulted. The relevance of the juvenile plumage to field identification therefore varies considerably. Some species reach adult plumage after their first post-juvenile moult (e.g. larks), whereas others go though a series of immature plumages. The term 'immature' has been employed more generally to denote plumages other than adult, and is used either where a more exact terminology has not been possible or where more precision would give rise to unnecessary complexity. Terms such as 'first-winter' (resulting from a partial moult from juvenile plumage) or 'first-summer' (plumage acquired prior to the breeding season of the year after hatching) have, however, been used where it was felt that this would be useful.

Many species assume a more colourful breeding plumage, which is often more striking in the male compared with the female. This can be realised either through a partial (or in some species complete) body moult (e.g. waders), or results from the wearing-off of pale or dark feather fringes (e.g. redstarts and buntings).

GEOGRAPHICAL SETTING

Climate

There are great contrasts in climate within the region. The extremes range from the almost rainless Great Indian, or Thar, Desert to the wet evergreen forests of the Himalayan foothills, and the Arctic conditions of the Himalayan peaks where only alpine flowers and cushion plants flourish at over 4900 m. There are similar contrasts in temperature ranges. In the Thar Desert summer temperatures soar as high as 50°C while winter temperatures drop to 0°C. On the coast the annual and daily range of temperatures are small, the temperature remaining at about 29°C to 32°C.

ACACIA SCRUBLAND, BHARATPUR.

Despite these variations, one feature dominates climate in the region and that is the monsoons. Most of the rain in the region falls between June and September during the southwest monsoon season. During this time, cool, moisture-laden winds from the Indian Ocean bring heavy, intermittent rains. Typically, the monsoon begins in Kerala and the far northeast in late May or early June and moves north and west to extend over northern India by the end of June. On reaching the great barrier of the Himalayas, the air rises, cools and the moisture condenses, providing abundant rainfall along this range. The air that has crossed the Himalayas is dry, causing a rain shadow on the northern side of the mountains in regions such as Ladakh. The monsoon begins to retreat from the northwest at the beginning of September and usually withdraws completely by mid-October. In much of the northern part of the subcontinent there is generally clear, dry weather in October, November and early December. Low-pressure systems from the west during this season do, however, bring some light to moderate precipitation to northern India. This falls as rain in the plains and as snow on the mountains.

The amount of rain varies from year to year, especially over areas of poor rainfall, such as Rajasthan, where it may be as little as 30 to 40 per cent of a normal year. Even when the total monsoon rain in an area is about average, it may fall over a very short period, bringing floods and drought in the same year.

MAIN HABITATS

The bird habitats of northern India can be roughly divided into forests, scrub, wetlands (inland and littoral), marine, grasslands, desert and agricultural land. There is overlap of some habitats – for example, mangrove forests can also be considered as wetlands, as can seasonally flooded grasslands. Many bird species require mixed habitat types.

Forests

There is a great variety of forest types in the region. Tropical forests range from coastal mangroves to wet, dense evergreen, dry deciduous and open desert thorn forests. In the Himalayas, temperate forests include those of mixed broadleaves, moist oak and rhododendron, and dry coniferous forests of pines and firs. Higher up are subalpine forests of birch, rhododendron and juniper.

CONIFEROUS FOREST.

The forests of the region are vitally important for many of its birds, including both globally threatened and restricted-range species.

Tropical deciduous forests once covered much of the plains and lower hills of the subcontinent, including moist and dry sal and teak forests, and riverine and dry thorn forests. Several widespread species endemic to the subcontinent are chiefly confined to these forests, including the Plum-headed Parakeet, which has a preference for moist deciduous forests, and the White-bellied Drongo, which favours open dry deciduous forests.

Scrub

Scrub has developed where trees are unable to grow in the region, either because soils are poor and thin, or because they are too wet, such as at the edges of wetlands or in seasonally inundated floodplains. Scrub also grows naturally in extreme climatic conditions, such as in semi-desert or at high altitudes in the Himalayas. In addition, there are now large areas of scrubland in the region where forests have been over-exploited for fodder and fuel collection or grazing.

Wetlands

Wetlands in the region are abundant and support a rich array of waterfowl. As well as providing habitats for breeding resident species, the subcontinent's wetlands include major staging and wintering grounds for waterfowl breeding in central and northern Asia. The region possesses a wide range of wetland types distributed almost throughout, including mountain glacial lakes, freshwater and brackish marshes, large water-storage reservoirs, village tanks, saline flats and coastal mangroves and mudflats. The results of the 1987–91 Asian Waterfowl Census (Perennou et al, 1994), published in 1994 by the Asian Wetland Bureau and the International Waterfowl and Wetlands Research Bureau (now Wetlands International), include detailed distribution maps for 200 Asian wetland species most commonly recorded during the period.

WETLANDS, BHARATPUR.

A detailed directory of Indian wetlands compiled by WWF India and the Asian Wetland Bureau describing the values, threats and conservation measures was published in 1993. Although no data are available, the coastal mudflats and estuaries are thought to be of great importance as staging and wintering areas. The extensive seasonally flooded manmade lagoons of Keoladeo Ghana National Park in Rajasthan are particularly diverse – over 400 species were recorded there. The vast saline flats of the Ranns of Kutch in northwest India are important for migratory waterfowl and support breeding colonies of the Lesser Flamingo, herons and egrets. Other wetlands in the region valuable for birds include the marshes, jheels and terai swamps of the Gangetic plain. Small water-storage reservoirs or tanks are a distinctive feature in India. Aggregations of these tanks provide important feeding and nesting areas for a wide range of waterbirds in some places.

Grasslands

The most important grasslands for birds in the subcontinent are the seasonally flooded grasslands occurring across the Himalayan foothills and in the floodplains of the Ganges river, the arid grasslands of the Thar Desert, and grasslands managed for animal fodder in Gujarat and Rajasthan. These lowland grasslands support distinctive bird communities, with a number of specialist endemic species.

Deserts

The Thar Desert is the largest desert in South Asia, covering an area of 200,000 km^2 in northwest India and Pakistan. Nearly 80 per cent of the Thar lies in Rajasthan and it also extends into parts of Punjab, Haryana and Gujarat. The far northern mountain regions, which the monsoon winds do not penetrate, experience a cold desert climate. Hot deserts in the region are extensions of the Saharan and Arabian deserts and are also connected with semi-arid parts of peninsular India.

Seas

Seabirds in the region comprise mainly gulls and terns. Surprisingly, few truly pelagic species have been recorded in the region (e.g. no petrels or shearwaters).

FLORICAN GRASSLAND, VELADAVAR, GUJARAT.

Agricultural Habitats

The region is remarkable for the abundance of birds in agricultural habitats in many areas, as a result of non-intensive agricultural systems and low levels of hunting and persecution. Shrikes, Indian Roller, Common Hoopoe, parakeets and birds of prey, for example, can appear abundant on road and rail journeys. This is changing though, as farming becomes more intensive and higher levels of pesticides are applied.

IMPORTANT BIRD SPECIES

Restricted-range Species

There is one Endemic Bird Area (EBA) in the region, the Western Himalayas Endemic Bird Area (which extends from western Nepal through the entire western Himalayas to the border between Afghanistan and Pakistan) (Stattersfield *et al.*, 1998). This EBA has 11 restricted-range species, as defined by BirdLife International. Six of these species are resident in temperate forests in the EBA (Western Tragopan, White-cheeked Tit, White-throated Tit, Kashmir Nuthatch, Spectacled Finch and Orange Bullfinch). Three other restricted-range forest birds are summer migrants to the EBA; Brooks's Leaf Warbler winters in the Himalayan foothills and plains of northern India, and Tytler's Leaf Warbler and Kashmir Flycatcher winter outside the region in the Western Ghats of the peninsula and, in the case of Kashmir Flycatcher, also in Sri Lanka. The remaining two restricted-range species (Cheer Pheasant and Himalayan Quail) are birds of steep grassy slopes, between 1400 and 3500 m.

Globally Threatened Species

Thirty-five species of northern Indian birds are classified by BirdLife International as globally threatened with extinction (BirdLife International, 2001). They include seven species that are categorised as Critical, and therefore at extremely high risk of extinction in the immediate future (White-rumped Vulture, Indian Vulture, Slender-billed Vulture, Siberian Crane and Forest Owlet, plus Pink-headed Duck and Himalayan Quail, which may already have met such a fate). A further five species are categorised as Endangered.

The plight of the three Critical vultures is a very recent phenomenon, with all three species suffering an extremely rapid population decline, probably as a result of disease, but perhaps compounded by the impact of poisons, pesticides, felling of trees, and changes in the processing of livestock carcasses. This decline is causing major problems in rural and urban areas because of the role vultures play in disposing of animal carcasses.

Remaining grasslands of the Gangetic plain, in Uttar Pradesh, are important for six threatened species (the Endangered Bengal Florican, plus Swamp Francolin, Hodgson's Bushchat – a rare winter visitor – Grey-crowned Prinia, Bristled Grassbird and Finn's Weaver). Grassland habitat once covered much of the floodplain of the Ganges, but almost all of this habitat has been cleared for agriculture and settlements, leaving only small fragments (such as Dudwa National Park, which is a particularly important site for Swamp Francolin and Bengal Florican), which are under considerable pressure from agriculture (especially conversion to sugarcane), livestock grazing, cutting and burning.

Elsewhere, dry grasslands, and the more arid regions of northern India, support ten threatened species, including the three vultures mentioned above, and the Endangered Indian Bustard and Lesser Florican. The range of the Indian Bustard is now highly fragmented, and remaining populations continue to be under pressure from agricultural intensification (often facilitated by the extension of irrigation) and overstocking of livestock. This species in particular requires a major national commitment, perhaps entitled

SALT PLAINS, RANN OF KUTCH.

'Project Bustard' (after the successful 'Project Tiger'), if it is to survive the current century. The vulnerable Stoliczka's Bushchat is now confined to northern India (and now feared extinct in Pakistan).

Two species, Forest Owlet and White-naped Tit, are birds of dry forest. In Gujarat, wood is collected for charcoal-making and bakeries. This process removes old trees and thereby many suitable nest-sites for the White-naped Tit.

Wetlands in the region support 13 threatened species. Important wetland habitats range from the high-altitude marshes of Ladakh, with a small population of Black-necked Cranes, to the seasonal wetlands of the Rann of Kutch at sea-level, with non-breeding populations of Dalmatian Pelican. The northern Indian region is the global stronghold for the Sarus Crane (on shallow wetlands) and Indian Skimmer (on the vast system of rivers). Sarus Crane, once almost ubiquitous, appears to be in steep decline owing to wetland drainage and agricultural intensification, whilst Indian Skimmer appears to be in serious trouble owing to the impact of dams, and the heavy human use of the riverine environment. Two *Aquila* eagles, Imperial and Greater Spotted, frequently inhabit wetlands in this region during winter. Keoladeo is internationally renowned, especially for its wintering flock of the Endangered Siberian Crane, the only known site for this species in the region but now sadly depleted.

Two of the restricted-range species of the Western Himalayan EBA, Western Tragopan and Kashmir Flycatcher, are threatened. The temperate forests in this region continue to be degraded by commercial forestry and livestock grazing.

The cage-bird trade is arguably the main threat to the Green Avadavat, which is sold in large numbers in domestic and even international markets. The bird trade is also having an impact on Finn's Weaver.

MIGRATION

Many Himalayan residents are altitudinal migrants, the level to which they descend in winter frequently depending on weather conditions. Pheasants, such as Western Tragopan and Himalayan Monal, and tits and nuthatches, for example, will descend to lower altitudes or seek south-facing slopes when conditions become harsh. Other 'resident' species regularly drop down to the foothills or plains (e.g. Wallcreeper and Black Redstart).

Many species are summer visitors to the western Himalayas. These includes species such as Ashy Drongo, Hume's Warbler and Olive-backed Pipit, which winter in the plains, as well as species such as Blue-capped Rock Thrush and Large-billed Leaf Warbler, which winter further south in the Indian peninsula. The Indian plains are also host to numerous winter visitors, originating from northern and central Asia, some of which are also passage migrants. These include vast numbers of ducks, waders, thrushes, *Acrocephalus* and *Phylloscopus* warblers, pipits and wagtails. A number of species breeding in the western Himalayas winter in Africa (e.g. European Roller and Pied Cuckoo). The winter quarters of some Himalayan breeders are very poorly known and it is possible that a few may largely winter in Southeast Asia (e.g. Large Hawk Cuckoo and Lesser Cuckoo).

BIRDWATCHING AREAS

There are numerous areas in Northern India that are excellent for birdwatching. For more details, refer to the highly recommended *A Birdwatcher's Guide to India* by Krys Kazmierczak and Raj Singh (1998). In addition to these sites, even a stop by the road, or a wander through agricultural land, can be very rewarding.

Yamuna River, Delhi

Location: On the eastern edge of Delhi, especially good around Okhla (including Okhla Island).
Habitat: Riverine habitats, including marshes, pools, sandbanks and seasonal agricultural land, with an abundance of waterbirds.
Best time to visit: November–March, although worth a visit at any time in the year.
Birds: White-tailed Lapwing, Small Pratincole, numerous ducks and waders including rarer species, Pallas's and Brown-headed gulls, Black-bellied and River terns, raptors including Imperial Eagle and Greater Spotted Eagle – although vultures (White-rumped and Indian) are now rare – Darter, Indian Cormorant, Painted Stork, Asian Openbill, White-tailed Stonechat, Bristled Grassbird, Striated Babbler, Streak-throated and Wire-tailed swallows.

Tughlaqabad, Delhi

Location: About 15 km south of Delhi.
Habitat: Ruined fort, with scrub, acacia woodland and seasonal agricultural land.
Best time to visit: November–March.
Birds: Sirkeer Malkoha, Yellow-wattled Lapwing, White-bellied Minivet, Marshall's Iora, Orange-headed Thrush, Brown Rock-chat, Rufous-fronted Prinia, Sulphur-bellied and Brooks's leaf warblers, Blyth's and Long-billed pipits, Large Grey Babbler and White-capped Bunting.

Sultanpur, Haryana

Location: About 45 km southwest of Delhi.
Habitat: Lake with scrub, acacia woodland and seasonal agricultural land.
Best time to visit: November–March.
Birds: Indian Courser, Yellow-wattled Lapwing, numerous species of raptor, numerous species of waterbird including Greater Flamingo, Black Ibis, Eurasian Spoonbill, Great White and Dalmatian pelicans, Woolly-necked and Black-necked storks, numerous species of warblers, larks and pipits.

Corbett National Park, Uttaranchal

Location: About 280 km northeast of Delhi.

Habitat: Sal forest, rivers and reservoir, and grasslands.

Best time to visit: Mid-November–May.

Birds: Kalij Pheasant, Great Slaty Woodpecker, Stork-billed and Crested kingfisher, Brown and Tawny fish owls, Ibisbill, Great Thick-knee, Mountain Hawk Eagle, Grey-headed and Lesser fish eagles, Indian Pitta (summer only) and Bright-headed Cisticola. Excellent for a wide range of sub-Himalayan forest birds and western Himalayan species in winter (e.g. a variety of woodpeckers, drongos, forktails, thrushes and chats, warblers and babblers). Over 400 species recorded.

Nainital, Uttaranchal

Location: About 320 km northeast of Delhi.

Habitat: Montane forest, agricultural fields, parks and gardens.

Best time to visit: October–May.

Birds: Black-headed Jay, Spotted Forktail, Altai, Rufous-breasted and Black-throated accentors and Collared Grosbeak. Good for thrushes and chats, warblers and rosefinches in winter.

Bharatpur (Keoladeo Ghana National Park), Rajasthan

Location: About 180 km south of Delhi.

Habitat: Lakes and marshes, woodland and grassland.

Best time to visit: October–March, although worth a visit at any time in the year.

Birds: Arguably the best birdwatching site in northern India. Excellent for waterbirds and birds of prey. Specialities include Bar-headed Goose, Comb Duck, Dusky Eagle Owl, Siberian and Sarus cranes, Pallas's Fish Eagle, Indian Spotted Eagle, Black-necked Stork and Spotted Creeper. Vultures, abundant here until the mid-1990s, are now scarce, but include White-rumped, Indian and Red-headed. Also good for wintering passerines, with Red-throated Flycatcher, Bluethroat and Hume's Warbler abundant. Brooks's Leaf Warbler and Booted Warbler also occur. Over 400 species recorded.

Ranthambhor, Rajasthan

Location: 350 km southwest of Delhi.

Habitat: Dry deciduous forest and lakes.

Best time to visit: November–March.

Birds: Good for raptors. Specialities include Painted Spurfowl, White-naped Woodpecker, Painted Sandgrouse, Indian Courser, Great Thick-knee, Indian Vulture, Indian Spotted Eagle, Black-necked Stork and Marshall's Iora.

Desert National Park, Rajasthan

Location: 40 km west of Jaisalmer.

Habitat: Sparsely vegetated semi-desert.

Best time to visit: November–February.

Birds: Specialities include Indian Bustard, Macqueen's Bustard, Cream-coloured Courser, Long-legged Buzzard, Stoliczka's Bushchat and Plain Leaf Warbler. Also good for various species of sandgrouse, wheatears and larks.

Harike Barrage, Punjab

Location: 60 km south of Amritsar.

CORBETT NATIONAL PARK, UTTARANCHAL.

Habitat: Lake with marshes, and surrounding acacia woodland and agricultural land.
Best time to visit: November–March.
Birds: Specialities include Sykes's Nightjar, Yellow-eyed Pigeon, Indian Skimmer, Black-bellied Tern, Pallas's Fish Eagle, Rufous-vented Prinia, Bristled Grassbird, Brooks's Leaf Warbler, White-crowned Penduline Tit and Sind Sparrow. Excellent for ducks, gulls, terns and raptors.

Velavadar, Gujarat
Location: 30 km north of Bhavnagar.
Habitat: Grassland and acacia scrub.
Best time to visit: August/September for Lesser Florican and winter for harriers.
Birds: Specialities include Lesser Florican and Stoliczka's Bushchat. Has a huge roost of harriers, mainly Montagu's, in winter.

Gir National Park, Gujarat
Location: 60 km southeast of Junagadh.
Habitat: Forest, grassland and riverine vegetation.
Best time to visit: November–March.
Birds: Rock Bush Quail, Painted Sandgrouse, Woolly-necked Stork, Black Ibis and Black-headed Cuckoo-shrike. Also the only site in Asia for Lion.

Bandhavgarh, Madhya Pradesh
Location: 30 km from Umaria.
Habitat: Forest, grassland and marshes
Best time to visit: November–March
Birds: Painted Francolin, Red Spurfowl, Painted Spurfowl, White-naped Woodpecker, Malabar Pied Hornbill, Sirkeer Malkoha, Painted Sandgrouse, Mottled Wood Owl, Indian Vulture and Lesser Adjutant.

NATIONAL ORGANISATIONS

Bombay Natural History Society (BNHS)
Hornbill House, Dr Salim Ali Chowk, Shaheed Bhagat Singh Road, Bombay 400 023.
Publications: *Journal of the Bombay Natural History Society; Hornbill* magazine (quarterly).
The BNHS was founded in 1883 and is the largest non-governmental organisation in the subcontinent engaged in the conservation of nature and natural resources, education and research in natural history. The Society has an invaluable collection of over 26,000 bird specimens held at its headquarters in Bombay. The Society's Nature Education Wing reaches over 10,000 students each year. The Salim Ali Nature Conservation Fund creates awareness, with training programmes for Indian Army officers, journalists and trekkers. Scientists have carried out vital ornithological research, including a national bird-ringing programme and studies on grassland birds.

Salim Ali Centre for Ornithology and Natural History (SACON)
Kalampalayam, Coimbatore, Tamil Nadu 641 010.
Publication: *SACON newsletter*
SACON came into being in 1990. SACON's objectives are to:

1. study India's biological diversity so as to promote its conservation and sustainable use;
2. study the ecology of the Indian avifauna with special reference to its conservation;
3. foster the development of professional wildlife research in India, by training post-graduates and forest managers; and
4. function as a regional nodal agency for the dissemination of information on bio-diversity and its conservation.

Current work includes biodiversity monitoring at Keoladeo Ghana National Park, and monitoring and conservation of the Lesser Florican.

Wildlife Institute of India (WII)
Post Bag No. 18, Chandrabani, Dehradun 248 001.
The WII was set up in 1982. Its objectives are to:

1. train biologists and managers for protected area management and wildlife research;
2. conduct and coordinate applied wildlife research, and evolve techniques relevant to the Indian situation;
3. train education and extension workers to acquire skills in eliciting public support for wildlife conservation;
4. provide consultancy services in conservation matters to government and non-official agencies;
5. create a database leading to a national wildlife information system; and
6. provide conservation orientation courses for those involved in land use management.

Zoological Survey of India (ZSI)
27, Jawaharlal Nehru Road, Calcutta 700 016.
Publications: *Newsletter of the Zoological Survey of India; Records of the Zoological Survey of India Annual Reports.*
The ZSI was established in 1916 and carries out surveys throughout the country. Its

collections cover the whole of India. The National Zoological Collection of India at Calcutta houses more than a million specimens belonging to all the animal groups. Fourteen collecting stations are maintained in different ecological biotopes, such as the Desert Regional Station at Jodhpur and the high-altitude station at Solan.

Indian Bird Conservation Network (IBCN)

The Indian Bird Conservation Network is a network of Indian organisations and individuals, coordinated by the Bombay Natural History Society, which collaborate to promote the conservation of birds in India and, through them, the conservation of biological diversity as a whole. The following are IBCN organisational partners in northern India:

Delhibird – The Northern India Bird Network
N-50, Panchsheel Park, New Delhi
Tel: 0129 5253294
email: nik@sapta.com
Mr Nikhil Devasar

Department of Wildlife Sciences
Aligarh Muslim University,
Aligarh 202 002
Tel: 0571 701052
Fax: 0571 701205

Forum for Forestry Furtherance (4-F)
B-159, Shahpura, Bhopal, Madhya Pradesh
Tel: 0755 773639
email: kos78@sancharnet.in
Mr Koustubh Sharma

Gujarat Ecological Education & Research Foundation (GEER)
Geer Foundation, Indroda Nature Park, Sector 9, Gandhinagar 382 009, Gujarat
Tel: 02712 21385
Fax: 02712 41128
email: geer@guj.nic.in
Dr Ketan Tatu

Nature Club Surat
81, Sarjan Society, Athwa Lines, Surat 395 007
Tel: 0261 3227596
Fax: 0261 8690807
email: sushafe@sify.com

NEED Organisation
Panchawati, Udaipur 313 004, Rajasthan
Tel: 0294 2526015
Fax: 0294 2524091
Dr Raza Tehsin

Vihang
19/414 Satyagrah Chhavni, Satellite Road, Ahmedabad 380 015
Tel: 079 6731878, 079 6740882
Dr Bakul N. Trivedi

World Pheasant Association
S-56/1, DLF-III, Gurgaon 122 002, Haryana
Tel: 0124 6562406
Fax: 0124 6562406
email: r_kaul@hotmail.com
Mr Rahul Kaul

INTERNATIONAL ORGANISATIONS

BirdLife International
Wellbrook Court, Girton Road, Cambridge CB3 0NA, UK.
email: birdlife@birdlife.org.uk
Website: www.birdlife.net
Publication: *World Birdwatch* magazine (quarterly).
BirdLife International (formerly the International Council for Bird Preservation) is a network of Partners and Affiliates represented in over 100 countries. BirdLife is the world's leading authority on the status of the world's birds, their habitats and the urgent problems that face them.
BirdLife aims to:

- prevent the extinction of any bird species;
- reduce the number of species that are globally threatened;
- enhance the conservation status of all bird species; and
- conserve crucial sites and habitats for birds.

BirdLife has recently completed the *Threatened Birds of Asia: The BirdLife International Red Data Book*, which provides a comprehensive assessment of the status, distribution and conservation needs of threatened birds in Asia. BirdLife is currently working on an inventory of Important Bird Areas in Asia. The Bombay Natural History Society is the BirdLife Partner Designate in India.

Oriental Bird Club (OBC)
P.O. Box 324, Bedford, MK42 0WG, UK.
email: mail@orientalbirdclub.org
Website: www.orientalbirdclub.org
Publications: *OBC Bulletin* (half-yearly); *Forktail* journal (annual).
The OBC was established in 1985. It aims to:

- encourage an interest in the birds of the oriental region and their conservation;
- liaise with and promote the work of existing regional societies; and
- collate and publish material on oriental birds.

The OBC offers grants to nationals in the region to encourage survey work useful for conservation and conservation awareness.

Wetlands International
South Asia Office, A-127, 2nd Floor, Defence Colony, New Delhi 110 024, India.
email: wisaind@del2.vsnl.net.in
Website: www.wetlands.org
Contact: Dr C.L. Trisal
Publication: *Wetlands* (Newsletter of Wetlands International).
Wetlands International was created in October 1995 following the merger of the Asian Wetland Bureau with the International Waterfowl and Wetlands Research Bureau. The organisation is committed to promoting the protection and sustainable utilisation of wetlands and wetland resources worldwide. It has been involved in surveys, monitoring and conservation of waterbirds and wetlands since 1954 and has coordinated the Asian Waterbird Census since 1987 (*see* www.wetlands.org/IWC/awc/awcmain.html). It coordinates the Asia-Pacific Migratory Waterbird Conservation Strategy: 2001–2005, which provides an international cooperative conservation framework involving governments, conventions, NGOs, development agencies and local people in the region. This aims to enhance the long-term conservation of migratory waterbirds and their habitats in the region (*see* www.wetlands.org/IWC/awc/waterbirdstrategy/default.htm).

World Pheasant Association South Asia Field Office (WPA-SARO)
DLF Phase 3 Gurgaon, Haryana, India.
Publication: *Mor*
WPA-SARO was established by the World Pheasant Association in April 1992. The main purpose of this office is to further the aims of WPA in the South Asian region. Over the last five years, the office is initiated many short- and long-term field research projects leading to the production of useful data, not only on Galliformes, but also on other birds, mammals and their habitats. The WPA-SARO has also been offering assistance by way of technical, material and financial help.

World Wide Fund for Nature (WWF)
WWF India
172-B Lodi Estate, New Delhi 110 023, India.
WWF India was established in 1969 and is the largest of the country's non-governmental conservation organisations. Today, the organisation's mission is 'to promote nature conservation and environmental protection as the basis for sustainable and equitable development'.

REFERENCES

Alström, P. (1998) Taxonomy of the *Mirafra assamica* complex. *Forktail* 13: 97–107.
Alström, P., and Olsson, U. (1999) The Golden-spectacled Warbler – a complex of sibling species, including a previously undescribed species. *Ibis* 141: 545–568.
Anon. (1991) Mangrove conservation. *Hornbill* 1991(4): 20.
Anon. (1996) *Asia-Pacific Migratory Waterbird Conservation Strategy: 1996–2000.* Wetlands International: Asia Pacific, Kuala Lumpur, Publication No. 117; and International Waterfowl and Wetlands Research Bureau, Japan Committee, Tokyo.
Bensch, S., and Pearson, D. (2002) The Large-billed Reed Warbler *Acrocephalus orinus* revisited. *Ibis* 144: 259–267.

IBISBILL SITE. RAMANAGAR. NORTHERN INDIA.

BirdLife International (2001) *Threatened Birds of Asia.* BirdLife International, Cambridge.

Collins, N.M., Sayer, J.A., and Whitmore, T.C. (1991) *The Conservation Atlas of Tropical Forests, Asia and the Pacific.* World Conservation Union. Macmillan, London.

Economic and Social Commission for Asia and the Pacific (1994) *Statistical Yearbook for Asia and the Pacific 1993.* Bangkok.

Gillham, E., and Gillham, B. (1996) *Hybrid Ducks – Contribution Towards an Inventory.* Privately published.

Grimmett, R., Inskipp, C., and Inskipp, T. (1998) *Birds of the Indian Subcontinent.* Christopher Helm.

Hussain, S.A. (1996) An overview of recent bird migration studies in India. Abstract. P.1 in Pan-Asian Ornithological Congress and XII BirdLife Asia Conference, Coimbatore, India, 9–16 November 1996.

Inskipp, T., Lindsey, N., and Duckworth, W. (1996) *An Annotated Checklist of the Birds of the Oriental Region.* Oriental Bird Club, Sandy.

Islam, M.Z., and Rahmani, A.R. (2002) Threatened birds of India. *Buceros* 7 (1&2). Compiled from *Threatened Birds of Asia*, BirdLife International, Red Data Book (2001), Cambridge: BirdLife International.

Kazmierczak, K., and Singh, R. (1998) *A Birdwatchers' Guide to India.* Prion Ltd, Sandy.

Knox, A.G. (1993) Richard Meinertzhagen – a case of fraud examined. *Ibis* 135: 320–325.

Ministry of Environment and Forests (1997) *State of Forest Report 1997.* Forest Survey of India, Dehra Dun.

Naoroji, R. (1995) Conservation issues of some raptor species in the Himalayan foothills with emphasis on Mountain Hawk-Eagle and Lesser Greyheaded Fishing Eagle. Pp. 32–34 in L. Vijayan, ed., *Avian Conservation in India.* SACON, Coimbatore.

Parry, S.J., Clark, W.S., and Prakash, V. (2002) On the taxonomic status of the Indian Spotted Eagle *Aquila hastata*. *Ibis* 144: 665–675.

Perennou, C., Mundkur, T., Scott, D.A., Folkestad, A., and Kvenild, L. (1994) *The Asian Waterfowl Census 1987–91: Distribution and Status of Asian Waterfowl.* AWB Publication 86. IWRB Publication 24. AWB, Kuala Lumpur, and IWRB, Slimbridge.

Rahmani, A.R., and Sankaran, R. (1995) The Indian Thar desert. Pp. 61–62 in L. Vijayan, ed., *Avian Conservation in India.* SACON, Coimbatore.

Rasmussen, P.C., and Parry, S.J. (2001) The taxonomic status of the 'Long-billed' Vulture *Gyps indicus*. *Vulture News*.

Rodgers, W.A., and Panwar, H.S. (1988) *Planning a Wildlife Protected Area Network in India.* Two volumes. Wildlife Institute of India, Dehra Dun.

Sankaran, R. (1995) A fresh initiative to conserve the Lesser Florican. *Oriental Bird Club Bulletin* 22: 42–44.

Shyamsunder, S., and Parameswarappa, S. (1987) Forestry in India – the forester's view. *Ambio* 16: 332–337.

Stattersfield, A.J., Crosby, M.J., Long, A.J., and Wege, D.C. (1998) *Endemic Bird Areas of the World, Priorities for Biodiversity Conservation.* BirdLife International, Cambridge.

WWF INDIA and AWB (1993) *Directory of Indian wetlands.* WWF INDIA, New Delhi and AWB, Kuala Lumpur.

ACKNOWLEDGEMENTS

The authors would like to thank once again those who contributed in a major way to the *Birds of the Indian Subcontinent* (Grimmett, Inskipp and Inskipp, 1998) and who are acknowledged in that work. Particular thanks go Carol Inskipp, the second author of this major work, who due to pressures of other work decided not to co-author the North India guide – this and the forthcoming South India guide could not have been produced without her earlier contribution. We are also extremely grateful to M. Zafar-ul Islam and Asad R. Rahmani, of the Bombay Natural History Society, for preparing the foreword and contributing material for the introductory sections. Thanks also go to Carl D'Silva, Alan Harris and Craig Robson who have prepared new illustrations for this edition. RG would like to thank Helen Taylor, and our two children George and Ella, as well as his parents, Frank and Molly Grimmett, for their continued encouragement and support. RG would also like to thank Ani Kartikasari and Meiske D. Tapilatu for their assistance in the preparation of the typescript. TI is very grateful to Bill Harvey for extensive comments on the distribution and status of birds in several states.

Once again we would also like to thank Robert Kirk, who commissioned the book and shared our vision to produce accessible guides for the birdwatching public, and to Nigel Redman and Mike Unwin of A & C Black, who have managed the project throughout and have skilfully handled the production process.

GLOSSARY

Altitudinal migrant: a species that breeds at high altitudes (in mountains) and moves to lower levels and valleys in non-breeding season.

Arboreal: tree-dwelling.

Arm: the basal part of the wing, from where it joins the body, outwards to the carpal joint.

Axillaries: the feathers in the armpit at the base of the underwing.

Biotope: a particular area that is substantially uniform in its environmental conditions and flora and fauna.

Cap: a well-defined patch of colour or bare skin on the top of the head.

Carpal: the bend of the wing or carpal joint.

Carpal patch: a well-defined patch of colour on the underwing in the vicinity of the carpal joint.

Casque: an enlargement on the upper surface of the bill, in front of the head, as in hornbills.

Cere: a fleshy (often brightly coloured) structure at the base of the bill and containing the nostrils.

Collar: a well-defined band of colour that encircles or partly encircles the neck.

Colonial: nesting or roosting in tight colonies; species that are loosely colonial have nests more widely spaced.

Commensalism: a rare situation where species A benefits from the presence of species B, but B is indifferent to the presence of A, neither gaining nor losing from that association.

Culmen: the ridge of the upper mandible.

Eclipse plumage: a female-like plumage acquired in some species (e.g. ducks and some sunbirds) during or after breeding.

Edgings or edges: outer feather margins that can frequently result in distinct paler or darker panels of colour in wings or tail.

Endemic: restricted or confined to a specific country or region.

Flight feathers: the primaries, secondaries and tail feathers.

Fringes: complete feather margins that frequently result in a scaly appearance to body feathers or coverts.

Frugivorous: fruit-eating.

Gape: the mouth and fleshy corner of the bill, which can extend back below the eye.

Gonys: a bulge in the lower mandible, usually distinct in gulls and terns.

Graduated tail: where the longest tail feathers are the central pair and the shortest the outermost, with those in between intermediate in length.

Granivorous: feeding on grain or seeds.

Gregarious: living in flocks or communities.

Gular pouch: a loose and pronounced area of skin extending from the throat (e.g. in pelicans or hornbills).

Hackles: long and pointed neck feathers that can extend across mantle and wing-coverts (e.g. in junglefowls).

Hand: the outer end of the wing, from the carpal joint to the tip of the wing.

Hepatic: used with reference to the rufous-brown morph of some cuckoos.

Iris (plural irides): the coloured membrane that surrounds the pupil of the eye, which can be brightly coloured.

Jheel: a shallow lake in a low-lying natural depression, usually with floating and submerged vegetation, reedbeds and partially submerged trees.

Lappet: a wattle, particularly one at the gape.

Leading edge: the edge of the forewing.

Local: occurring or common within a small or restricted area.

Mandible: the lower or upper half of the bill.

Mask: a dark area of plumage surrounding the eye and often covering the ear-coverts.

Melanistic: when the plumage is dominated by black pigmentation.

Morph: a distinct plumage type, which occurs alongside one or more other distinct plumage types.

Nomadic: of a wandering or erratically occurring species that has no fixed territory when not breeding.

Nominate: the first-named race of a species, that which has its racial name the same as the specific name.

Nuchal: the hind-neck, used with reference to a patch or collar.

Nullah: a watercourse or ravine, usually dry.

Ocelli: eye-like spots of iridescent colour; a distinctive feature in the plumage of peafowls.

Orbital ring: a narrow circular ring of feathering or bare skin surrounding the eye.

Pelagic: of the open sea.

pH: a measure of acidity: low pH indicates high acidity, high pH low acidity.

Plantation: group of trees (usually exotic or non-native species) planted in close proximity to each other for timber or as a crop.

Primary projection: the extension of the primaries beyond the longest tertial on a closed wing; this can be of critical use (e.g. in the identification of larks or *Acrocephalus* warblers).

Race: subspecies, a geographical population whose members all show constant differences (e.g. in plumage or size) from those of other populations of the same species.

Rectrices: the tail feathers.

Remiges: the primaries and secondaries.

Rictal bristles: bristles, often prominent, at the base of the bill.

Shaft streak: a fine pale or dark line of colour that follows the feather shaft.

Speculum: refers to the often glossy panel across the secondaries of dabbling ducks, which is often bordered by pale tips to these feathers and a greater-covert wing-bar.

Subspecies: *see* race.

Subterminal band: a dark or pale band, usually broad, which lies behind the terminal band of the tail.

Terai: the undulating alluvial, often marshy, strip of land 25–45 km wide lying north of the Gangetic plain in Uttaranchal. Naturally supports tall elephant grass interspersed with dense forest, but large areas have been drained and converted to cultivation.

Terminal band: a dark or pale band, usually broad, at the end of the tail.

Terrestrial: living or occurring mainly on the ground.

Trailing edge: a darker or paler rear edge of the wing.

Vent: the area around the cloaca (anal opening), just behind the legs (should not be confused with the undertail-coverts).

Vermiculated: finely barred or marked with fine or narrow wavy lines, usually visible only at close range.

Wattle: a lobe of bare, often brightly coloured, skin attached to the head (frequently at the bill base), as in the mynas or wattled lapwings.

Wing linings: underwing-coverts.

Wing-bar: generally a narrow and well-defined dark or pale bar across the wing, and often refers to a band formed by pale tips to the greater or median coverts (or both as in 'double wing-bar').

Wing-panel: a pale or dark band across the wing that is broader and generally more diffuse than a wing-bar (often formed by pale edges to the remiges or coverts).

SELECTED BIBLIOGRAPHY

A large number of references were analysed for the information on occurrence and status of birds in the individual states. However, the initial lists were built up from a few key references, which are listed below with the relevant states appended in brackets.

Abdulali, H., and Panday, J.D. (1978) *Checklist of the Birds of Delhi, Agra and Bharatpur with Notes on their Status in the Neighbourhood.* Published by the author, Bombay. [Delhi, Rajasthan, Uttar Pradesh]

Agoramoorthy, G., and Mohnot, S.M. (1989) Checklist of birds around Jodhpur. *TigerPaper* 16(1): 11–13. [Rajasthan]

Ali, Sálim (1945) *The Birds of Kutch.* Oxford University Press, Bombay. [Gujarat]

Ali, Sálim (1954–1955) The birds of Gujarat. *J. Bombay Nat. Hist. Soc.* 52: 374–458, 735–802. [Gujarat]

Ali, Sálim, and Whistler, H. (1939–1940) The birds of central India. *J. Bombay Nat. Hist. Soc.* 41: 82–106, 470–488. [Madhya Pradesh]

Bates, R.S.P., and Lowther, E.H.N. (1952) *Breeding Birds of Kashmir.* Oxford University Press, Bombay. [Jammu & Kashmir]

Briggs, F.S. (1931) A note on the birds in the neighbourhood of Mhow. *J. Bombay Nat. Hist. Soc.* 35: 382–404. [Madhya Pradesh]

Briggs, F.S. (1934) A note on the birds of Ghazipur. *J. Bombay Nat. Hist. Soc.* 37: 378–390. [Uttar Pradesh]

D'Abreu, E.A. (1935) A list of the birds of the Central Provinces. *J. Bombay Nat. Hist. Soc.* 38: 95–116. [Madhya Pradesh, Maharashtra]

Devarshi, D., and Trigunayat, M.M. (1989) Checklist of the birds of Mount Abu (Rajasthan). *Pavo* 27: 59–63. [Rajasthan]

Dharmakumarsinhji, R.S. (1955) *The Birds of Saurashtra*. Times of India Press, Bombay. [Gujarat]

Dhindsa, M.S., Sandhu, P.S., and Sandhu, J.S. (1991) Some additions to the checklist of birds of Punjab. *Pavo* 28: 23–28. [Punjab]

Ganguli, U. (1975) *A Guide to the Birds of the Delhi Area*. Indian Council of Agricultural Research, New Delhi. [Delhi, Haryana]

Gaston, A.J., Garson, P.J., and Pandey, S. (1993) Birds recorded in the Great Himalayan National Park, Himachal Pradesh, India. *Forktail* 9: 45–57. [Himachal Pradesh]

Gill, E.H.N. (1923–1925) A description of the nest and eggs of the common birds occurring in the plains of the United Provinces. *J. Bombay Nat. Hist. Soc.* 28: 1069–1074; 29: 107–116, 334–344, 757–768, 963–970; 30: 273–284. [Uttar Pradesh]

Green, M.J.B. (1987) The birds of the Kedarnath Sanctuary, Chamoli district, Uttar Pradesh: status and distribution. *J. Bombay Nat. Hist. Soc.* 83: 603–617. [Uttaranchal]

Hewetson, C.E. (1956) Observations on the bird life of Madhya Pradesh. *J. Bombay Nat. Hist. Soc.* 53: 595–645. [Madhya Pradesh, Maharashtra]

Hudson, C. (1930) A list of some birds of the seven hills of Naini Tal, U.P. *J. Bombay Nat. Hist. Soc.* 34: 821–827. [Uttaranchal]

Javed, S., and Rahmani, A.R. (1998) Conservation of the avifauna of Dudwa National Park, India. *Forktail* 14: 55–64. [Uttar Pradesh]

Jesse, W. (1902–1903) A list of the birds of Lucknow. *Ibis* (8)2: 470–490, 531–566; (8)3: 49–81, 148–178. [Uttar Pradesh]

Jones, A.E. (1919a) A list of birds found in the Simla hills 1908–1918. *J. Bombay Nat. Hist. Soc.* 26: 601–620. [Himachal Pradesh]

Jones, A.E. (1919b) Further notes on the birds of the Ambala district, Punjab. *J. Bombay Nat. Hist. Soc.* 26: 675–676. [Haryana]

Jones, A.E. (1947–1948) The birds of the Simla and adjacent hills. *J. Bombay Nat. Hist. Soc.* 47: 117–125, 219–249, 409–432. [Himachal Pradesh]

Kalpavriksh (1991) *What's that Bird? A Guide to Birdwatching, with Special Reference to Delhi*. Kalpavriksh, New Delhi. [Delhi, Haryana]

Klein, R., and Buchheim, A. (1997) Die westliche Schwarzmeerküste als Kontaktgebiet zweier Großmöwenformen der *Larus cachinnans*-Gruppe. *Vogelwelt* 118: 61–70.

Koelz, W. (1937) Notes on the birds of Spiti, a Himalayan province of the Punjab. *Ibis* (14)1: 86–104. [Himachal Pradesh]

Koelz, W. (1940a) Notes on the birds of Zankskar and Purig, with appendixes giving new records for Ladakh, Rupshu and Kulu. *Pap. Michigan Acad. Sci.* 25: 297–322. [Jammu & Kashmir, Himachal Pradesh]

Koelz, W. (1940b) Notes on the winter birds of the lower Punjab. *Pap. Michigan Acad. Sci.* 25: 323–356. [Haryana, Punjab]

Lavkumar, K.S. (1956) A contribution to the ornithology of Garhwal. *J. Bombay Nat. Hist. Soc.* 53: 315–329. [Uttaranchal]

Liebers, D., Helbig, A.J., and de Knijff, P. (2001) Genetic differentiation and phylogeography of gulls in the *Larus cachinnans-fuscus* group (Aves: Charadriiformes). *Molecular Ecology* 10: 2447–2462.

Monga, S.G., and Naoroji, R.K. (1984) Birds of the Rajpipla forests – south Gujarat. *J. Bombay Nat. Hist. Soc.* 80: 575–612. [Gujarat]

Musavi, A.H., and Urfi, A.J. (1987) *Avifauna of Aligarh Region*. Nature Conservation Society of India. [Uttar Pradesh]

Newton, P.N., Breeden, S., and Norman, G.J. (1987) The birds of Kanha Tiger Reserve,

Madhya Pradesh, India. *J. Bombay Nat. Hist. Soc.* 83: 477–498. [Madhya Pradesh]

Osmaston, A.E. (1913) The birds of Gorakhpur. *J. Bombay Nat. Hist. Soc.* 22: 532–549. [Uttar Pradesh]

Osmaston, B.B. (1925) The birds of Ladakh. *Ibis* (12)1: 663–719. [Jammu & Kashmir]

Osmaston, B.B. (1926) The birds of Ladakh. *Ibis* (12)2: 446–448. [Jammu & Kashmir]

Osmaston, B.B. (1927) Notes on the birds of Kashmir. *J. Bombay Nat. Hist. Soc.* 31: 975–999; 32: 134–153. [Jammu & Kashmir]

Osmaston, B.B., and Sale, J.B. (1989) *Wildlife of Dehra Dun and Adjacent Hills.* Natraj, Dehra Dun. [Uttaranchal]

Pfister, O. (2001) Birds recorded during visits to Ladakh, India, from 1994 to 1997. *Forktail* 17: 81–90. [Jammu & Kashmir]

Rahmani, A.R. (1992) Birds of the Karera Bustard Sanctuary, Madhya Pradesh. *J. Bombay Nat. Hist. Soc.* 88: 172–194. [Madhya Pradesh]

Rahmani, A.R. (1997) *Wildlife in the Thar.* WWF India, New Delhi. [Rajasthan]

Sankar, K., Mohan, D., and Pandey, S. (1993) Birds of Sariska Tiger Reserve, Rajasthan, India. *Forktail* 8: 133–141. [Rajasthan]

Sharma, S.C., and Harvey, B. (2002) Haryana checklist. www.delhibird.org/checklists/check-lists_haryana.htm

Sharma, S.K., and Tehsin, R. (1994) Birds of southern Rajasthan. *Newsletter for Birdwatchers* 34: 109–113. [Rajasthan]

Singh, G. (1993) *A Checklist of Birds of Punjab.* Punjab Govt. Press. [Punjab]

Singh, S., Kothari, A., and Pande, P., eds (1990) *Directory of National Parks and Sanctuaries in Himachal Pradesh, Management Status and Profiles.* Indian Institute of Public Administration, New Delhi. [Himachal Pradesh]

Toor, H.S., Chakravarthy, A.K., Dhindsa, M.S., Sandhu, P.S., and Ananda Rao, P.K. (1982) *A Check List of Birds of Punjab and Chandigarh.* Published by the authors. [Punjab]

Vyas, R. (1992) Checklist of the birds of Kota district in south-east Rajasthan. *Newsletter for Birdwatchers* 32(11 & 12): 8–10. [Rajasthan]

Vyas, S. (1996) Checklist of the birds of the Delhi region: an update. *J. Bombay Nat. Hist. Soc.* 93: 219–237. [Delhi, Haryana] With a further update on www.64.6.246.114/checklists/check-lists_delhi.htm

Ward, A.E. (1907) Birds of the provinces of Kashmir and Jammu and adjacent districts. *J. Bombay Nat. Hist. Soc.* 17: 108–113, 479–485, 723–729, 943–949. [Jammu & Kashmir]

Ward, A.E. (1908) Further notes on birds of the provinces of Kashmir and Jammu and adjacent districts. *J. Bombay Nat. Hist. Soc.* 18: 461–464. [Jammu & Kashmir]

Whistler, H. (1918) Notes on the birds of Ambala dist., Punjab. *J. Bombay Nat. Hist. Soc.* 25: 665–681; 26: 172–191. [Haryana, Punjab]

Whistler, H. (1919) Some birds of Ludhiana district, Punjab. *J. Bombay Nat. Hist. Soc.* 26: 585–598. [Punjab]

Whistler, H. (1922) A contribution to the ornithology of Cashmere. *J. Bombay Nat. Hist. Soc.* 28: 990–1006. [Jammu & Kashmir]

Whistler, H. (1925) The birds of Lahul, N.W. Himalaya. *Ibis* (12)1: 152–208. [Himachal Pradesh]

Whistler, H. (1926a) A note on the birds of Kulu. *J. Bombay Nat. Hist. Soc.* 31: 458–485. [Himachal Pradesh]

Whistler, H. (1926b) The birds of Kangra district, Punjab. *Ibis* (12)2: 521–581, 724–783. [Himachal Pradesh]

Whistler, H. (1938) The ornithological survey of Jodhpur state. *J. Bombay Nat. Hist. Soc.* 40: 213–235. [Rajasthan]

Whitehead, C.H.T. (1911) Notes on the birds of Sehore, Central India, with special reference to migration. *J. Bombay Nat. Hist. Soc.* 21: 153–170. [Madhya Pradesh]

Yadav, J.S., and Maleyvar, R.P. (1978) The birds of Haryana: a classified list. *J.H.S. (Kurukshetra)* 10: 37–51. [Haryana]

Yadav, J.S., and Maleyvar, R.P. (1982) The birds of Haryana: a few more spottings. *Pavo* 19: 51–55. [Haryana]

FAMILY SUMMARIES

Some families are divided into subfamilies and some of these are further divided into tribes.

■ ■ **Partridges, Francolins, Snowcocks, Quails and Pheasants** Phasianidae ■ ■

Terrestrial, feeding and nesting on the ground, but many species roost in trees at night. They are good runners, often preferring to escape on foot rather than taking to the air. Their flight is powerful and fast, but, except in the case of the migratory quails, it cannot be sustained for long periods. Typically, they forage by scratching the ground with their strong feet to expose food hidden among dead leaves or in the soil. They mainly eat seeds, fruit, buds, roots and leaves, complemented by invertebrates. **pp.46–55**

■ ■ **Whistling-Ducks** Dendrocygnidae **and Swans, Geese and Ducks** Anatidae ■ ■

Aquatic and highly gregarious, typically migrating, feeding, roosting and resting together, often in mixed flocks. Most species are chiefly vegetarian when adult, feeding on seeds, algae, plants and roots, often supplemented by aquatic invertebrates. Their main foraging methods are diving, surface-feeding or dabbling, and grazing. They also upend, wade, filter and sieve water and debris for food, and probe with the bill. They have a direct flight with sustained fast wingbeats, and characteristically they fly in V-formation. **pp.56–65**

■ ■ ■ **Buttonquails** Turnicidae ■ ■ ■

Small, plump terrestrial birds. They are found in a wide variety of habitats with a dry, often sandy substrate and low ground cover under which they can readily run or walk. Buttonquails are very secretive and fly with great reluctance, with weak whirring beats low over the ground, dropping quickly into cover. They feed on grass and weed seeds, grain, greenery and small insects, picking food from the ground surface, or scratching with the feet. **pp.48–49**

■ ■ ■ **Honeyguides** Indicatoridae ■ ■ ■

Small, inconspicuous birds that inhabit forest or forest edge. All species eat insects, but a peculiarity shared by the family is that they also eat wax, usually as bee combs. They spend long periods perched upright and motionless, and they feed by clinging to bee combs, often upside-down, and by making aerial sallies. **pp.66–67**

■ ■ ■ **Wrynecks, Piculets and Woodpeckers** Picidae ■ ■ ■

Chiefly arboreal birds, and usually seen clinging to, and climbing up, vertical trunks and lateral branches. Typically, they work up trunks and along branches in jerky spurts, directly or in spirals. Some species feed regularly on the ground, searching mainly for termites and ants. The bill of many species is powerful, for boring into wood to extract insects and for excavating nest holes. Woodpeckers feed chiefly on ants, termites, and grubs and pupae of wood-boring beetles. Most woodpeckers also hammer rapidly against tree trunks with their bill, producing a loud rattle, known as 'drumming', which is used to advertise territories and warn off intruders. Their flight is strong and direct, with marked undulations. Many species can be located by their characteristic loud calls. **pp.66–71**

■ ■ ■ **Asian Barbets** Megalaimidae ■ ■ ■

Arboreal birds, and usually found in the tree-tops. Despite their bright coloration, they can be very difficult to see, especially when silent, their plumage blending remarkably well with tree foliage. They often sit motionless for long periods. Barbets call persistently and monotonously in the breeding season, sometimes throughout the day; in the non-breeding season they are usually silent. They are chiefly frugivorous, many species favouring figs *Ficus*. Their flight is strong and direct, with deep woodpecker-like undulations. **pp.72–73**

▪ ▪ ▪ Hornbills Bucerotidae ▪ ▪ ▪

Medium-sized to large birds with massive bills and variable-sized casques. They are mainly arboreal, and feed chiefly on wild figs *Ficus*, berries and drupes, supplemented by small animals and insects. Flight is powerful and slow, and for most species consists of a few wing-beats followed by a sailing glide with the wing-tips upturned. In all but the smaller species, the wingbeats make a distinctive loud puffing sound audible for some distance. Hornbills often fly one after another in follow-my-leader fashion. They are usually found in pairs or small parties, sometimes in flocks of up to 30 or more where food is abundant. **pp.74–75**

▪ ▪ ▪ Hoopoes Upupidae ▪ ▪ ▪

Hoopoes have a distinctive appearance, with a long, decurved bill, short legs and rounded wings. They are insectivorous, and forage by pecking and probing the ground. Flight is undulating, slow and butterfly-like. **pp.76–77**

▪ ▪ ▪ Trogons Trogonidae ▪ ▪ ▪

Brightly coloured, short-necked, medium-sized birds with a long tail, short rounded wings and a rather short, broad bill. They usually occur singly or in widely separated pairs. Characteristically, they perch almost motionless in upright posture for long periods in the middle or lower storey of dense forests. Trogons are mainly insectivorous and also eat leaves and berries. They capture flying insects on the wing when moving from one vantage point to another, twisting with the agility of a flycatcher. **pp.76–77**

▪ ▪ ▪ Rollers Coraciidae ▪ ▪ ▪

Stoutly built, medium-sized birds with large head and short neck. They eat mainly large insects. Typically, they occur singly or in widely spaced pairs. Flight is buoyant, with rather rapid, deliberate wingbeats. **pp.76–77**

▪ ▪ ▪ Small Kingfishers Alcedinidae, **Large Kingfishers** Halcyonidae **and Pied Kingfishers** Cerylidae ▪ ▪ ▪

Small to medium-sized birds, with large head, long strong beak and short legs. Most king-fishers spend long periods perched singly or in well-separated pairs, watching intently before plunging swiftly downwards to seize prey with bill; they usually return to the same perch. They eat mainly fish, tadpoles and invertebrates; larger species also eat frogs, snakes, crabs, lizards and rodents. Their flight is direct and strong, with rapid wingbeats, and often close to the water surface. **pp.78–79**

▪ ▪ ▪ Bee-Eaters Meropidae ▪ ▪ ▪

Brightly coloured birds with long, decurved beak, pointed wings and very short legs. They catch large flying insects on the wing, by making short, swift sallies like a flycatcher from an exposed perch such as a treetop, branch, post or telegraph wire; insects are pursued in a lively chase with a swift and agile flight. Some species also hawk insects in flight like swallows. Most species are sociable. Their flight is graceful and undulating, a few rapid wingbeats followed by a glide. **pp.80–81**

▪ ▪ ▪ Old World Cuckoos Cuculidae ▪ ▪ ▪

Birds with an elongated body and fairly long neck, a tail varying from medium length to long and graduated, and quite long, decurved bill. Almost all Cuculidae are arboreal and eat hairy caterpillars. Apart from Green-billed Malkoha, male cuckoos are very noisy in the breeding season, calling frequently during the day, especially if cloudy, and often into the night. When not breeding they are silent and unobtrusive, and as a result their status and distribution at this season are very poorly known. Cuckoos (apart from Green-billed Malkoha) are notorious for their nest parasitism. **pp.82–83**

▪ ▪ ▪ Coucals Centropodidae ▪ ▪ ▪

Large, skulking birds with long graduated tail and weak flight. Coucals are terrestrial, frequenting dense undergrowth, bamboo, tall grassland or scrub jungle. They eat small animals and invertebrates. **pp.84–87**

■ ■ ■ Parrots Psittacidae ■ ■ ■

Parrots have a short neck and short, stout, hooked bill, with the upper mandible strongly curved and overlapping the lower mandible. Most parrots are noisy and highly gregarious. They associate in family parties and small flocks and gather in large numbers at concentrations of food, such as paddy-fields. Their diet is almost entirely vegetarian: fruit, seeds, buds, nectar and pollen. The flight of *Psittacula* parrots is swift, powerful and direct. **pp.86–87**

■ ■ ■ Swifts Apodidae **and Treeswifts** Hemiprocnidae ■ ■ ■

Birds with long, pointed wings, compact body, short bill with a wide gape and very short legs. Swifts spend most of the day swooping and wheeling in the sky with great agility and grace. Typical swift flight is a series of rapid shallow wingbeats interspersed with short glides. They feed entirely in the air, drink and bathe while swooping low over water, and regularly pass the night in the air. Swifts eat mainly tiny insects, caught by flying back and forth among aerial concentrations of these with their large mouth open; they also pursue individual insects. **pp.88–89**

■ ■ ■ Barn Owls and Grass Owls Tytonidae **and Typical Owls** Strigidae ■ ■ ■

Birds with a large and rounded head, big forward-facing eyes surrounded by a broad facial disc, and a short tail. Most are nocturnal and cryptically coloured and patterned, making them inconspicuous when resting during the day. When hunting, owls either quarter the ground or scan and listen for prey from a perch. Their diet consists of small animals and invertebrates. Owls are usually located by their distinctive and often weird calls, which are diagnostic of the species and advertise their presence and territories. **pp.90–95**

■ ■ ■ Nightjars Caprimulgidae ■ ■ ■

Small to medium-sized birds with long, pointed wings, and gaping mouth with long bristles that help to catch insects in flight. Nightjars are crepuscular and nocturnal in habit, with soft, owl-like, cryptically patterned plumage. By day they perch on the ground or lengthwise on a branch, and are difficult to detect. They eat flying insects that are captured in flight. Typically, they fly erratically to and fro over and among vegetation, occasionally wheeling, gliding and hovering to pick insects from foliage. They are most easily located by their calls. **pp.96–97**

■ ■ ■ Pigeons and Doves Columbidae ■ ■ ■

Birds with a stout, compact body, rather short neck, and small head and bill. Their flight is swift and direct, with fast wingbeats. Most species are gregarious outside the breeding season. Seeds, fruits, buds and leaves form their main diet, but many species also eat small invertebrates. They have soft plaintive cooing or booming voices, and their calls are often monotonously repeated. **pp.98–103**

■ ■ ■ Bustards Otididae ■ ■ ■

Medium-sized to large terrestrial birds that inhabit grasslands, semi-desert and desert. They have fairly long legs, a stout body, long neck, and crests and neck plumes, which are exhibited in display. The wings are broad and long, and in flight the neck is outstretched. Their flight is powerful and can be very fast. When feeding, bustards have a steady, deliberate gait. They are more or less omnivorous, and feed opportunistically on large insects, such as grasshoppers and locusts, young birds, shoots, leaves, seeds and fruits. Males perform elaborate and spectacular displays in the breeding season. **pp.104–105**

▪ ▪ ▪ Cranes Gruidae ▪ ▪ ▪

Stately, long-necked, long-legged birds with tapering body, and long inner secondaries that hang over the tail. The flight is powerful, with the head and neck extended forwards and legs and feet stretched out behind. Flocks of cranes often fly in V-formation; they sometimes soar at considerable heights. Most cranes are gregarious outside the breeding season, and flocks are often very noisy. Cranes have a characteristic resonant and far-reaching musical trumpet-like call. A wide variety of plant and animal food is taken. The bill is used to probe and dig for plant roots and to graze and glean vegetable material above the ground. Both sexes have a spectacular and beautiful dance that takes place throughout the year. **pp.106–107**

▪ ▪ ▪ Rails, Gallinules and Coots Rallidae ▪ ▪ ▪

Small to medium-sized birds, with moderate to long legs for wading and short, rounded wings. With the exception of the Common Moorhen and Common Coot, which spend much time swimming in the open, rails are mainly terrestrial. Many occur in marshes. They fly reluctantly and feebly, with legs dangling, for a short distance and then drop into cover again. The majority are heard more often than seen, and are most voluble at dusk and at night. Their calls consist of strident or raucous repeated notes. They eat insects, crustaceans, amphibians, fish and vegetable matter. **pp.108–111**

▪ ▪ ▪ Sandgrouse Pterococlidae ▪ ▪ ▪

Cryptically patterned terrestrial birds resembling pigeons in size and shape. The wings are long and pointed. Most sandgrouse are wary and, when disturbed, rise with a clatter of wings, flying off rapidly and directly with fast, regular wingbeats. They walk and run well, foraging mainly for small hard seeds picked up from the ground and sometimes also eating green leaves, shoots, berries, small bulbs and insects. They need to drink every day, and will sometimes travel distances to waterholes. Most sandgrouse have regular drinking times that are characteristic of each species, and they often visit traditional watering places, sometimes gathering in large numbers. Most species are gregarious except when breeding. **pp.112–113**

▪ ▪ ▪ Woodcocks, Snipes, Godwits, Sandpipers, Curlews and Phalaropes Scolopacidae ▪ ▪ ▪

Woodcocks and Snipes Subfamily Scolopacinae

Woodcocks and snipes are small to medium-sized waders with a very long bill, fairly long legs and cryptically patterned plumage. They feed mainly by probing in soft ground and also by picking from the surface. Their diet consists mostly of small aquatic invertebrates. If approached, they usually first crouch on the ground and 'freeze', preferring to rely on their protective plumage pattern to escape detection. They inhabit marshy ground. **pp.114–115**

Godwits, Sandpipers, Curlews, Phalaropes Subfamily Tringinae

The Tringinae are wading birds with quite long to very long legs and a long bill. They feed on small aquatic invertebrates. **pp.116–121**

▪ ▪ ▪ Painted-snipes Rostratulidae ▪ ▪ ▪

Painted-snipes frequent marshes and superficially resemble snipes, but have spectacular plumages. **pp.114–115**

▪ ▪ ▪ Jacanas Jacanidae ▪ ▪ ▪

Jacanas characteristically have very long toes, which enable them to walk over floating vegetation. They inhabit freshwater lakes, ponds and marshes. **pp.122–123**

▪ ▪ ▪ Thick-Knees Burhinidae ▪ ▪ ▪

Medium-sized to large waders, with cryptically patterned plumage. They are mainly crepuscular or nocturnal, and eat invertebrates and small animals. **pp.122–123**

■ ■ **Oystercatchers, Ibisbill, Avocets, Plovers and Lapwings** Charadriidae ■ ■

Oystercatchers, Ibisbill and Avocets Subfamily Recurvirostrinae

Oystercatchers are waders that usually inhabit the seashore and are only vagrants inland. They have all-black or black and white plumage. The bill is long, stout, orange-red and adapted for opening shells of bivalve molluscs. Stilts and avocets have a characteristic long bill, and longer legs in proportion to the body than any other birds except flamingos. They inhabit marshes, lakes and pools. The Ibisbill has a distinctive decurved bill and frequents rivers and streams. Both feed on aquatic invertebrates. **pp.122–123**

Plovers and Lapwings Subfamily Charadriinae

Plovers and lapwings are small to medium-sized waders with rounded head, short neck and short bill. Typically, they forage by running in short spurts, pausing and standing erect, then stooping to pick up invertebrate prey. Their flight is swift and direct. **pp.124–126**

■ ■ ■ **Crab-plover, Pratincoles and Coursers** Glareolidae ■ ■ ■

Crab-plover Subfamily Dromadinae

The Crab-plover is the only species in this subfamily. Usually found singly, in pairs and in small parties, but hundreds occurring at traditional roost sites. Mainly crepuscular. Feeds chiefly on crabs, mudskippers and crustaceans, which it hunts in plover-like manner. **pp.122–123**

Pratincoles and Coursers Subfamily Glareolinae

Coursers and pratincoles have an arched and pointed bill, wide gape and long, pointed wings. Coursers are long-legged and resemble plovers; they feed on the ground. Most pratincoles are short-legged; they catch most of their prey in the air, although they also feed on the ground. All pratincoles live near water, whereas coursers frequent dry grassland and dry, stony areas. **pp.128–129**

■ ■ ■ **Skimmers, Gulls and Terns** Laridae ■ ■ ■

This family comprises the subfamilies Larinae and Alcinae. Only the subfamily Larinae occurs in Northern India, with representatives from three tribes occurring in the region. **pp.128–135**

Skimmers Tribe Rynchopini

Skimmers have very long wings, a short forked tail, a long bill and short red legs and toes, and are black above and white below. They frequent rivers and lakes. **pp.128–129**

Gulls Tribe Larini

Medium-sized to large birds with relatively long, narrow wings, usually a stout bill, moderately long legs and webbed feet. Immatures are brownish and cryptically patterned. In flight, gulls are graceful and soar easily in updraughts. All species swim buoyantly and well. They are highly adaptable, and most species are opportunistic feeders with a varied diet including invertebrates. Most species are gregarious. **pp.130–131**

Terns Tribe Sternini

Small to medium-sized aerial birds with a gull-like body but, generally, more delicately built. The wings are long and pointed, typically narrower than those of the gulls, and the flight is buoyant and graceful. Terns are highly vocal and most species are gregarious. Two main groups of terns occur in Northern India: the Sterna terns and the Chlidonias, or marsh terns. The Sterna terns have a deeply forked tail. Sterna terns mainly eat small fish, tadpoles and crabs caught by hovering and then plunge-diving from the air, often submerging completely, and also by picking prey from the surface. Marsh terns lack a prominent tail-fork and, compared with Sterna terns, are smaller, more compact and short-tailed, and have a more erratic and rather stiff-winged flight. Typically, marsh terns hawk insects or swoop down to pick small prey from the water surface. **pp.132–135**

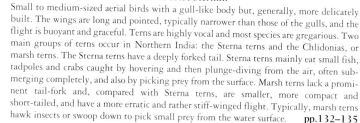

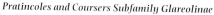

■ ■ ■ Osprey, Hawks, Eagles, Harriers and Vultures etc. Accipitridae ■ ■ ■

A large and varied family of raptors, ranging from the Besra to the huge Himalayan Griffon. In most species, the vultures being an exception, the female is larger than the male and is often duller and brownish. The Accipitridae feed on mammals, birds, reptiles, amphibians, fish, crabs, molluscs and insects – dead or alive. All have a hooked, pointed bill and very acute sight, and all except the vultures have powerful feet with long curved claws. They frequent all habitat types, ranging from dense forest, deserts and mountains to fresh waters.　**pp.136–157**

■ ■ ■ Falcons Falconidae ■ ■ ■

Small to medium-sized birds of prey, which resemble the Accipitridae in having a hooked beak, sharp, curved talons, and remarkable powers of sight and flight. Like other raptors they are mainly diurnal, although a few are crepuscular. Two genera occur: the falconets (*Microhierax*) and the falcons (*Falco*). The falconets prey mainly on insects. Some falcons (e.g. Peregrine) kill flying birds in a surprise attack, often by stooping at great speed; others (e.g. Common Kestrel) hover and then swoop on prey on the ground; and several species (e.g. Eurasian Hobby) hawk insects in flight.　**pp.158–161**

■ ■ ■ Grebes Podicipedidae ■ ■ ■

Aquatic birds adapted for diving from the surface and swimming under the water to catch fish and aquatic invertebrates. Their strong legs are placed near the rear of their almost tailless body, and the feet are lobed. In flight, grebes have an elongated appearance, with the neck extended, and feet hanging lower than the humped back. They usually feed singly, but may form loose congregations in the non-breeding season.　**pp.162–163**

■ ■ ■ Anhingas Anhingidae ■ ■ ■

Large aquatic birds adapted for hunting fish underwater. Anhingas have a long, slender neck and head, long wings and a very long tail.　**pp.162–163**

■ ■ ■ Cormorants Phalacrocoracidae ■ ■ ■

Medium-sized to large aquatic birds, with long neck, hooked bill of moderate length and a long, stiff tail. Cormorants swim with the body low in the water, with the neck straight and the head and bill pointing a little upwards. They eat mainly fish, which are caught by underwater pursuit. In flight, the neck is extended and the head is held slightly above the horizontal. Typically, they often perch for long periods in upright posture on trees, posts or rocks, with spread wings and tail.　**pp.162–163**

■ ■ ■ Herons and Bitterns Ardeidae ■ ■ ■

Medium-sized to large birds with long legs for wading. The diurnal herons have a slender body and long head and neck; the night herons are more squat, with shorter neck and legs. They fly with leisurely flaps, with the legs outstretched and projecting beyond the tail, and nearly always with head and neck drawn back. They frequent marshes and the shores of lakes and rivers. Typically, herons feed by standing motionless at the water's edge, waiting for prey to swim within reach, or by slow stalking in shallow water or on land. Bitterns usually skulk in reedbeds, although occasionally one may forage in the open, and they can clamber about reed stems with agility. Normally they are solitary and crepuscular, and most often seen flying low over reedbeds with slow wingbeats, soon dropping into cover again. When in danger, bitterns freeze, pointing the bill and neck upwards and compressing their feathers so that the whole body appears elongated. The bitterns are characterised by their booming territorial calls. Herons and bitterns feed on a wide variety of aquatic prey.　**pp.164–166**

■ ■ ■ Flamingos Phoenicopteridae ■ ■ ■

Large wading birds with long neck, very long legs, webbed feet and pink plumage. The bill is highly specialised for filter-feeding. Flamingos often occur in huge numbers and are found mainly on salt lakes and lagoons.　**pp.168–169**

■ ■ ■ Ibises and Spoonbills Threskiornithidae ■ ■ ■

Large birds with long neck and legs, partly webbed feet and long, broad wings. Ibises have a long decurved bill, and forage by probing in shallow water, mud and grass. Spoonbills have a long spatulate bill, and catch floating prey in shallow water.　**pp.168–169**

▪ ▪ ▪ Pelicans Pelecanidae ▪ ▪ ▪

Large, aquatic, gregarious fish-eating birds. The wings are long and broad, and the tail is short and rounded. They have a characteristic long, straight, flattened bill, hooked at the tip, and with a large expandable pouch suspended beneath the lower mandible. Many pelicans often fish cooperatively by swimming forward in a semicircular formation, driving the fish into shallow waters; each bird then scoops up fish from the water into its pouch, before swallowing the food. Pelicans fly either in V-formation or in lines, and often soar for considerable periods in thermals. They are powerful fliers, proceeding by steady flaps and with the head drawn back between the shoulders. When swimming, the closed wings are typically held above the back.   **pp.170–171**

▪ ▪ ▪ Storks Ciconiidae ▪ ▪ ▪

Large or very large birds with long bill, neck and legs, long and broad wings, and a short tail. In flight, the legs are extended behind and the neck is outstretched. They have a powerful slow-flapping flight and frequently soar for long periods, often at great heights. They capture fish, frogs, snakes, lizards, large insects, crustaceans and molluscs while walking slowly in marshes, at edges of lakes and rivers, and in grassland.   **pp.172–174**

▪ ▪ ▪ Pittas Pittidae ▪ ▪ ▪

Brilliantly coloured, terrestrial, forest passerines. They are of medium size, stocky and long-legged, with short square tail, stout bill and an erect carriage. Most of their time is spent foraging for invertebrates on the forest floor, flicking leaves and other vegetation, and probing with their strong bill into leaf litter and damp earth. Pittas usually progress on the ground by long hopping bounds. Typically, they are skulking and are often most easily located by their high-pitched whistling calls or songs. They sing in trees or bushes.   **pp.176–177**

▪ ▪ ▪ Broadbills Eurylaimidae ▪ ▪ ▪

Small to medium-sized, plump birds with rounded wings and short legs. Most species have a distinctively broad bill. Typically, they inhabit the middle storey of forest and feed mainly on invertebrates gleaned from leaves and branches. Broadbills are active when foraging, but are often unobtrusive and lethargic at other times.   **pp.176–177**

▪ ▪ ▪ Fairy Bluebirds and Leafbirds Irenidae ▪ ▪ ▪

Small to medium-sized passerines with fairly long, slender bill with the upper mandible decurved at the tip. All are arboreal, typically frequenting thick foliage in the canopy. They search leaves for insects and also feed on berries and nectar. Their flight is swift, but usually only over a short distance.   **pp.176–177**

▪ ▪ ▪ Shrikes Laniidae ▪ ▪ ▪

Medium-sized, predatory passerines with a strong, stout bill, hooked at the tip of the upper mandible, strong legs and feet, a large head, and a long tail with graduated tip. Shrikes search for prey from a vantage point, such as the top of a bush or small tree or post. They swoop down to catch invertebrates or small animals from the ground or in flight. Over long distances their flight is typically undulating. Their calls are harsh, but most have quite musical songs and are good mimics. Shrikes typically inhabit open country with scattered bushes or light scrub.   **pp.178–179**

▪ ▪ ▪ Corvids Corvidae ▪ ▪ ▪

This is very large family, represented in Northern India by four subfamilies (in some cases further subdivided into tribes).   **pp.180–191**

Subfamily Corvinae

Jays, Magpies, Treepies, Choughs, Nutcrackers, Crows, Ravens Tribe Corvini
These are all robust perching birds that differ considerably from each other in appearance, but that have a number of features in common: a fairly long straight bill, very strong feet and legs, and a tuft of nasal bristles extending over the base of the upper mandible. The sexes are alike or almost alike in plumage. They are strong fliers. Most are gregarious, especially when feeding and roosting. Typically, they are noisy birds, uttering loud and discordant squawks, croaks or screeches. The Corvini are highly inquisitive and adaptable.   **pp.180–183**

Woodswallows Tribe Artamini

Plump birds with long, pointed wings, short tail and legs, and a wide gape. They feed on insects, usually captured in flight, and spend prolonged periods on the wing. They perch close together on a bare branch or wire, and often waggle the tail from side to side. **pp.184–185**

Orioles, Cuckooshrikes, Minivets, Flycatcher-Shrikes Tribe Oriolini

Orioles Genus *Oriolus* Medium-sized arboreal passerines that usually keep hidden in the leafy canopy. Orioles have beautiful, fluty, whistling songs and harsh, grating calls. They are usually seen singly, in pairs or in family parties. Their flight is powerful and undulating, with fast wingbeats. They feed mainly on insects and fruit. **pp.184–185**

Cuckooshrikes Genus *Coracina* Arboreal, insectivorous birds that usually keep high in the trees. They are of medium size, with long, pointed wings, a moderately long, rounded tail, and an upright carriage when perched. **pp.184–185**

Minivets Genus *Pericrocotus* Small to medium-sized, brightly coloured passerines with a moderately long tail and an upright stance when perched. They are arboreal, and feed on insects by flitting about in the foliage to glean prey from leaves, buds and bark, sometimes hovering in front of a sprig or making short aerial sallies. They usually keep in pairs in the breeding season, and in small parties when not breeding. When feeding and in flight, they continually utter contact calls. **pp.186–187**

Subfamily Dicrurinae

Fantails Tribe Rhipidurini

Small, confiding, arboreal birds, perpetually on the move in search of insects. Characteristically, they erect and spread the tail like a fan, and droop the wings, while pirouetting and turning from side to side with jerky, restless movements. When foraging, they flit from branch to branch, making frequent aerial sallies after winged insects. They call continually. Fantails are usually found singly or in pairs, and often join mixed hunting parties with other insectivorous birds. **pp.186–187**

Drongos Tribe Dicrurini

Medium-sized passerines with characteristic black and often glossy plumage, long, often deeply forked tail, and a very upright stance when perched. They are mainly arboreal and insectivorous, catching larger, winged insects by aerial sallies from a perch. They are usually found singly or in pairs. Their direct flight is swift, strong and undulating. Drongos are rather noisy, and have a varied repertoire of harsh calls and pleasant whistles; some species are good mimics. **pp.188–189**

Monarchs Tribe Monarchini

Most species are small to medium-sized, with long, pointed wings and a medium-length to long tail. They feed mainly on insects. **pp.190–191**

Ioras Subfamily Aegithininae

Small, fairly lively passerines that feed in trees, mainly on insects and especially caterpillars. **pp.190–191**

Woodshrikes Subfamily Malaconotinae

Medium-sized, arboreal, insectivorous passerines. The bill is stout and hooked, the wings are rounded and the tail is short. **pp.190–191**

■ ■ ■ Dippers Cinclidae ■ ■ ■

Dippers have short wings and tail, and are adapted for feeding on invertebrates in or under running water. They fly low over the water surface on rapidly whirring wings. **pp.190–191**

■ ■ **Thrushes, Shortwings, Old World Flycatchers and Chats** Muscicapidae ■ ■
A large and varied family represented in Northern India by two subfamilies, the second of
which is subdivided into two tribes.   **pp.192–211**

Subfamily Turdinae

Thrushes Genera *Monticola, Myophonus, Zoothera* and *Turdus*   Medium-sized passerines with rather long, strong legs, a slender bill and fairly long wings. On the ground they
progress by hopping. All are insectivorous, and many eat fruit as well. Some species are
chiefly terrestrial and others arboreal. Most thrushes have loud and varied songs, which are
used to proclaim and defend their territories when breeding. Many species gather in flocks
outside the breeding season.   **pp.192–197**

Shortwings Genus *Brachypteryx*   Small, chat-like thrushes with short, rounded wings,
almost square tail and strong legs. They are mainly terrestrial, and inhabit low bushes,
undergrowth or thickets. Shortwings are chiefly insectivorous. They are found singly or in
pairs.   **pp.196–197**

Subfamily Muscicapinae

Old World Flycatchers Tribe Muscicapini

Small insectivorous birds with a small, flattened bill, and bristles at the gape that help in
the capture of flying insects. They normally have a very upright stance when perched.
Many species frequently flick the tail and hold the wings slightly drooped. Generally, flycatchers frequent trees and bushes. Some species regularly perch on a vantage point, from
which they catch insects in mid-air in short aerial sallies or by dropping to the ground,
often returning to the same perch. Other species capture insects while flitting among
branches or by picking them from foliage. Flycatchers are usually found singly or in pairs;
a few join mixed hunting parties of other insectivorous birds.   **pp.198–201**

Chats Tribe Saxicolini

A diverse group of small/medium-sized passerines that includes the chats, bush robins,
magpie robins, redstarts, forktails, cochoas and wheatears. Most are terrestrial or partly terrestrial, some are arboreal, and some are closely associated with water. Their main diet is
insects, and they also consume fruits, especially berries. They forage mainly by hopping
about on the ground in search of prey, or by perching on a low vantage point and then
dropping to the ground on to insects or making short sallies to catch them in the air. They
are found singly or in pairs.   **pp.202–211**

■ ■ ■ **Starlings and Mynas** Sturnidae ■ ■ ■

Robust, medium-sized passerines with strong legs and bill, moderately long wings and a
square tail. The flight is direct; strong and fast in the more pointed-winged species
(*Sturnus*), and rather slower with more deliberate flapping in the more rounded-winged
ones. Most species walk with an upright stance in a characteristic, purposeful, jaunty fashion, broken by occasional short runs and hops. Their calls are often loud, harsh and grating, and the song of many species is a variety of whistles; mimicry is common. Most are
highly gregarious at times. Some starlings are mainly arboreal and feed on fruits and
insects; others are chiefly ground-feeders, and are omnivorous. Many are closely
associated with human cultivation and habitation.   **pp.212–213**

■ ■ ■ **Nuthatches and Wallcreeper** Sittidae ■ ■ ■

Nuthatches and the Wallcreeper are small, energetic passerines with compact body, short
tail, large strong feet and a long bill. The Wallcreeper is adept at clambering over rock
faces. Nuthatches are agile tree climbers. They can move with ease upwards, downwards,
sideways and upside-down over trunks or branches, progressing by a series of jerky hops.
Unlike woodpeckers and treecreepers, they usually begin near the top of a tree and work
down the main trunk or larger branches, often head-first, and do not use the tail as a prop.
Their flight is direct over short distances, and undulating over longer ones. Nuthatches
capture insects and spiders, and also feed on seeds and nuts. They are often found singly
or in pairs; outside the breeding season, they often join foraging flocks of other
insectivorous birds.   **pp.214–215**

■ ■ ■ Treecreepers and Wrens Certhiidae ■ ■ ■

A family of mainly small, rather similar-looking species with two subfamilies.

Treecreepers and Spotted Creeper Subfamily Certhiinae

Small, quiet, arboreal passerines with a slender, decurved bill and, with the exception of Spotted Creeper, a stiff tail, like that of the woodpeckers, that is used as a prop when climbing. Treecreepers forage by creeping up vertical trunks and along the underside of branches, spiralling upwards in a series of jerks in search of insects and spiders; on reaching the top of a tree, they fly to the base of the next one. Their flight is undulating and weak, and is usually only over short distances. Treecreepers are non-gregarious, but outside the nesting season they usually join mixed hunting parties of other insectivorous birds. They inhabit broadleaved and coniferous forest, woodland, groves, and gardens with trees. Thin high-pitched contact calls are used continually. **pp.214–215**

Wrens Subfamily Troglodytinae

Small, plump, insectivorous passerines with rather short, blunt wings, strong legs and tail characteristically held erect. **pp.218–219**

■ ■ ■ Tits Paridae and Long-Tailed Tits Aegithalidae ■ ■ ■

Small, active, highly acrobatic passerines with a short bill and strong feet. Their flight over long distances is undulating. They are mainly insectivorous, although many species also depend on seeds, particularly from trees in winter, and some also eat fruit. They probe bark crevices, search branches and leaves, and frequently hang upside-down from twigs. Tits are chiefly arboreal, but also descend to the ground to feed, hopping about and flicking aside leaves and other debris. They are very gregarious; in the non-breeding season most species join roving flocks of other insectivorous birds. **pp.216–219**

■ ■ ■ Swallows and Martins Hirundinidae ■ ■ ■

Gregarious, rather small passerines with a distinctive slender, streamlined body, long, pointed wings and a small bill. The long-tailed species are often called swallows, and the shorter-tailed species martins. All hawk day-flying insects in swift, agile, sustained flight, sometimes high in the air. Many species have a deeply forked tail, which affords better manoeuvrability. Hirundines catch most of their food while flying in the open. They perch readily on exposed branches and wires. **pp.220–223**

■ ■ ■ Kinglets Regulidae ■ ■ ■

Tiny passerines with bright crown feathers, represented by only one species in the region, Goldcrest. Typically inhabits the canopy of coniferous forest, frequently hovering to catch insects. They often join mixed feeding parties. **pp.240–241**

■ ■ ■ Bulbuls Pycnonotidae ■ ■ ■

Medium-sized passerines with soft, fluffy plumage, rather short and rounded wings, medium-long to long tail, slender bill and short, weak legs. Bulbuls feed on berries and other fruits, often supplemented by insects, and sometimes also nectar and buds of trees and shrubs. Many species are noisy, especially when feeding. Typically, bulbuls have a variety of cheerful, loud, chattering, babbling and whistling calls. Most species are gregarious in the non-breeding season. **pp.224–225**

■ ■ ■ Grey Hypocolius Hypocoliidae ■ ■ ■

Grey Hypocolius is the only member of this family. Feeds mainly on berries, and forages by hopping and clambering about within trees and bushes,. Flight is strong and direct, with rapid wingbeats and occasional swooping glides or high circling. Settles on the tops of bushes and remains still for long periods. It raises its nape feathers when excited or alarmed. Often forms flocks in winter. **pp.224–225**

■ ■ ■ Cisticolas and Prinias Cisticolidae ■ ■ ■

Cisticolas Genus *Cisticola* Tiny, short-tailed, insectivorous passerines. The tail is longer in winter than in summer. They are often found in grassy habitats, and many have distinctive aerial displays. **pp.226–229**

Prinias Genus *Prinia*   Prinias have a long, graduated tail that is longer in winter than in summer. Most inhabit grassland, marsh vegetation or scrub. They forage by gleaning insects and spiders from vegetation, and some species also feed on the ground. When perched, the tail is often held cocked and slightly fanned. Flight is weak and jerky.   **pp.226–229**

■ ■ ■ **White-eyes** Zosteropidae ■ ■ ■

Small or very small insectivorous passerines with a slightly decurved and pointed bill, a brush-tipped tongue, and a white ring around each eye. White-eyes frequent forest, forest edge, and bushes in gardens.   **pp.228–230**

■ ■ ■ **Warblers, Laughingthrushes and Babblers** Sylviidae ■ ■ ■

A huge and varied family of mostly small species.   **pp.230–251**

Warblers Subfamily Acrocephalinae

A large group of small, active perching birds with a fine pointed bill. Insects and spiders form their main diet; some species also consume berries, seeds and nectar. They usually capture their prey by gleaning from foliage, but sometimes also from the ground. Warblers inhabit all types of vegetation, often in dense habitats.   **pp.230–241**

Tesias   Tiny, active, almost tailless warblers. They inhabit forest and are mainly terrestrial.   **pp.228–229**

Bush Warblers   Medium-sized warblers with rounded wings and tail. They inhabit marshes, grassland and forest undergrowth, and are usually found singly. Bush warblers call frequently, and are usually heard more often than seen. *Cettia* species have surprisingly loud voices, and some can be identified by their distinctive melodious songs. Bush warblers seek insects and spiders by actively flitting and hopping about in vegetation close to the ground. They are reluctant to fly, and usually cover only short distances at low level before dropping into dense cover again. When excited, they flick their wings and tail.   **pp.230–231**

Warblers Genus *Locustella*   Very skulking, medium-sized warblers with a rounded tail, usually found singly. Characteristically, they keep low down or on the ground among dense vegetation, walking furtively and scurrying off when startled. They fly at low level, flitting between plants, or rather jerkily over longer distances, ending in a sudden dive into cover.   **pp.232–233**

Warblers Genus *Acrocephalus*   Medium-sized to large warblers with prominent bill and rounded tail. They usually occur singly. Many species are skulking, typically keeping low down in dense vegetation. Most frequent marshy habitats, and are able to clamber about readily on reeds and other vertical stems of marsh plants. Their songs are harsh and often monotonous.   **pp.234–235**

Warblers Genus *Hippolais*   Medium-sized warblers with a large bill, square-ended tail, and rather sloping forehead and peaked crown giving a distinctive domed head shape. Their songs are harsh and varied. They clamber about vegetation with a rather clumsy action.   **pp.236–237**

Tailorbirds   Birds with a long, decurved bill, short wings, and a graduated tail held characteristically cocked.   **pp.228–229**

Tit Warblers   Small warblers with soft, copious plumage. Tit warblers inhabit scrub or coniferous forest.   **pp.228–229**

Warblers Genus *Phylloscopus* Rather small, slim and short-billed warblers. Useful identification features are: voice; strength of supercilium; colour of underparts, rump, bill and legs; and presence or absence of wing-bars, of coronal bands or of white on the tail. The coloration of upperparts and underparts and the presence or prominence of wing-bars are affected by wear. Leaf warblers are fast-moving and restless, hopping and creeping about actively and often flicking the wings. They mostly glean small insects and spiders from foliage, twigs and branches, often first disturbing prey by hovering and fluttering; they also make short fly-catching sallies. **pp.236–241**

Warblers Genera *Seicercus* and *Abroscopus* Small and active warblers. They feed in a similar manner to *Phylloscopus* warblers, by gleaning insects from foliage and twigs and making frequent aerial sallies, but have a broader bill and brighter plumage than those species. **pp.240–241**

Grassbirds Subfamily Megalurinae
Brownish warblers with a longish tail. They inhabit damp tall grassland. The males perform song flights in the breeding season. **pp.234–235**

Laughingthrushes Subfamily Garrulacinae
Medium-sized, long-tailed passerines that are gregarious even in the breeding season. At the first sign of danger, they characteristically break into a concert of loud hissing, chattering and squealing. They often feed on the ground, moving along with long, springy hops, rummaging among leaf litter, flicking leaves aside and into the air, and digging for food with their strong bill. Their flight is short and clumsy, the birds flying from tree to tree in follow-my-leader fashion **pp.242–243**

Babblers Subfamily Sylviinae, Tribe Timaliini
A large and diverse group of small to medium-sized passerines. They have soft, loose plumage, short or fairly short wings, and strong feet and legs. The sexes are alike in most species. With the exception of most wren babblers, the members of this tribe associate in flocks outside the breeding season, and some species do so throughout the year. Babbler flocks are frequently a component of mixed-species feeding parties. Most babblers have a wide range of chatters, rattles and whistles; some have a melodious song. Many are terrestrial or inhabit bushes or grass close to the ground, while other species are arboreal. Babblers are chiefly insectivorous, and augment their diet with fruits, seeds and nectar. Arboreal species collect food from leaves, moss, lichen and bark; terrestrial species forage by probing, digging and tossing aside dead foliage. **pp.244–251**

Sylvia Warblers Subfamily Sylviinae, Tribe Sylviini
Small to medium-sized passerines with a fine bill, closely resembling the true warblers. Typically, they inhabit bushes and scrub, and feed chiefly by gleaning insects from foliage and twigs; they sometimes also consume berries in autumn and winter. **pp.232–233**

■ ■ ■ Larks Alaudidae ■ ■ ■
Terrestrial, generally small-sized, cryptically coloured passerines. They usually walk and run on the ground and often have a very elongated hindclaw. Their flight is strong and undulating. Larks take a wide variety of food, including insects, molluscs, arthropods, seeds, flowers, buds and leaves. Many species have a melodious song, which is often delivered in a distinctive, steeply climbing or circling aerial display, but also from a conspicuous low perch. They live in a wide range of open habitats, including grassland and cultivation. **pp.252–255**

■ ■ ■ Flowerpeckers, Sunbirds and Spiderhunters
Nectariniidae, *Subfamily Nectariniinae* ■ ■ ■

These birds are represented in Northern India by two discrete tribes.

Flowerpeckers Tribe Dicaeini

Very small passerines with short beak and tail, and with a tongue adapted for nectar-feeding. They usually frequent the tree canopy and feed mainly on soft fruits, berries and nectar, but also on small insects and spiders. Many species are especially fond of mistletoe (*Loranthus*) berries. Flowerpeckers are very active, continually flying about restlessly, and twisting and turning in different attitudes when perched, while calling frequently with high-pitched notes. Normally they live singly or in pairs; some species form small parties in the non-breeding season.

pp.256–257

Sunbirds and Spiderhunters Tribe Nectariniini

Sunbirds and spiderhunters have a bill and tongue adapted to feed on nectar; they also eat small insects and spiders. The bill is long, thin and curved for probing the corollas of flowers. The tongue, which is very long, tubular and extensible far beyond the bill, is used to draw out nectar.

pp.256–259

Sunbirds   Small to very small passerines that feed mainly at the blossoms of flowering trees and shrubs. They flit and dart actively from flower to flower, clambering over the blossoms, often hovering momentarily in front of them, and clinging acrobatically to twigs. Sunbirds usually keep singly or in pairs, although several may congregate in flowering trees and some species join mixed foraging flocks. They have sharp, metallic calls and high-pitched trilling and twittering songs.

pp.256–259

Spiderhunters   Similar in foraging behaviour to the sunbirds, but are larger and bulkier, have a longer bill and utter explosive chattering calls. The sexes are alike. They are usually found singly or in pairs.

pp.258–259

■ ■ ■ Passeridae ■ ■ ■

Sparrows and Snowfinches Subfamily Passerinae

Small passerines with a thick conical bill. There are four genera: *Passer*, the true sparrows, some of which are closely associated with human habitation; *Petronia*, the rock sparrows, which inhabit dry rocky country or light scrub; and *Montifringilla* and *Pyrgilauda*, the snowfinches, which occur in mountainous areas. They are mainly brown and grey in coloration, sometimes with black, except for the snowfinches, which always have some conspicuous white in the plumage. Most species feed on seeds, taken on or near the ground; snowfinches also consume a high proportion of insects when available. The *Passer* sparrows are rather noisy, uttering a variety of harsh, chirping notes; the others have more varied songs and rather harsh calls.

pp.260–261

Wagtails and Pipits Subfamily Motacillinae

Small, slender, terrestrial birds with long legs, relatively long toes and a thin, pointed bill. Some wagtails exhibit wide geographical plumage variation. All walk with a deliberate gait and run rapidly. The flight is undulating and strong. Most wagtails wag the tail up and down, and so do some pipits. They feed mainly by picking insects from the ground as they walk along, or by making short rapid runs to capture insects they have flushed; they also catch prey in mid-air. Song flights are characteristic of many pipits. Both wagtails and pipits call in flight, and this is often a useful identification feature. They are usually found singly or in pairs in the breeding season and in scattered flocks in autumn and winter.

pp.262–267

Accentors Subfamily Prunellinae

Small, compact birds resembling *Passer* sparrows in appearance, but with a more slender and pointed bill. Accentors forage quietly and unobtrusively on the ground, moving by hopping or in a shuffling walk; some species also run. In summer accentors are chiefly insectivorous, and in winter they feed mainly on seeds. Their flight is usually low over the ground and sustained only over short distances.

pp.268–269

Weavers Subfamily Ploceinae

Small, rather plump, finch-like passerines with a large, conical bill. Adults feed chiefly on seeds and grain, supplemented by invertebrates; the young are often fed on invertebrates. Weavers inhabit grassland, marshes, cultivation and very open woodland. They are highly gregarious, roosting and nesting communally, and are noted for their elaborate, roofed nests. **pp.270–271**

Estrildine Finches Subfamily Estrildinae

Small, slim passerines with a short, stout, conical beak. They feed chiefly on small seeds, which they pick up from the ground or gather by clinging to stems and pulling them directly from seedheads. Their gait is a hop or occasionally a walk. Outside the breeding season all species are gregarious. Flight is fast and undulating. **pp.270–271**

▪ ▪ ▪ Finches and Buntings Fringillidae ▪ ▪ ▪

Finches Subfamily Fringillinae

Small to medium-sized passerines with a strong conical bill used for eating seeds. They forage on the ground, although some species also feed on seedheads of tall herbs, and blossoms or berries of bushes and trees. Their flight is fast and undulating. Finches are highly gregarious outside the breeding season. **pp.272–279**

Buntings Subfamily Emberizinae

Small to medium-sized, terrestrial passerines with a strong, conical bill designed for shelling seeds, usually of grasses; adults also eat insects in summer. They forage by hopping or creeping on the ground. Their flight is undulating. Buntings are usually gregarious outside the breeding season, feeding and roosting in flocks. They occur in a wide variety of open habitats. **pp.280–283**

1 Snow Partridge *Lerwa lerwa* 38 cm

ADULT Vermiculated dark brown and white upperparts, chestnut streaking on underparts, and red bill and legs. Often occurs in large parties, and can be very tame. High-altitude rocky and grassy slopes with scrub. Resident; summers mainly 4000–5000 m, winters down to 3050 m. HP: nr, JK: nr, UR: nr.

2 Himalayan Snowcock *Tetraogallus himalayensis* 72 cm

ADULT Very large, with chestnut neck stripes, whitish breast contrasting with dark grey underparts, and chestnut flank stripes. In flight, shows extensive white in primaries, little or no white in secondaries, and greyish rump. Call is not markedly different from Tibetan, a far-carrying *cour-lee-whi-whi*. High-altitude rocky slopes and alpine meadows. Resident; 4250–5500 m (–5900 m). HP: nr, JK: nr, UR: nr.

3 Tibetan Snowcock *Tetraogallus tibetanus* 51 cm

ADULT Large size, white ear-covert patch, grey bands across breast, and white underparts with black flank stripes. In flight, shows only a small amount of white in primaries, extensive white patch in secondaries, and chestnut rump. Call is a far-carrying *keep-kweep-kweep*. High-altitude rocky slopes and alpine meadows. Resident; summers mainly 4500–5500 m, winters down to 3650 m. HP: nr, JK: lcr.

4 Chukar *Alectoris chukar* 38 cm

ADULT Black gorget encircling throat, barring on flanks, and red bill and legs. Call is a rapidly repeated *chuck, chuck-aa*. Open rocky or grassy hills; dry terraced cultivation. Resident; mainly 2100–3960 m. HP: nr, JK: cr, UR: lcr.

5 Grey Francolin *Francolinus pondicerianus* 33 cm

ADULT Buffish throat with fine dark necklace. Finely barred upperparts with shaft streaking, and finely barred underparts. Sexes similar, but female lacks spurs. Male usually calls from vantage point; a rapidly repeated *khateeja-khateeja-khateeja*. Dry grass and thorn scrub. Resident. DE: cr, GU: cr, HA: cr, HP: nr, JK: nr, MP: cr, PU: cr, RA: lcr, UP: cr, UR: lcr.

6 Black Francolin *Francolinus francolinus* 34 cm

a MALE and **b** FEMALE Male has black face with white ear-covert patch, rufous neck band, and black underparts with white spotting. Female has rufous hind-neck, buffish supercilium and dark eye-stripe, streaked appearance to upperparts, and heavily barred or spotted underparts. Male usually calls from vantage point; a loud, harsh *kar-kar, kee, ke-kee*. Cultivation, tall grass and scrub in plains and hills. Resident; up to 2050 m. DE: cr, GU: lcr, HA: nr, HP: nr, JK: nr, MP: nr, PU: cr, RA: lcr, UP: lcr, UR: lcr.

7 Painted Francolin *Francolinus pictus* 31 cm

a MALE and **b** FEMALE Rufous-orange face (and often throat), and bold white spotting on upperparts and underparts. Sexes rather similar. Call is a *click...cheek-cheek-keray*, very similar to that of Black Francolin. Tall grassland and cultivation with scattered trees; open thin forest. Resident. GU: cr, MP: cr, RA: nr, UP: nr.

8 Swamp Francolin *Francolinus gularis* 37 cm

ADULT Rufous-orange throat, finely barred upperparts, and bold white streaking on underparts. Sexes similar, but female lacks spurs. Call is a long series of sharp notes, *chuill-chuill-chuill...* Often wades in water, or climbs onto reeds in deep water. Tall wet grassland and marshes. Globally threatened (Vulnerable). Resident. UP: lcr.

9 Tibetan Partridge *Perdix hodgsoniae* 31 cm

ADULT Black patch on white face, rufous collar, and black and rufous barring on underparts. Occurs in large coveys outside breeding season. Call is a rattling and repeated *scherrrrreck-scherrrrreck*. High-altitude semi-desert, rock and scrub slopes. Resident in the trans-Himalayas; winters 3700–4100 m, summers up to 5000 m. HP: nr, JK: nr, UR: nr.

1

Common Quail *Coturnix coturnix* 20 cm
a MALE and **b** FEMALE Male has black 'anchor' mark on throat (which may be lacking), and buff or rufous breast with pale streaking. Female lacks 'anchor' mark and has blackish spotting on buffish breast. Song is a far-carrying *whit, whit-tit*, repeated in quick succession. Crops and grassland. DE: np, GU: nr, HA: nwp, HP: np, JK: np, MP: lcr, PU: cr, RA: nr, UP: lcr, UR: cwp.

2

Rain Quail *Coturnix coromandelica* 18 cm
a MALE and **b** FEMALE Male has strongly patterned head and neck, black on breast, and streaking on flanks. Female smaller than female Common, with unbarred primaries. Crops, grassland, grass and scrub jungle. DE: ns, GU: cr, HA: ns, HP: ns, MP: cr, PU: nr, RA: ns, UP: cs, UR: cs.

3

Blue-breasted Quail *Coturnix chinensis* 14 cm
a MALE and **b** FEMALE Small size. Male has black-and-white head pattern, slaty-blue flanks, and chestnut belly. Female has rufous forehead and supercilium, and barred breast and flanks. Song is a high-pitched, descending *ti-yu* or *quee-kee-kew*. Wet grassland, field edges and scrub. MP: nr, RA: nr, UP: nr, UR: nr.

4

Jungle Bush Quail *Perdicula asiatica* 17 cm
a MALE and **b** FEMALE Male has barred underparts, rufous-orange throat, rufous supercilium edged with white, white moustachial stripe, brown ear-coverts and orange-buff vent. Female has vinaceous-buff underparts, with head pattern similar to male. Rufous throat of female distinct from underparts. Dry grass and scrub, deciduous forest. DE: lcr, GU: lcr, HA: lcr, HP: nr, JK: nr, MP: lcr, PU: cr, RA: lcr, UP: lcr, UR: lcr.

5

Rock Bush Quail *Perdicula argoondah* 17 cm
a MALE and **b** FEMALE Male has barred underparts, and vinaceous-buff ear-coverts and throat; lacks white moustachial stripe. Female has vinaceous-buff underparts, including throat and ear-coverts, and short, whitish supercilium. Head pattern of female much plainer than in female Jungle. Dry rocky and sandy areas with thorn scrub in plains and foothills. GU: cr, HA: nr?, MP: nr, RA: lcr, UP: nr.

6

Painted Bush Quail *Perdicula erythrorhyncha* 18 cm
a MALE and **b** FEMALE Black spotting on upperparts and flanks, and red bill and legs. Male has white supercilium and throat, and black chin and mask. Female has rufous supercilium, ear-coverts and throat. Scrub in plains and foothills. MP: nr.

7

Small Buttonquail *Turnix sylvatica* 13 cm
MALE Very small size and pointed tail. Buff edges to scapulars form prominent lines, and rufous mantle and coverts are boldly fringed in buff, creating scaly appearance. Underparts are similar to many Yellow-legged, but very different to those of Barred. Has repetitive booming call. Bill grey and legs are pinkish. Tall grassland. DE: v, GU: lcr, HA: nr, HP: nr, MP: nr, PU: nr, RA: nr, UP: nr, UR: nr.

8

Yellow-legged Buttonquail *Turnix tanki* 15–16 cm
a MALE and **b** FEMALE Yellow legs and bill. Comparatively uniform upperparts (lacking scaly or striped appearance), and buff coverts with bold black spotting. Pattern and coloration of underparts very different from Barred. Utters a low-pitched hoot, repeated with increasing strength to become human-like moan. Scrub and grassland and crops. DE: v, GU: lcr, HA: nr, HP: nr, MP: nr, PU: nr, RA: nr, UP: nr.

9

Barred Buttonquail *Turnix suscitator* 15 cm
a MALE and **b** FEMALE Grey bill and legs, and bold black barring on sides of neck, breast and wing-coverts. Orange-rufous flanks and belly clearly demarcated from barred breast. Female has black throat and centre of breast. Utters a motorcycle-like *drr-r-r-r-r-r-r*, and a far-carrying *hoon-hoon-hoon-hoon*. Scrub, grassland, and field edges. DE: lcr, GU: cr, HA: nr, HP: nr, MP: nr, PU: nr, RA: nr, UP: nr, UR: nr.

1 Hill Partridge *Arborophila torqueola* 28 cm

a MALE and **b** FEMALE Male has rufous crown and ear-coverts, black eye-patch and eye-stripe, white neck sides streaked with black, and white collar. Female has black barring on mantle, and rufous-orange fore-neck lacks black lower border (which is present in Rufous-throated). Grey or brown legs and feet. Call is a single mournful, drawn-out whistle, repeated two or three times, followed by a series of three to six double whistles; call often preceded by a shrill, continuous *kwik kwik kwik kwik kwik*. thought to be female's call. Broadleaved evergreen forest; mainly 1830–3200 m (–3550 m). HP: nr, UR: nr.

2 Rufous-throated Partridge *Arborophila rufogularis* 27 cm

a MALE and **b** FEMALE Greyish-white supercilium, diffuse whitish moustachial stripe, unbarred mantle, and black border between rufous-orange fore-neck and grey breast. Pinkish or red legs and feet. Sexes similar. Call is a mournful double whistle *wheea-whu* repeated constantly and on slightly ascending scale, the first note prolonged and the second short and sharp. Broadleaved evergreen forest; mainly 1450–1830 m (250–2050 m). UR: nr.

3 Red Spurfowl *Galloperdix spadicea* 36 cm

a MALE and **b** FEMALE Red facial skin and legs/feet. Male has brownish-grey head and neck, and rufous body. Female has black mottling on upperparts, and barred underparts. Scrub, bamboo thickets and secondary growth. GU: nr, MP: cr, RA: nr, UP: nr, UR: nr.

4 Painted Spurfowl *Galloperdix lunulata* 32 cm

a MALE and **b** FEMALE Dark bill and legs/feet. Male has greenish-black head and neck barred with white, chestnut-red upperparts and yellowish-buff underparts with spotting and barring. Female is dark brown, with chestnut supercilium and forehead, and buff throat and malar stripe; lacks red orbital skin. Thorn scrub and bamboo thickets. MP: nr, RA: nr.

5 Himalayan Quail *Ophrysia superciliosa* 25 cm

a MALE and **b** FEMALE Red bill and legs/feet. Male has black-and-white head pattern. Female is boldly spotted and streaked with black. Long grass and brush on steep slopes. Globally threatened (Critical). UR: presumed extinct.

1 Western Tragopan *Tragopan melanocephalus* M 68–73 cm, F 60 cm

a MALE and **b** FEMALE Male has orange fore-neck, blackish underparts, that are boldly spotted with white, red hind-neck, and red facial skin. Female is dull greyish-brown in coloration, with white spotting on underparts. Female Satyr is more rufous in coloration. Call is a nasal, wailing *khuwaah*, repeated in bouts of 7–15 calls, likened to the wailing of a child or goat. Also a more abrupt *waa, waa, waa* when alarmed. Temperate and subalpine forest. Globally threatened (Vulnerable). HP: nr, JK: nr, UR: nr.

2 Satyr Tragopan *Tragopan satyra* M 67–72 cm, F 57.5 cm

a MALE and **b** FEMALE Male has red underparts with black-bordered white spots, and olive-brown coloration to upperparts. Female is rufous-brown with white streaking and spotting. Call is a deep, wailing, drawn-out *wah, waah! oo-ah! oo-aaaaa!* uttered 12–14 times mainly at dawn, the series rising in volume and becoming more protracted; also a *wah wah* at any time. Moist evergreen forest with dense undergrowth; summers mainly 2500–3800 m, winters down to 2100 m. UR: nr.

3 Koklass Pheasant *Pucrasia macrolopha* M 58–64 cm, F 52.5–56 cm

a MALE and **b** FEMALE Male has bottle-green head and ear-tufts, chestnut on underparts, and streaked appearance to upperparts. Female has white throat, short buff ear-tufts and heavily streaked body. Both sexes have wedge-shaped tail. Call of male is a far-carrying, raucous *kok, kark, kuku...kukuk*. Conifer, oak and rhododendron forests; summers mainly 2680–3200 m (–3500 m), winters down to 213 m. HP: cr, JK: cr, UR: lcr.

4 Himalayan Monal *Lophophorus impejanus* M 70 cm, F 63.5 cm

a MALE and **b** FEMALE Male is iridescent green, copper and purple, with white patch on back and cinnamon-brown tail. Female has white throat, short crest, boldly streaked underparts, white crescent on uppertail-coverts and narrow white tip to tail. Both sexes utter a series of upward-inflected whistles, *kur-leiu* or *kleeh-vick*, which are often strung together, alternated with higher-pitched *kleeh* calls. Summers on rocky and grass-covered slopes; winters in forest; summers chiefly 3300–4570 m (–2500 m), winters down to 2500 m. HP: nr, JK: nr, UR: nr.

1 Red Junglefowl *Gallus gallus* M 65–75 cm, F 42–46 cm

a MALE and **b** FEMALE Male has red comb and wattles, orange and golden-yellow neck hackles, blackish-brown underparts, and long greenish-black sickle-shaped tail. In eclipse plumage, male lacks neck hackles and elongated central tail feathers. Female has naked, reddish face, black-streaked golden 'shawl', and rufous-brown underparts streaked with buff. Male's call at dawn and dusk is a loud *cock-a-doodle-doo*, very similar to the crowing of a domestic cockerel. Forest undergrowth and scrub; usually below 300 m (–1280 m). GU: nr, HA: nr, HP: lcr, JK: nr, MP: lcr, PU: nr, UP: lcr, UR: lcr.

2 Grey Junglefowl *Gallus sonneratii* M 70–80 cm, F 38 cm

a MALE and **b** FEMALE Male has 'shawl' of white and pale yellow spotting, and golden-yellow spotting on scapulars. Eclipse male lacks neck hackles and elongated tail feathers. Female has white streaking on underparts. Male's call is a loud *kuk-ka-kurruk-ka*, repeated at regular intervals. Forest undergrowth, secondary growth and bamboo thickets. GU: nr, MP: lcr, RA: nr.

3 Kalij Pheasant *Lophura leucomelanos* M 65–73 cm, F 50–60 cm

a MALE and **b** FEMALE Both sexes have red facial skin and down-curved tail. The race occurring in the western Himalayas is *L. l. hamiltonii*. Male has white or grey-brown crest, broad white barring on rump and heavily scaled upperparts. Female is reddish brown, with greyish-buff fringes producing scaly appearance. Calls include a crowing, described as a loud whistling chuckle or *chirrup*. All types of forest with dense undergrowth; 245–3050 m (–3700 m). HA: nr?, HP: cr, JK: nr, PU: nr, UR: lcr.

4 Cheer Pheasant *Catreus wallichii* M 90–118 cm, F 61–76 cm

a c MALE and **b** FEMALE Long, broadly barred tail, pronounced crest and red facial skin. Male is more cleanly and strongly marked than female, with pronounced barring on mantle, unmarked neck and broader barring across tail. Utters distinctive pre-dawn and dusk contact calls, including high piercing whistles, *chewewoo*. Steep, craggy hillsides with scrub, secondary growth. Globally threatened (Vulnerable). 1800–3050 m. HP: nr, UR: nr.

5 Indian Peafowl *Pavo cristatus* M 180–230 cm, F 90–100 cm

a MALE and **b** FEMALE Male has blue neck and breast, and spectacular glossy green train of elongated uppertail-covert feathers with numerous ocelli. Female has whitish face and throat, white belly, and lacks elongated uppertail-coverts. Call is a trumpeting, far-carrying and mournful *kee-ow, kee-ow, kee-ow*. Dense riverine vegetation and open sal forest; mainly below 300 m. DE: cr, GU: cr, HA: cr, HP: lcr, JK: nr, MP: cr, PU: cr, RA: lcr, UP: cr, UR: lcr.

1a

1b

2a

2b

3a

3b

4a

4b

4c

5a

5b

2125 | 14
JAIPUR

1 Fulvous Whistling-duck *Dendrocygna bicolor* 51 cm

a **b** ADULT and **c** JUVENILE Larger than Lesser, with bigger, squarer head and larger bill. Adult distinguished from adult Lesser by warmer rufous-orange head and neck, dark blackish line down hind-neck, dark striations on neck, more prominent streaking on flanks, indistinct chestnut-brown patch on forewing and white band across uppertail-coverts. Freshwater wetlands. DE: v, MP: nr, UP: nr.

2 Lesser Whistling-duck *Dendrocygna javanica* 42 cm

a **b** ADULT and **c** JUVENILE Smaller than Fulvous Whistling-duck, and separated from that species by greyish-buff head and neck, dark-brown crown, lack of well-defined dark line down hind-neck, bright chestnut patch on forewing, and chestnut uppertail-coverts. Both species of whistling-duck have rather weak, deep-flapping flight, when they show dark upperwing and underwing, and are very noisy with much whistling. Wetlands. DE: lcs, GU: cr, HA: lcs, HP: np, MP: lcr, PU: nw, RA: nr, UP: lcr, UR: lcs.

3 White-headed Duck *Oxyura leucocephala* 43–48 cm

a MALE and **b** FEMALE Swollen base to bill, and pointed tail, which is often held erect. Male has blue bill, white head with black cap. Female has grey bill and striped head. Large fresh waters, lakes and brackish lagoons. Globally threatened (Endangered). DE: v, HA: v, JK: v, PU: v, RA: v, UP, v.

4 Comb Duck *Sarkidiornis melanotos* 56–76 cm

a **b** MALE, **c** FEMALE and **d** JUVENILE Whitish head, speckled with black, and whitish underparts with incomplete narrow black breast-band. Upperwing and underwing blackish. Male has fleshy comb. Comb lacking in female and she is much smaller with duller upperparts. Pools in well-wooded country. DE: nr, GU: nr, HA: nr, MP: nr, PU: ns, RA: nr, UP: lcr, UR: nr.

5 Pink-headed Duck *Rhodonessa caryophyllacea* 60 cm

a MALE and **b** FEMALE Male has pink head and bill, and dark brown body. Female has greyish-pink head and duller brown body. In flight, pale fawn secondaries contrast with dark forewing, and pinkish underwing contrasts with dark body. Pools and marshes in elephant-grass jungle. Globally threatened (Critical) PU: probably extinct, UP: probably extinct.

2128 114
RANTHURNBOR

1a

1b

2b

2a

1c

2c

4a

4c

4b

4d

3a

3b

5b

5a

1

Greylag Goose *Anser anser* 75–90 cm
a **b** ADULT and **c** JUVENILE Large grey goose with pink bill and legs. Shows pale grey forewing in flight. *See* Appendix for comparison with Greater White-fronted Goose and Lesser White-fronted Goose. Crops, lakes and large rivers. DE: cw, GU: nw, HA: cw, HP: nw, JK: nw, MP: nw, PU: cw, RA: nw, UP: cw, UR: lcw.

2

Bar-headed Goose *Anser indicus* 71–76 cm
a **b** ADULT and **c** JUVENILE Adult has white head with black banding, and white line down grey neck. Has black-tipped yellowish bill, and yellowish legs. Juvenile has white face and dark-grey crown and hind-neck. Plumage paler steel-grey, with paler grey forewing, compared with Greylag. Large rivers and lakes. DE: cw, GU: nw, HA: cw, HP: nw, JK: ns, MP: lcw, PU: lcw, RA: lcw, UP: cw, UR: lcw.

3

Ruddy Shelduck *Tadorna ferruginea* 61–67 cm
a **b** MALE and **c** FEMALE Rusty-orange, with buffish head; white upperwing- and underwing-coverts contrast with black remiges in flight. Breeding male has black neck-band. Wetlands. DE: cw, GU: cw, HA: cw, HP: nw, JK: ns, MP: lcw, PU: lcw, RA: lcw, UP: cw, UR: cw.

4

Common Shelduck *Tadorna tadorna* 58–67 cm
a **b** MALE, **c** FEMALE and **d** **e** JUVENILE Adult has greenish-black head and neck, and largely white body with chestnut breast-band and black scapular stripe. Female is very similar to male, but slightly duller, and lacks knob on bill. Juvenile lacks breast-band and has sooty-brown upperparts. White upperwing- and underwing-coverts contrast with black remiges in flight in all plumages. Wetlands. DE: nw, GU: nw, HA: nw, MP: v, PU: nw, RA: nw, UP: nw, UR: nw.

1a

1b

1c

2a

2b

2c

3a

3b

3c

4a

4b

4c

4d

4e

ZIZZLILI RAHTHANTBOR

1

Gadwall *Anas strepera* 39–43 cm

a **b** MALE and **c** **d** FEMALE White patch on inner secondaries in all plumages. Male is mainly grey with white belly and dark patch at rear; bill is dark grey. Female similar to female Mallard, but has orange sides to dark bill and clear-cut white belly. Wetlands. DE: cw, GU: cw, HA: cw, HP: nw, JK: np, MP: cw, PU: cw, RA: lcw, UP: cw, UR: cw.

2

Falcated Duck *Anas falcata* 48–54 cm

a **b** MALE and **c** **d** FEMALE Male has bottle-green head with maned hind-neck, and elongated black-and-grey tertials; shows pale grey forewing in flight. Female has rather plain greyish head, a dark bill, dark spotting and scalloping on brown underparts, and greyish-white fringes to exposed tertials; shows greyish forewing and white greater-covert bar in flight, but does not show striking white belly (*compare with* female Eurasian Wigeon). Lakes and large rivers. DE: v, GU: v, HA: v, PU: v, RA: v, UP: v, UR: v.

3

Eurasian Wigeon *Anas penelope* 45–51 cm

a **b** MALE and **c** **d** FEMALE Male has yellow forehead and fore-crown, chestnut head and pinkish breast; shows white forewing in flight. Female has rather uniform head, breast and flanks. In all plumages, shows white belly and rather pointed tail in flight. Male has distinctive whistled *wheeooo* call. Wetlands. DE: cw, GU: cw, HA: cw, HP: np, JK: np, MP: nw, PU: nw, RA: lcw, UP: nw, UR: cw.

4

Mallard *Anas platyrhynchos* 50–65 cm

a **b** MALE and **c** **d** FEMALE In all plumages, has white-bordered purplish speculum. Male has yellow bill, dark green head and purplish-chestnut breast. Female is pale brown and boldly patterned with dark brown; bill variable, patterned mainly in dull orange and dark brown. Wetlands. DE: nw, GU: nw, HA: nw, HP: nw, JK: ns/cw, MP: nw, PU: nw, RA: nw, UP: lcw, UR: nw.

5

Spot-billed Duck *Anas poecilorhyncha* 58–63 cm

a **b** MALE and **c** FEMALE Yellow tip to bill, dark crown and eye-stripe, spotted breast and boldly scalloped flanks, and white tertials. Sexes similar, but male has red loral spot and is more strongly marked than female. Wetlands. DE: cr, GU: cr, HA: cr, HP: nr, JK: nr, MP: nr, PU: cr, RA: lcr, UP: cr, UR: lcr.

1

Cotton Pygmy-goose *Nettapus coromandelianus* 30–37 cm

a **b** MALE, **c** ECLIPSE MALE and **d** **e** FEMALE Small size. Male has broad white band across wing, and female has white trailing edge to wing. Male has white head and neck, black cap, and black breast-band. Eclipse male and female have dark stripe through eye. Vegetation-covered wetlands. DE: ns, GU: lcr, HA: ns, HP: nw, JK: v, MP: cr, PU: ns, RA: lcr, UP: cr, UR: ns.

2

Common Teal *Anas crecca* 34–38 cm

a **b** MALE and **c** **d** FEMALE Male has chestnut head with green band behind eye, white stripe along scapulars and yellowish patch on undertail-coverts. Female has rather uniform head, lacking pale loral spot of female Garganey. In flight, both sexes have broad white band along greater coverts, and green speculum with narrow white trailing edge; forewing of female is brown. *See* Appendix for comparison with Baikal Teal. Wetlands. DE: cw, GU: cw, HA: cw, HP: nw, JK: cp, MP: cw, PU: cw, RA: lcw, UP: cw, UR: cw.

3

Garganey *Anas querquedula* 37–41 cm

a **b** MALE and **c** **d** FEMALE Male has white stripe behind eye, and brown breast contrasting with grey flanks; shows blue-grey forewing in flight. Female has more patterned head than female Common Teal, with more prominent supercilium, whitish loral spot, pale line below dark eye-stripe and dark cheek-bar; shows pale grey forewing and broad white trailing edge to wing in flight. Wetlands. DE: cp, GU: cw, HA: cp, HP: np, JK: np, MP: cw, PU: cp, RA: lcw, UP: cw, UR: lcp.

4

Northern Pintail *Anas acuta* 51–56 cm

a **b** MALE and **c** **d** FEMALE Long neck and pointed tail. Male has chocolate-brown head, with white stripe down sides of neck. Female has comparatively uniform buffish head and slender grey bill; in flight she shows combination of indistinct brownish speculum, prominent white trailing edge to secondaries, and greyish underwing. Wetlands. DE: cw, GU: cw, HA: cw, HP: nw, JK: np, MP: lcw, PU: nw, RA: lcw, UP: cw, UR: lcw.

5

Northern Shoveler *Anas clypeata* 44–52 cm

a **b** MALE and **c** **d** FEMALE Long, spatulate bill. Male has dark-green head, white breast, chestnut flanks and blue forewing. Female recalls female Mallard in plumage but has blue-grey forewing. Wetlands. DE: cw, GU: cw, HA: cw, HP: np, JK: np, MP: nw, PU: cw, RA: lcw, UP: cw, UR: lcw.

2a
1a
1e
1c
1b
1d
2c
2d
2b
3b
3d
3c
3a
4d
4c
4b
4a

2/27/14
RANTWAN BOR

5d
5a
5b

2/27/14

5c

RANTHAN BOR

1 Red-crested Pochard *Rhodonessa rufina* 53–57 cm

a **b** MALE and **c** **d** FEMALE Large, with square-shaped head. Shape at rest and in flight more like dabbling duck. Male has rusty-orange head, black neck and breast, and white flanks. Female has pale cheeks contrasting with brown cap. Both sexes have largely white flight feathers on upperwing, and whitish underwing. Lakes and large rivers. DE: lcw, GU: cw, HA: lcw, HP: nw, JK: np, MP: nw, PU: lcw, RA: lcw, UP: lcw, UR: lcw.

2 Common Pochard *Aythya ferina* 42–49 cm

a **b** MALE, **c** **d** FEMALE and **e** IMMATURE MALE Large with domed head. Pale grey flight feathers and grey forewing result in different upperwing pattern from other *Aythya*. Male has chestnut head, black breast, and grey upperparts and flanks. Female has brownish head and breast contrasting with paler brownish-grey upperparts and flanks; lacks white undertail-coverts; eye is dark, and bill has grey central band. Lakes and large rivers. DE: cw, GU: cw, HA: cw, HP: nw, JK: np, MP: nw, PU: cw, RA: lcw, UP: cw, UR: lcw.

3 Ferruginous Pochard *Aythya nyroca* 38–42 cm

a **b** MALE and **c** FEMALE Smallest *Aythya* duck, with dome-shaped head. Chestnut head, breast and flanks, and white undertail-coverts. Female is duller than male, with dark iris. *See* Appendix for comparison with Baer's Pochard. In flight, shows extensive white wing-bar and white belly. Lakes and large rivers. DE: lcw, GU: cw, HA: lcw, HP: np, JK: ns, MP: cw, PU: lcw, RA: lcw, UP: cw, UR: lcw.

4 Tufted Duck *Aythya fuligula* 40–47 cm

a **b** MALE, **c** IMMATURE MALE, **d** **e** FEMALE and **f** FEMALE WITH SCAUP-LIKE HEAD Breeding male is glossy black, with prominent crest and white flanks. Eclipse/immature males are duller, with greyish flanks. Female is dusky brown, with paler flanks; some females may show white face patch, recalling Greater Scaup, but they usually also show tufted nape and squarer head shape. Female has yellow iris. Lakes and large rivers. DE: cw, GU: cw, HA: cw, HP: nw, JK: np, MP: nw, PU: cw, RA: lcw, UP: nw, UR: cw.

5 Greater Scaup *Aythya marila* 40–51 cm

a **b** MALE, **c** IMMATURE MALE, **d** **e** FEMALE and **f** IMMATURE FEMALE Larger and stockier than Tufted, and lacking any sign of crest. Male has grey upperparts contrasting with black rear end. Immature male is duller. Female has broad white face patch, which is less extensive on juvenile/immature. Female usually has greyish-white vermiculations ('frosting') on upperparts and flanks. Large lakes and rivers. DE: v, GU: v, HA: v, HP: v, JK: v, MP: v, PU: v, RA: v, UP: v, UR: v.

6 Common Merganser *Mergus merganser* 58–72 cm

a **b** MALE and **c** **d** FEMALE Male has dark green head, and whitish breast and flanks (with variable pink wash). Female and immature male have chestnut head and greyish body. Lakes, rivers and streams. HP: nw, JK: ns, MP: v, UP: nw, UR: nr?

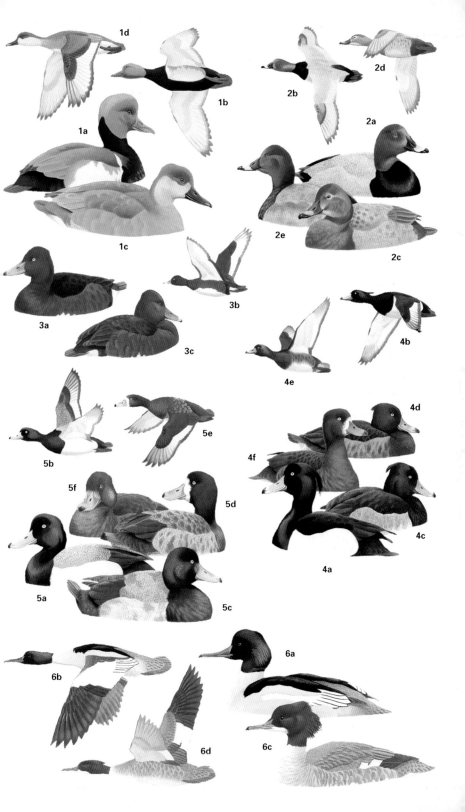

1 Yellow-rumped Honeyguide *Indicator xanthonotus* 15 cm
a MALE and b FEMALE Golden-yellow forehead, back and rump, streaked underparts and square, blackish tail. Inner edges of tertials are white, and form parallel lines down back. Male has pronounced, yellow malar stripes. Near Giant Rock Bee nests on cliffs, and adjacent forest; mainly 1800–3300 m, winters down to 610 m. HP: nr, JK: nr, UR: nr.

2 Eurasian Wryneck *Jynx torquilla* 16–17 cm
ADULT Cryptically patterned with grey, buff and brown. Has dark stripe down nape and mantle, and long, barred tail. Scrub, secondary growth and cultivation edges. DE: lcw, GU: nw, HA: nw, HP: nw, JK: lcs, MP: nw, PU: nw, RA: nw, UP: nw, UR: nw.

3 Speckled Piculet *Picumnus innominatus* 10 cm
a MALE and b FEMALE Tiny size. Whitish underparts with black spotting, black ear-covert patch and malar stripe, and white in black tail. Male has orange on forehead, which is lacking in female. Bushes and bamboo in broadleaved forest and secondary growth; mainly 915–1830 m. HP: nr, JK: nr, PU: nr, UR: nr.

4 White-browed Piculet *Sasia ochracea* 9–10 cm
a MALE and b FEMALE Tiny size. Rufous underparts and white supercilium behind eye. Male has golden-yellow on forehead, which is lacking in female. Bushes and bamboo in broadleaved forest and secondary growth; 250–2130 m. UR: nr.

5 Rufous Woodpecker *Celeus brachyurus* 25 cm
a MALE and b FEMALE Short black bill and shaggy crest. Rufous-brown, with prominent black barring. Male has scarlet patch on ear-coverts. Broadleaved forest and secondary growth. GU: nr, MP: nr, RA: nr, UP: nr, UR: nr.

6 White-bellied Woodpecker *Dryocopus javensis* 48 cm
a MALE and b FEMALE Large black woodpecker with white belly. Male has red crown and moustachial stripe; red restricted to hind-crown on female. In flight, shows white rump, white underwing-coverts and small white patch at base of primaries. Forest and secondary growth with tall trees. GU: nr.

7 Heart-spotted Woodpecker *Hemicircus canente* 16 cm
a MALE and b FEMALE Prominent crest; very short tail. Black-and-white plumage, with heart-shaped black spots on tertials. Male has black crown female has white crown and juvenile has black spotting on white crown. Broadleaved forest and coffee plantations. GU: nr, MP: nr.

8 Great Slaty Woodpecker *Mulleripicus pulverulentus* 51 cm
a MALE and b FEMALE Huge, slate-grey woodpecker with long bill and long neck and tail. Male has pinkish-red moustachial patch. Mature trees in sal forest and forest clearings; below 240 m. HP: nr, UP: nr, UR: nr.

Brown-capped Pygmy Woodpecker *Dendrocopos nanus* 13 cm

a MALE and **b** FEMALE Very small. Has fawn-brown crown and eye-stripe, brown coloration to upperparts, greyish- to brownish-white underparts (streaked with brown), and white spotting on central tail feathers. Light forest and trees in cultivation. GU: nr, HA: nr, MP: lcr, PU: cr, RA: nr, UP: lcr, UR: nr.

Grey-capped Pygmy Woodpecker *Dendrocopos canicapillus* 14 cm

a MALE and **b** FEMALE Very small. Has grey crown, blackish eye-stripe, blackish coloration to upperparts, diffuse blackish malar stripe and dirty fulvous underparts streaked with black, and lacks white spotting on central tail feathers. Open broadleaved forest. HA: nr, HP: nr, PU: nr, UP: lcr, UR: lcr.

Brown-fronted Woodpecker *Dendrocopos auriceps* 19–20 cm

a MALE and **b** FEMALE Brownish forehead and fore-crown, yellowish central crown, white-barred upperparts, prominent black moustachial stripe, well-defined streaking on underparts, pink undertail-coverts and unbarred central tail feathers. Coniferous and dry broadleaved forest; 1065–2440 m. HA: nr, HP: cr, JK: lcr, PU: v, UR: lcr.

Fulvous-breasted Woodpecker *Dendrocopos macei* 18–19 cm

a MALE and **b** FEMALE White barring on mantle and wing-coverts, and diffusely streaked buffish underparts. Male has red crown, which is black on female (*compare with* Brown-fronted). Forest edges and open forest. HA: nr, HP: nr, PU: nr, UR: nr.

Yellow-crowned Woodpecker *Dendrocopos mahrattensis* 17–18 cm

a MALE and **b** FEMALE Yellowish forehead and fore-crown, white-spotted upperparts, poorly defined moustachial stripe, dirty underparts with heavy but diffuse streaking, red patch on lower belly and bold white barring on central tail feathers. Open woodland, open country with scattered trees. DE: cr, GU: cr, HA: cr, HP: nr, JK: nr, MP: cr, PU: cr, RA: lcr, UP: cr, UR: lcr.

Rufous-bellied Woodpecker *Dendrocopos hyperythrus* 20 cm

a MALE and **b** FEMALE Whitish face and rufous underparts. Lacks white wing-patch. Male has red crown. Female has black crown with white spots. Juvenile has barred underparts. Oak/rhododendron and coniferous forest; 2135–2400 m. HP: nr, JK: nr, UR: nr.

Himalayan Woodpecker *Dendrocopos himalayensis* 23–25 cm

a MALE and **b** FEMALE White wing-patch, unstreaked underparts and black rear border to ear-coverts. *See* Appendix for comparison with Sind Woodpecker. Coniferous and broadleaved forest; 1980–3050 m. HP: lcr, JK: lcr, UR: lcr.

1

Lesser Yellownape *Picus chlorolophus* 27 cm
a MALE and **b** FEMALE Tufted yellow nape, scarlet and white markings on head, and barring on underparts. Smaller than Greater Yellownape, with less prominent crest and smaller bill. Broadleaved forest and secondary growth. GU: nr, HP: nr, JK: nr, MP: nr, UP: lcr, UR: nr.

2

Greater Yellownape *Picus flavinucha* 33 cm
a MALE and **b** FEMALE Tufted yellow nape, yellow (male) or rufous-brown (female) throat, dark-spotted white fore-neck, unbarred underparts and rufous barring on secondaries. Broadleaved forest and forest edges. UP: lcr, UR: nr.

3

Streak-throated Woodpecker *Picus xanthopygaeus* 30 cm
a MALE and **b** FEMALE Scaling on underparts. Smaller than Scaly-bellied, with dark bill and pale eye, streaked throat and upper breast, and indistinct barring on tail. Broadleaved forest and secondary growth. HA: nr, HP: nr, MP: nr, PU: nr, RA: nr, UP: lcr, UR: lcr.

4

Scaly-bellied Woodpecker *Picus squamatus* 35 cm
a MALE and **b** FEMALE Scaling on underparts. Larger than Streak-throated, with pale bill and reddish eye, prominent black eye-stripe and moustachial stripe, unstreaked throat and upper breast (although these parts are streaked in juvenile), and barred tail. Coniferous and oak/coniferous forest; 1850–3700 m, mainly below 3300 m. HP: lcr, JK: nr, UR: lcr.

5

Grey-headed Woodpecker *Picus canus* 32 cm
a MALE and **b** FEMALE Plain grey face, black nape and moustachial stripe, and uniform greyish-green underparts. Male has scarlet fore-crown. Broadleaved forest; below 2000 m. HA: nr, HP: nr, JK: nr, UP: lcr, UR: nr.

6

Himalayan Flameback *Dinopium shorii* 30–32 cm
a MALE and **b** FEMALE Smaller bill than Greater Flameback, with unspotted black hindneck, and brownish-buff centre of throat (and breast on some) with black spotting forming irregular border. Centre of divided moustachial stripe is brownish buff (with touch of red on some males). Breast less heavily marked with black than on Greater. Has reddish or brownish eyes, and three toes. Female has white streaking to black crest. Mature broadleaved forest; below 270 m. HA: nr, UP: lcr, UR: nr.

7

Black-rumped Flameback *Dinopium benghalense* 26–29 cm
a MALE and **b** FEMALE Black eye-stripe and throat (lacking dark moustachial stripe), spotting on wing-coverts, and black rump. Light forest, groves and trees in open country. DE: cr, GU: lcr, HA: cr, HP: nr, JK: nr, MP: cr, PU: cr, RA: nr, UP: cr, UR: lcr.

8

Greater Flameback *Chrysocolaptes lucidus* 33 cm
a MALE and **b** FEMALE Large size and long bill. White- or black-and-white-spotted hindneck and upper mantle, clean black line down centre of throat and neck, and white spotting on black breast. Moustachial stripe is clearly divided (with obvious white oval centre). Has pale eyes and four toes. Female has white spotting to black crest. Forest and groves. GU: nr, HA: cr, UP: lcr, UR: nr.

9

White-naped Woodpecker *Chrysocolaptes festivus* 29 cm
a MALE and **b** FEMALE White hind-neck and mantle, and black scapulars and back forming V-shape. Moustachial stripe is clearly divided. Rump is black. Female has yellow crown. Light broadleaved forest and scattered trees. GU: nr, MP: nr, RA: nr, UP: lcr, UR: nr.

1 Great Barbet *Megalaima virens* 33 cm

ADULT Large yellow bill, bluish head, brown breast and mantle, olive-streaked yellowish under-parts, and red undertail-coverts. Has a monotonous, incessant and far-reaching *piho, piho* uttered throughout the day; a repetitive *tuk tuk tuk* is often uttered in a duet, presumably by female. Subtropical and temperate forest; mainly 900–2200 m (305–2600 m). HA: nr, HP: lcr, JK: nr, PU: v, UR: lcr.

2 Brown-headed Barbet *Megalaima zeylanica* 27 cm

ADULT Fine streaking on brown head and breast, brown throat, orange circumorbital skin and bill (when breeding), and white-spotted wing-coverts. Streaking almost absent on belly and flanks. Call is a monotonous *kotroo, kotroo, kotroo* or *kutruk, kutruk, kutruk*. Forest, wooded areas and trees near habitation. DE: cr, GU: lcr, HA: cr, HP: nr, JK: nr, MP: lcr, PU: cr, RA: nr, UP: cr, UR: lcr.

3 Lineated Barbet *Megalaima lineata* 28 cm

a ADULT and **b** PALER VARIANT Bold white streaking on head and breast, whitish throat and uniform unspotted wing-coverts. Less extensive circumorbital skin than Brown-headed and which is usually separated from bill. Call is a monotonous *kotur kotur kotur* (slightly mellower and softer than Brown-headed's) uttered throughout the day. Open sal forest and well-wooded areas. HP: nr, UR: lcr.

4 Blue-throated Barbet *Megalaima asiatica* 23 cm

a ADULT and **b** JUVENILE Blue 'face' and throat, red forehead and hind-crown, and black band across crown. Juvenile has duller head pattern. Voice is a harsh and loud *took-a-rook, took-a-rook* uttered very rapidly. Open forest, groves and gardens; common below 1500 m, frequent up to 2100 m. HP: lcr, JK: nr, PU: nr, UP: nr, UR: lcr.

5 Coppersmith Barbet *Megalaima haemacephala* 17 cm

a ADULT and **b** JUVENILE Small barbet with crimson forehead and breast-patch, yellow patches above and below eye, yellow throat and streaked underparts. Juvenile lacks red on head and breast. Voice is a loud, metallic, repetitive and monotonous *tuk, tuk, tuk*. Open wooded country, groves and trees in cultivation, and gardens. DE: cr, GU: cr, HA: cr, HP: nr, JK: nr, MP: lcr, PU: cr, RA: lcr, UP: cr, UR: lcr.

1

Indian Grey Hornbill *Ocyceros birostris* 50 cm

a b MALE and **c** IMMATURE Small hornbill with sandy brownish-grey upperparts, long tail that has dark subterminal band and elongated central feathers, and white trailing edge to wing. Prominent black casque and extensive black at base of bill. Female and immature similar to male, but with smaller bill and casque. Territorial call is a loud cackling and squealing *k-k-k-ka-e* or rapid piping *pi-pi-pi-pi-pipipieu* etc.; normal contact call is a kite-like *chee-ooww*. Open broadleaved forest, groves and gardens with fruiting trees. DE: lcr, GU: nr, HA: lcr, HP: nr, JK: nr, MP: cr, PU: cr, RA: nr, UP: cr, UR: lcr.

2

Malabar Pied Hornbill *Anthracoceros coronatus* 65 cm

a b MALE and **c** FEMALE Compared with Oriental has axe-shaped casque with large black patch along upper ridge, white outer tail feathers (immatures have black at base, but not so extensive as in Oriental), broader white trailing edge to wing, and pink throat-patches. Orbital skin is blue-black on male, pinkish on female. Female's casque similar in shape and patterning to male's, although lacks black at posterior end; bill of female lacks black at tip. Open forest and large fruit trees near villages. MP: nr, UP: nr.

3

Oriental Pied Hornbill *Anthracoceros albirostris* 55–60 cm

a b MALE and **c** FEMALE Much smaller than Great Hornbill. Head and neck black. Tail mainly black with white tips to outer feathers. Both sexes have cylindrical casque, blue orbital skin and throat-patch. Female has smaller casque than male, and has black at tip of bill. Calls include a variety of loud, shrill, nasal squeals and raucous chucks. Mature broadleaved forest with fruiting trees. DE: v, HA: nr?, UP: lcr, UR: nr.

4

Great Hornbill *Buceros bicornis* 95–105 cm

a b MALE Huge size, with massive yellow casque and bill, and white tail with black sub-terminal band. Has white neck, wing-bars and trailing edge to wings, which are variably stained with yellow (by preen-gland oils). Sexes alike, although female has white iris (red in male) and lacks black at ends of casque. Calls are loud and raucous, frequently given as a duet, *grongk-gonk, grongk-gongk*, and often becoming louder and more agitated prior to flight; flight call is a loud *ger-onk*. Mature broadleaved forest with fruiting trees. HA: nr, UP: lcr, UR: nr.

2|25|14
JAIPUR

1a

1b

2b

1c

2a

3c

2c

3b

4a

3a

4b

1 Common Hoopoe *Upupa epops* 31 cm

a **b** ADULT Orange-buff, with black-and-white wings and tail, and black-tipped fan-like crest. Voice is a repetitive and mellow *poop, poop, poop* similar to that of Oriental Cuckoo. Open country, cultivation and villages. DE: cr, GU: cw, HA: cr, HP: lcr, JK: cs, MP: cr, PU: cr, RA: lcr, UP: cr, UR: cr.

2 Malabar Trogon *Harpactes fasciatus* 31 cm

a MALE and **b** FEMALE Male has black head and breast, pink underparts, and black-and-grey vermiculated wing-coverts. Female has dark cinnamon head and breast, pale cinnamon underparts, and brown-and-buff vermiculated coverts. Immature male has cinnamon underparts. Dense broadleaved forest. GU: nr.

3 Red-headed Trogon *Harpactes erythrocephalus* 35 cm

a MALE and **b** FEMALE Male has crimson head and breast, pink underparts, and black-and-grey vermiculated wing-coverts. Female has dark-cinnamon head and breast, and brown-and-buff vermiculated coverts. Immature resembles female but has whitish underparts. Call is a descending series of notes, *tyaup, tyaup, tyaup, tyaup, tyaup....* Dense broadleaved forest; mainly 250–1000 m (–1830 m). UR: nr.

4 European Roller *Coracias garrulus* 31 cm

a **b** ADULT and **c** JUVENILE Turquoise head and underparts, and rufous-cinnamon mantle. Has black flight feathers and tail corners. Juvenile is much duller, and has whitish streaking on throat and breast; patterning of wings and tail helps separate it from Indian Roller. Open woodland and cultivation. DE: v, GU: lcw, HA: np, HP: np, JK: ns, MP: v, PU: np, RA: np, UP: np.

5 Indian Roller *Coracias benghalensis* 33 cm

a **b** ADULT and **c** JUVENILE Has rufous-brown on nape and underparts, white streaking on ear-coverts and throat, and greenish mantle. In flight, shows turquoise band across primaries and dark blue terminal band to tail. Juvenile is similar to adult but duller, with more heavily streaked throat and breast. Cultivation, open woodland, groves and gardens. DE: cr, GU: lcr, HA: cr, HP: lcr, MP: cr, PU: cr, RA: lcr, UP: lcr, UR: lcr.

6 Dollarbird *Eurystomus orientalis* 28 cm

a **b** ADULT Dark greenish, appearing black at distance, with red bill and eye-ring. In flight, shows turquoise patch on primaries. Tropical forest and forest clearings. HA: ns, UR: ns.

3/ KTLRK
KHAJURAHO
3/5/14

1   Common Kingfisher *Alcedo atthis*   16 cm

ADULT Orange ear-coverts. Greenish blue on head, scapulars and wings, and turquoise line down back. Fresh waters in open country. DE: cr, GU: cr, HA: nr, HP: lcr, JK: lcr, MP: lcr, PU: cr, RA: lcr, UP: lcr, UR: nr.

2   Blue-eared Kingfisher *Alcedo meninting*   16 cm

a MALE and **b** JUVENILE Blue ear-coverts. Deeper blue upperparts and richer rufous underparts compared with Common Kingfisher. Confusingly, juvenile has orange ear-coverts, but otherwise overall coloration is as adult. Streams in dense forest. UR: nr.

3   Stork-billed Kingfisher *Halcyon capensis*   38 cm

ADULT Huge size and massive red bill. Has brown cap, orange-buff collar and underparts, and blue upperparts. Has an explosive laugh, *ke-ke-ke-ke-ke*; song is a long series of paired melancholy whistles. Shaded slow-moving rivers and streams. GU: nr, HA: np?, MP: nr, PU: nr, RA: nr, UP: lcr, UR: nr.

4   White-throated Kingfisher *Halcyon smyrnensis*   28 cm

ADULT White throat and centre of breast, brown head and most of underparts, and turquoise upperparts. Shows prominent white wing-patch in flight. Call is a loud rattling laugh; song is drawn-out musical whistle, *kililili*. Cultivation, forest edges, gardens and wetlands. DE: cr, GU: cr, HA: cr, HP: lcr, JK: lcr, MP: cr, PU: cr, RA: lcr, UP: cr, UR: lcr.

5   Black-capped Kingfisher *Halcyon pileata*   30 cm

ADULT Black cap, white collar, purplish-blue upperparts and pale orange underparts. Shows white wing-patch in flight. Call is a ringing cackle, *kikikikikiki*. Wetlands. GU: nw, MP: v, RA: v, UP: v.

6   Crested Kingfisher *Megaceryle lugubris*   41 cm

ADULT Much larger than Pied, with evenly barred wings and tail. Lacks supercilium, and has spotted breast that is sometimes mixed with rufous. Mountain rivers, large rivers in foothills. Resident; 250–1800 m (–3000 m). HA: nr?, HP: nr, JK: lcr, PU: nr, UR: nr.

7   Pied Kingfisher *Ceryle rudis*   31 cm

a MALE and **b** FEMALE Smaller than Crested, with white supercilium, white patches on wings and black band(s) across breast. Female has single breast-band (double in male). Slow-moving rivers and streams, lakes and pools in open country. DE: nr, GU: cr, HA: cr, HP: lcr, JK: lcr, MP: lcr, PU: cr, RA: lcr, UP: cr, UR: lcr.

1

Blue-bearded Bee-eater *Nyctyornis athertoni* 31–34 cm

ADULT Large bee-eater with square-ended tail and blue 'beard'. Has yellowish-buff belly and flanks with greenish streaking. Edges of broadleaved forest and open forest. GU: nr, HA: nr?, HP: nr, MP: nr, UP: nr, UR: nr.

2

Green Bee-eater *Merops orientalis* 16–18 cm **3/4/14**

a **b** ADULT and **c** JUVENILE *M. o. beludschicus*; **d** ADULT *M. o. orientalis* Small bee-eater, with blue cheeks, black gorget and golden coloration to crown (stronger in *orientalis*, which has a more easterly distribution). Green tail with elongated central feathers. Juvenile has green crown and nape, yellowish throat, lacks black gorget, and has square-ended tail. Open country with scattered trees. DE: cs, GU: cr, HA: cs, HP: lcs, JK: ns, MP: cr, PU: cr, RA: lcr, UP: cr, UR: lcs.

3

Blue-cheeked Bee-eater *Merops persicus* 24–26 cm

a **b** ADULT Larger than Green Bee-eater, with chestnut lower throat, whitish forehead, and turquoise-and-white supercilium. Green upperparts, underparts and tail, although may show touch of turquoise on rump, belly and tail-coverts. *See below* for differences from Blue-tailed. Near water in arid areas. DE: lcs, GU: nr, HA: cs, JK: np, MP: v, PU: np, RA: lcs, UR: ns.

4

Blue-tailed Bee-eater *Merops philippinus* 23–26 cm

a **b** ADULT and **c** JUVENILE Larger than Green Bee-eater, with chestnut throat, green crown and nape, and blue tail. Compared with Blue-cheeked, forehead and supercilium are mainly green, sometimes with a touch of blue on supercilium; chestnut of throat is more extensive and extends onto ear-coverts, and blue streak below mask is less extensive. Upperparts and underparts are washed with brown and blue (greener in Blue-cheeked). Juvenile is like washed-out version of adult; lacks elongated central tail feathers. Near water in open wooded country. DE: lcs, GU: np, HA: cs, HP: lcs, JK: ns, MP: np, PU: ns, RA: np, UP: lcr, UR: nr.

5

European Bee-eater *Merops apiaster* 23–25 cm

a **b** **c** ADULT and **d** JUVENILE Yellow throat, black gorget, blue underparts, chestnut crown and mantle, and golden-yellow scapulars. Juvenile is duller than adult, but still shows chestnut on crown and well-defined yellowish throat. Open country. GU: v, JK: ns, PU: v, RA: v, UR: v.

6

Chestnut-headed Bee-eater *Merops leschenaulti* 18–20 cm

a **b** ADULT and **c** JUVENILE Chestnut crown, nape and mantle, and yellow throat with diffuse black gorget. Tail has slight fork; lacks elongated central tail feathers. Juvenile is like washed-out version of adult, but crown and nape are dark green on some. Open broadleaved forest, often near water. GU: nr, HA: nr, HP: nr, JK: v, MP: nr, UP: lcr?, UR: nr.

314 / 14
KALAKHO

1

Pied Cuckoo *Clamator jacobinus* 33 cm

ADULT Adult is black and white with prominent crest. Crest smaller, upperparts browner and underparts more buffish on juvenile. Call is metallic, pleasant *piu…piu…pee-pee piu, pee-pee piu.* Broadleaved forest and well-wooded areas. DE: lcs, GU: cs, HA: cs, HP: ns, JK: ns, MP: ns, PU: cs, RA: ns, UP: cs, UR: lcs.

2

Chestnut-winged Cuckoo *Clamator coromandus* 47 cm

ADULT Prominent crest, whitish collar and chestnut wings. Immature has rufous fringes to upperparts. Makes a series of double metallic whistles, *breep breep.* Broadleaved forest. UR: ns.

3

Large Hawk Cuckoo *Hierococcyx sparverioides* 38 cm

a MALE and **b** JUVENILE Larger than Common Hawk Cuckoo, with browner upperparts strongly barred underparts and broader tail-banding. Juvenile has barred flanks and broad tail-banding; head dark grey on older birds. Call is a shrill *pee-pee-ah…pee-pee-ah,* which is repeated, rising in pitch and momentum, climaxing in hysterical crescendo. Broadleaved forest. Mainly 1830–3000 m. DE: v, HP: ns, JK: ns, MP: v, PU: nw, UR: cs.

4

Common Hawk Cuckoo *Hierococcyx varius* 34 cm

a MALE and **b** JUVENILE Smaller than Large Hawk Cuckoo, with grey upperparts, more rufous on underparts, indistinct barring on belly and flanks, and narrow tail-banding. Juvenile has spotted flanks and narrow tail-banding. Call like that of Large Hawk Cuckoo. Well-wooded country. DE: cs, GU: lcr, HA: cs, HP: ns, JK: ns, MP: cr, PU: nr, RA: ns, UP: cr, UR: lcs.

5

Indian Cuckoo *Cuculus micropterus* 33 cm

a MALE and **b** JUVENILE Brown coloration to grey upperparts and tail, broad barring on underparts, and pronounced white barring and spotting on tail. Juvenile has broad and irregular white tips to feathers of crown and nape, and white tips to scapulars and wing-coverts. Call is a descending, four-noted whistle, *kwer-kwah…kwah-kurh.* Forest and well-wooded country. DE: v, GU: v, HA: ns, HP: ns, JK: ns, MP: cs, PU: np, RA: v, UP: ns, UR: lcs.

6

Eurasian Cuckoo *Cuculus canorus* 32–34 cm

a MALE and **b** HEPATIC FEMALE Finer barring on whiter underparts than Oriental. Male's call is a loud, repetitive *cuck-oo…cuck-oo*; both sexes have a bubbling call. Forest, well-wooded country and scrub. DE: np, GU: cp, HA: np, HP: cs, JK: cs, MP: ns, PU: np, RA: v, UP: ns, UR: lcs.

7

Oriental Cuckoo *Cuculus saturatus* 30–32 cm

a MALE and **b** HEPATIC FEMALE Broader barring on buffish-white underparts compared with Eurasian; upperparts are a shade darker and head is paler. Hepatic female is slightly more heavily barred than Eurasian. Call is a resonant *ho…ho…ho…ho,* easily confused with the call of Common Hoopoe. Forest and well-wooded country. DE: np, HP: ns, JK: lcs, RA: v, UP: v, UR: lcs.

8

Lesser Cuckoo *Cuculus poliocephalus* 25 cm

a MALE and **b** HEPATIC FEMALE Smaller than Oriental; hepatic female can be bright rufous and indistinctly barred on crown and nape. Call is a strong, cheerful *pretty-peel-lay-ka-beet.* Forest, well-wooded country. DE: v, GU: v, HP: ns, JK: lcs, UR: ns.

Banded Bay Cuckoo *Cacomantis sonneratii* 24 cm

ADULT White supercilium, finely barred white underparts, and fine and regular dark barring on upperparts. Song is a shrill, whistled *pi-pi-pew-pew*, the first two notes at the same pitch, the last two descending. Dense broadleaved forest. GU: ns, HP: ns, JK: ns, MP: ns, UR: ns.

Grey-bellied Cuckoo *Cacomantis passerinus* 23 cm

a ADULT, **b** HEPATIC FEMALE and **c** JUVENILE Adult is grey with white vent and under-tail-coverts. On hepatic female, underparts are whitish with dark barring, upperparts are bright rufous with crown and nape only sparsely barred, and rufous tail is unbarred. Juvenile is either grey, with pale barring on underparts, or similar to hepatic female, or intermediate. *See* Appendix for comparison with Plaintive Cuckoo. Song is a clear, interrogative *pee-pipee-pee…pipee-pee*, ascending in scale and pitch; also a single plaintive repeated whistle. Groves and open forest. DE: ns, GU: ns, HA: ns, HP: lcs, JK: ns, MP: cs, PU: np, RA: ns, UP: lcs, UR: lcs.

Drongo Cuckoo *Surniculus lugubris* 25 cm

a ADULT and **b** JUVENILE Black, with white-barred undertail-coverts. Bill fine and down-curved, and tail has indentation. Juvenile is spotted with white. Song is an ascending series of repeated whistles, *pee-pee-pee-pee-pee*. Edges and clearings of forest and groves. DE: v, HA: v, HP: ns, JK: ns, MP: ns, PU: v, UP: nr, UR: ns.

Asian Koel *Eudynamys scolopacea* 43 cm

a MALE and **b** FEMALE Male is greenish black, with green bill. Female is spotted and barred with white. Song is a loud rising, repeated *ko-el…ko-el…ko-el…ko-el*. Open woodland, gardens and cultivation. DE: ns, GU: cr, HA: cs, HP: ns, JK: ns, MP: cr, PU: ns, RA: ns, UP: cr, UR: lcs.

Green-billed Malkoha *Phaenicophaeus tristis* 38 cm

ADULT Greyish-green coloration, green and red bill, red eye-patch, white-streaked supercilium and white-tipped tail. Dense forest and thickets. UP: nr, UR: nr.

Blue-faced Malkoha *Phaenicophaeus viridirostris* 39 cm

ADULT Greenish coloration, green bill, blue eye-patch and bold white tips to tail. Scrub and secondary growth. GU: nr.

Sirkeer Malkoha *Phaenicophaeus leschenaultii* 42 cm

ADULT Sandy coloration, yellow-tipped red bill, dark mask with white border, and bold white tips to tail. Thorn scrub and acacia trees in dry areas. DE: nr, GU: cr, HA: nr, HP: nr, JK: nr, MP: lcr, PU: cr, RA: nr, UP: lcr, UR: nr.

Greater Coucal *Centropus sinensis* 48 cm

a ADULT and **b** JUVENILE Larger than Lesser Coucal, with brighter and more uniform chestnut wings and black underwing-coverts. Juvenile is heavily barred. Call is a deep primate-like *hoop-hoop-hoop-hoop-hoop-hoop-hoop*, descending and then rising towards the end of the series. Tall grassland and thickets near cultivation. DE: cr, GU: cr, HA: nr, HP: nr, JK: nr, MP: cr, PU: cr, RA: lcr, UP: cr, UR: lcr.

Lesser Coucal *Centropus bengalensis* 33 cm

a ADULT BREEDING, **b** ADULT NON-BREEDING and **c** IMMATURE Smaller than Greater Coucal, with duller chestnut wings, and chestnut underwing-coverts; often with buff streaking on scapulars and wing-coverts. Non-breeding has pronounced buff shaft-streaking on head and body, chestnut wings and black tail; immature similar but with barred wings and tail. Song is a series of deep, resonant *pwoop-pwoop-pwoop* notes; similar to Greater, but usually slightly faster and more interrogative. Tall grassland, reedbeds and scrub. DE: v, UP: lcr, UR: nr.

Alexandrine Parakeet *Psittacula eupatria* 53 cm

a MALE and **b** FEMALE Very large, with maroon shoulder-patch. Male has black chin-stripe and pink collar. Call is a loud, guttural *keeak* or *kee-ah*, much deeper than that of Rose-ringed. Sal and riverine forest. DE: cr, GU: nr, HA: lcr, HP: lcr, JK: nr, MP: cr, PU: cr, RA: nr, UP: lcr, UR: lcr.

Rose-ringed Parakeet *Psittacula krameri* 42 cm

a MALE and **b** FEMALE Green head and blue-green tip to tail. Male has black chin-stripe and pink collar. Call is a loud, shrill *kee-ah*. Broadleaved forest, wooded areas and cultivation. DE: cr, GU: cr, HA: cr, HP: nr, JK: nr, MP: cr, PU: cr, RA: lcr, UP: cr, UR: lcr.

Slaty-headed Parakeet *Psittacula himalayana* 41 cm

a MALE, **b** FEMALE and **c** IMMATURE Dark grey head, dark green upperparts, red-and-yellow bill, and yellow-tipped tail. Female lacks maroon shoulder-patch of male. Immature lacks slaty head. Call is a shrill *tooi-tooi*. Broadleaved forest and well-wooded areas; breeds 1200–2500 m, winters down to 250 m. HA: nr, HP: lcr, JK: nr, PU: nr, UR: lcr.

Plum-headed Parakeet *Psittacula cyanocephala* 36 cm

a MALE, **b** FEMALE and **c** IMMATURE Head is plum-red on male, pale grey on female. Yellow upper mandible and white-tipped blue-green tail. Head of female is paler grey than Slaty-headed, and lacks black chin-stripe and half-collar of that species; shows yellow collar and upper breast. Call higher-pitched than Slaty-headed's. Broadleaved forest and well-wooded areas. DE: lcr, GU: nr, HA: lcr, HP: lcr, JK: nr, MP: cr, PU: cr, RA: nr, UP: cr, UR: lcr.

Red-breasted Parakeet *Psittacula alexandri* 38 cm

a MALE, **b** FEMALE and **c** IMMATURE Lilac-grey head with broad black chin-stripe, pink underparts and yellowish-green patch on wing-coverts. Female has all-black bill. Immature has green underparts. Call is a sharp, nasal *kaink*. Open broadleaved forest and secondary growth. UR: lcr.

1a

2a

2b

1b

2c

3b

4a

2/23/14 DELHI

4b

3a

5a

5b

4c

5c

6c

7b

6a

3/5/14 TONHA G.R.

7a

7c

6b

1 **Himalayan Swiftlet** *Collocalia brevirostris* 14 cm
a **b** ADULT Stocky brownish swiftlet with paler grey-brown underparts and diffuse greyish rump-band. Shows distinct indentation to tail. Banking and gliding flight, interspersed with bat-like fluttering. Open areas near forest; foothills up to 3600 m. HP: lcr, PU: v, UR: nr.

2 **White-rumped Needletail** *Zoonavena sylvatica* 11 cm
a **b** ADULT Small and stocky, with oval-shaped wings. Has white rump, and whitish belly and undertail-coverts help distinguish it from House Swift. Flight is fast with rapid wing beats, much banking from side to side, interspersed with short glides on slightly bowed wings. Broadleaved forest. Up to 1700 m. MP: nr, UP: nr?, UR: nr.

3 **White-throated Needletail** *Hirundapus caudacutus* 20 cm
a **b** ADULT Large swift, with very fast and powerful flight. Has striking white throat and white horseshoe crescent on underparts. Also shows prominent pale 'saddle' and white patch on tertials. Ridges, cliffs, upland grassland and river valleys. 1200–4000 m. HP: ns, JK: v, UR: nr.

4 **Asian Palm Swift** *Cypsiurus balasiensis* 13 cm
a **b** ADULT Small and very slim, with scythe-shaped wings and long, forked tail (which is usually held closed). Fluttering flight, interspersed with short glides. Mainly brown with paler throat. Open country and cultivation with palms. DE: v, GU: lcr, PU: cr, RA: nr, UP: nr, UR: nr.

5 **Alpine Swift** *Tachymarptis melba* 22 cm
a **b** ADULT Large, powerful swift with white throat, brown breast-band and white patch on belly. Mainly hills and mountains. DE: np, GU: nr, HA: np?, HP: lcp, JK: nr, MP: nr, PU: nr, RA: np, UR: nr.

6 **Common Swift** *Apus apus* 17 cm
a **b** ADULT Uniform dark brown swift, with white throat; lacks white rump. Has prominently forked tail. *See* Appendix for comparison with Pallid Swift. Chiefly mountains. Mainly 1500–3300 m. GU: v, HP: ns, JK: lcs, PU: np.

7 **Fork-tailed Swift** *Apus pacificus* 15–18 cm
a **b** ADULT Blackish swift with white rump and white scaling on underparts. Slimmer bodied and longer-winged than House Swift, with deeply forked tail. Open ridges and hilltops. Up to 3600 m. GU: v, HA: v, HP: lcs, JK: ns, PU: np, RA: v, UR: nr.

8 **House Swift** *Apus affinis* 15 cm
a **b** ADULT *A. a. affinis*; **c** **d** ADULT *A. a. nipalensis* Small blackish swift with broad white rump-band. Compared with Fork-tailed is rather stocky, with relatively short wings, and tail appears square-ended or has only a slight fork. Himalayan *nipalensis* has narrower white rump-band and more pronounced tail fork than *affinis* in the lowlands, which is known as 'Little Swift'. Towns and villages. DE: cr, GU: cr, HA: cr, HP: lcr, JK: nr, MP: lcr, PU: cr, RA: lcr, UP: cr, UR: lcr.

9 **Crested Treeswift** *Hemiprocne coronata* 23 cm
a **b** MALE and **c** FEMALE Large size and long, forked tail. Blue-grey upperparts and paler underparts, becoming whitish on belly and vent. Male has dull orange ear-coverts (dark grey in female). Forest. GU: lcr, MP: cr, RA: v, UP: nr, UR: lcr.

1 Barn Owl *Tyto alba* 36 cm

ADULT Unmarked white face, whitish underparts, and golden-buff and grey upperparts. Eyes are dark. Utters a variety of eerie screeching and hissing noises. Generally nocturnal. Usually hunts in flight, quartering the ground and often banking or hovering to locate prey. Roosts in old buildings and hunts in cultivation. DE: lcr, GU: nr, HA: nr, HP: nr, JK: nr, MP: nr, PU: cr, RA: nr, UP: nr, UR: nr.

2 Grass Owl *Tyto capensis* 36 cm

a **b** ADULT Similar to Barn Owl, with whitish face and underparts, but upperparts are darker and heavily marked with dark brown. Also shows dark barring on flight feathers, golden-buff patch at base of primaries contrasting with dark primaries, and dark-barred tail. Mottled rather than streaked upperparts, lack of prominent streaking on breast and black eyes are useful distinguishing features from Short-eared Owl, which may be found in similar habitat. Generally nocturnal, and usually only seen when flushed. Tall grassland. MP: nr, UP: nr, UR: nr.

3 Mountain Scops Owl *Otus spilocephalus* 20 cm

ADULT Very small ear-tufts. Upperparts mottled with buff and brown; underparts indistinctly spotted with buff and barred with brown. Occurs as grey or fulvous-brown morphs. Call is a double whistle, *toot-too*. Dense broadleaved forest; 1500–2600 m. HP: nr, UR: nr.

4 Pallid Scops Owl *Otus brucei* 22 cm

ADULT Compared with grey morph Oriental Scops, is paler, greyer and more uniform. Has less-distinct scapular spots, and narrower dark streaking on underparts, which lack pale horizontal panels. *See* Appendix for comparison with Eurasian Scops Owl. Call is a resonant *whoop-whoop-whoop...*. Stony foothills in semi-desert. GU: v, HA: v, UP: v.

5 Oriental Scops Owl *Otus sunia* 19 cm

a ADULT RUFOUS and **b** BROWN MORPH Prominent ear-tufts. Prominent white scapular spots, streaked underparts and upperparts; lacks prominent nuchal collar. Iris yellow. *See* Appendix for comparison with Eurasian Scops Owl. Nocturnal. Call is frog-like *wut-chu-chraati*. Forest, secondary growth and groves. Plains up to 1800 m. DE: xr, GU: nw, HP: lcr, MP: nr, RA: v, UP: nr, UR: lcr.

6 Collared Scops Owl *Otus bakkamoena* 23–25 cm

a ADULT GREY and **b** RUFOUS-BROWN MORPH Larger than other scops owls, with buff nuchal collar, finely streaked underparts and indistinct buffish scapular spots. Iris dark orange or brown. Nocturnal. Call is a subdued, frog-like *whuk*, repeated at irregular intervals. Forest, well-wooded areas and groves. DE: nr, GU: nr, HA: nr, HP: lcr, MP: nr, PU: nr, RA: nr, UP: nr, UR: nr.

1 Eurasian Eagle Owl *Bubo bubo* 56–66 cm

a ADULT *B. b. hemachalana*; **b** ADULT *B. b. bengalensis* Very large owl, with upright ear-tufts. Upperparts mottled dark brown and tawny-buff; underparts heavily streaked. Himalayan *hemachalana* is larger and paler than *bengalensis* of the lowlands and hills. Mainly nocturnal, but usually perches before sunset and after sunrise in a prominent position on cliff or rock. Call is a resonant *tu-whooh*. Cliffs, rocky hills, ravines and wooded areas. Plains up to 4300 m. DE: nr, GU: nr, HA: nr, HP: nr, JK: lcr, MP: nr, PU: nr, RA: nr, UP: lcr, UR: nr.

2 Spot-bellied Eagle Owl *Bubo nipalensis* 63 cm

a ADULT and **b** IMMATURE Very large owl, with prominent ear-tufts and bold chevron-shaped spots on underparts. Upperparts dark brown, barred with buff. Eyes dark brown. Juvenile is striking, with much white in underparts. Nocturnal. Call is a deep hoot and a mournful scream. Dense broadleaved forest; 150–2130 m. UR: nr.

3 Dusky Eagle Owl *Bubo coromandus* 58 cm

ADULT Large grey owl with prominent ear-tufts. Upperparts greyish-brown with fine whitish vermiculations and diffuse darker brown streaking. Underparts greyish white with brown streaking. Call is a deep, resonant *wo, wo, wo, wo-o-o-o-o*. Generally nocturnal, but emerges from roost about an hour before sunset; sometimes hunts during day in cloudy weather. Often calls during the day. Well-watered areas with extensive tree cover. DE: xr, GU: nr, HA: nr, HP: nr, MP: nr, PU: nr, RA: nr, UP: nr, UR: nr.

4 Brown Fish Owl *Ketupa zeylonensis* 56 cm

ADULT Compared with Tawny Fish Owl, has close dark barring on dull buff underparts, which also show finer streaking, and upperparts are duller brown with finer streaking. Partly diurnal, emerging from roost long before sunset; sometimes hunts during the day. Calls include a soft, deep *hup-hup-hu* and a wild *hu-hu-hu-hu...hu ha*. Forest and well-wooded areas near water. DE: xr, GU: nr, HA: nr, HP: lcr, MP: nr, PU: nr, RA: nr, UP: lcr, UR: nr.

5 Tawny Fish Owl *Ketupa flavipes* 61 cm

ADULT Larger and more richly coloured than Brown Fish Owl. Upperparts are pale orange with bold black streaking; wing-coverts and flight feathers have bold orange-buff barring. Shows broad black streaking on pale rufous-orange underparts, which lack fine, dark cross-barring shown by Brown Fish Owl. Has prominent whitish patch on forehead that is generally lacking in Brown. Mainly nocturnal, but sometimes fishes during the day. Call is a deep *whoo-hoo* and a cat-like mewing. Ravines in broadleaved forest near water; 250–360 m. HP: nr, JK: nr, UR: nr.

6 Mottled Wood Owl *Strix ocellata* 48 cm

ADULT Concentric barring on facial discs, and white, rufous and dark brown mottling on upperparts; dark brown barring mixed with rufous on whitish underparts. Call is a spooky, quavering *whaa-aa-aa-aa-ah*. Open wooded areas, groves around villages and cultivation. DE: v, GU: nr, HA: nr, HP: nr, JK: nr, MP: nr, RA: nr, UP: nr.

7 Brown Wood Owl *Strix leptogrammica* 47–53 cm

ADULT Uniform facial discs, uniform brown upperparts with fine white barring on scapulars, and buffish-white underparts with fine brown barring. Nocturnal. Calls include a *hoo-hoohoohoo(hoo)* and a loud eerie scream. Dense broadleaved forest; 750 m up to at least 2500 m. HP: nr, JK: nr, UP: nr, UR: nr.

8 Tawny Owl *Strix aluco* 45–47 cm

a ADULT *S. a. nivicola*; **b** ADULT *S. a. biddulphi* Rufous to grey-brown, with heavily streaked underparts, white markings on scapulars, dark centre to crown and pale fore-crown stripes. The larger and greyer form *biddulphi* occurs in the north-west of the region. Nocturnal. Call is a *too-tu-whoo*, sometimes shortened to a two-noted *turr-whooh*; also a low-pitched *ku-wack-ku-wack*. Oak/rhododendron and coniferous forest; 1800 m up to the treeline. HP: lcr, JK: lcr, UR: nr.

1a

2a

1b

2b

3

4

5

6

7/28/14

RANTHMBOR

6

7

8a

8b

1

Collared Owlet *Glaucidium brodiei* 17 cm

ADULT Very small and heavily barred. Spotted crown, streaking on flanks and owl-face pattern on upper mantle. Diurnal and crepuscular. Call is a repeated bell-like whistle, *toot...tootoot...toot*. Broadleaved forest; 1900–3050 m. HA: nr, HP: nr, JK: lcr, UR: lcr.

2

Asian Barred Owlet *Glaucidium cuculoides* 23 cm

ADULT Heavily barred. Best told from Jungle Owlet by larger size, buff (rather than rufous) barring on wing-coverts and flight feathers, and streaked flanks. Mainly diurnal, often perching in prominent position during day. Open forest; foothills up to 2100 m. HP: lcr, JK: nr, PU: nr, UP: lcr, UR: nr.

3

Jungle Owlet *Glaucidium radiatum* 20 cm

ADULT Small and heavily barred. Smaller than Asian Barred, with more closely barred upperparts and underparts, and with barred flanks and rufous barring on wings. Mainly crepuscular. Open forest and secondary growth. Below 2000 m. GU: nr, HA: nr, HP: nr, MP: cr, RA: nr, UP: cr, UR: lcr.

4

Little Owl *Athene noctua* 23 cm

ADULT Sandy-brown, with streaked breast and flanks, and streaked crown. Crepuscular and partly diurnal; often perches prominently in daylight. Cliffs and ruins in semi-desert; 3000–5000 m. JK: nr.

5

Spotted Owlet *Athene brama* 21 cm

ADULT White spotting on upperparts, including crown, and diffuse brown spotting on underparts. Mainly crepuscular and nocturnal. Call is a harsh, screechy *chirurr-chirurr-chirurr...* followed by/alternated with *cheevak, cheevak, cheevak*. Habitation and cultivation. DE: cr, GU: cr, HA: cr, HP: nr, JK: nr, MP: cr, PU: cr, RA: lcr, UP: cr, UR: lcr.

6

Forest Owlet *Athene blewitti* 23 cm

ADULT Compared with Spotted Owlet, has rather dark grey-brown crown and nape, only faintly spotted with white, and lacks prominent white collar. Wings (apart from inner-coverts) and tail are broadly banded blackish-brown and white, with white-tipped remiges and a broad white tail-tip. Breast dark brown, and barring on upper flanks is broader and more prominent; rest of underparts white, much cleaner than on Spotted. Globally threatened (Critical). MP: nr.

7

Boreal Owl *Aegolius funereus* 24–26 cm

ADULT Greyish facial discs bordered with black, and with angular upper edge. Subalpine forest. Call is a soft *Po-po-po....* HP: nr.

8

Brown Hawk Owl *Ninox scutulata* 32 cm

ADULT Hawk-like profile. Dark face, and rufous-brown streaking on underparts. Nocturnal, often hunting from prominent perch. Call is a repeated, soft, pleasant *oo...ok, oo...ok,....* Forest and well-wooded areas. Foothills up to 1000 m. GU: nr, MP: nr, RA: v, UP: nr, UR: nr.

9

Long-eared Owl *Asio otus* 35–37 cm

a **b** ADULT Long ear-tufts, orange-brown facial discs and orange eyes. Additional differences from Short-eared are more heavily streaked belly and flanks, orange-buff base coloration to primaries and tail feathers, and lack of white trailing edge to wing. On passage and in winter frequents stunted trees and poplar plantations. Recorded breeding in well-wooded coniferous areas and groves. GU: v, HP: v, JK: nr, PU: v, RA: v, UR: v.

10

Short-eared Owl *Asio flammeus* 37–39 cm

a **b** ADULT Streaked underparts and short ear-tufts. Buffish facial discs and yellow eyes. In flight, rather long and narrow wings show buffish patch at base of primaries and dark carpal patches. Often seen hunting during the day, quartering low over the ground in a leisurely manner, when often hovering or gliding with wings in V. Grassland and open scrub country. DE: nw, GU: nw, HA: nw, HP: nw, JK: np, MP: nw, PU: nw, RA: nw, UP: lcw, UR: nw.

1

2

3

2/27/14
RANTHAMBOR

4

RANTHAMBOR

5

2/27/14
RANTHAMBOR

6

7

8

9b

9a

10b

10a

1 Grey Nightjar *Caprimulgus indicus* 27–32 cm

a b MALE and **c** FEMALE Greyer in overall coloration compared with Large-tailed, and less strikingly patterned (absent or less pronounced pale edges to scapulars, and less prominent pale tips to coverts). (*See also* Table 1 on p.291.) Song is a loud, resonant *chunk-chunk-chunk-chunk....* Forest clearings and scrub-covered slopes. DE: nr?, GU: nr, HA: nr?, HP: ns, MP: lcr, PU: nr, RA: nr, UP: nr?, UR: lcr.

2 Eurasian Nightjar *Caprimulgus europaeus* 25 cm

a b MALE and **c** FEMALE Medium-sized, grey nightjar with regular, bold lanceolate streaking on crown, nape and scapulars (latter with buffish outer edges). Similar in coloration to Grey Nightjar, but more cleanly streaked and with pronounced pale edges to scapulars, and more prominent pale tips to coverts. (*See also* Table 1 on p.291.) Song is a continuous churring; soft *quoit quoit* in flight. Rocky slopes with scattered bushes. GU: np, JK: v, MP: v, RA: np.

3 Sykes's Nightjar *Caprimulgus mahrattensis* 23 cm

a b MALE and **c** FEMALE Small, grey or sandy-coloured nightjar. Rather uniform in appearance, with finely streaked crown, irregular black marks on scapulars, irregular buff spotting on nape forming indistinct collar and irregular buff spotting on coverts. (*See also* Table 1 on p.291.) Has continuous churring song; low, soft *chuck-chuck* in flight. Breeds in semi-desert; wide variety of habitats in winter. DE: np?, GU: nw, HA: nr?, MP: v, PU: ns, RA: nw.

4 Large-tailed Nightjar *Caprimulgus macrurus* 33 cm

a b MALE and **c** FEMALE More warmly coloured and strongly patterned than Grey, with longer and broader tail. Has diffuse, pale rufous-brown nuchal collar, well-defined buff edges to scapulars, and prominent buff tips to wing-coverts usually forming pronounced wing-bars. (*See also* Table 1 on p.291.) Song is a series of loud, resonant calls: *chaunk-chaunk-chaunk* notes, repeated at the rate of about 100 per minute. Edges and clearings of subtropical forest. Foothills up to 1800 m. DE: v, HA: nr?, HP: lcs, MP: nr, PU: nr, RA: v, UP: cr, UR: lcr.

5 Indian Nightjar *Caprimulgus asiaticus* 24 cm

a b MALE Like a small version of Large-tailed. Has boldly streaked crown, rufous-buff nuchal collar, bold black centres and broad buff edges to scapulars, and relatively unmarked central tail feathers. (*See also* Table 1 on p.291.) Song is a far-carrying *chuk-chuk-chuk-chuk-tukaroo*; short sharp *qwit-qwit* in flight. Open scrub and cultivation. DE: np?, GU: lcr, HA: nr?, HP: nr, JK: nr?, MP: lcr, PU: nr, RA: nr, UP: nr, UR: np.

6 Savanna Nightjar *Caprimulgus affinis* 23 cm

a b MALE and **c** FEMALE Crown and mantle finely vermiculated; often appears rather plain except for scapulars, which are edged with rufous-buff. Male has largely white outer tail feathers, although this can be difficult to see since tail is often not fully spread when in flight. (*See also* Table 1 on p.291.) Song is a strident *dheet*. Open forest and scrubby hillsides. DE: np?, GU: lcr, HA: nr?, HP: nr?, MP: lcr, PU: nr, RA: nr?, UP: nr, UR: lcr.

1

Rock Pigeon *Columba livia* 33 cm

a **b** ADULT *C. l. intermedia*; **c** ADULT *C. l. neglecta* Grey tail with blackish terminal band, and broad black bars across greater coverts and tertials/secondaries. Northern *neglecta* race has whitish back (note difference in tail pattern compared with Hill Pigeon). Feral birds vary considerably in coloration and patterning. Often in large flocks. Feral birds live in villages and towns, wild birds around cliffs and ruins. DE: cr, GU: cr, HA: cr, HP: lcr, JK: lcr, MP: cr, PU: cr, RA: lcr, UP: cr, UR: lcr.

2

Hill Pigeon *Columba rupestris* 33 cm

a **b** ADULT Similar in appearance to Rock Pigeon, but has white band across tail contrasting with blackish terminal band. Often in large flocks. High-altitude villages and cliffs, mainly in Tibetan plateau country. Summers 3000–5500 m, winters above 1650 m. HP: lcr, JK: lcr, UR: nr.

3

Snow Pigeon *Columba leuconota* 34 cm

a **b** **c** ADULT Slate-grey head, creamy-white collar and underparts, fawn-brown mantle, and white band across black tail. Keeps in pairs and small parties in summer and in large flocks in winter. Cliffs and gorges in mountains. Summers 3000–5100 m, winters above 1500 m. HP: lcr, JK: nr, UR: lcr.

4

Yellow-eyed Pigeon *Columba eversmanni* 30 cm

a **b** ADULT Smaller than Rock, with narrower and shorter black wing-bars. Yellow orbital skin and iris, yellow tip to bill, brownish cast to upperparts, purplish cast to grey crown and nape, and extensive greyish-white back and upper rump. Also slight differences in tail pattern from Rock: dark terminal band is less clear cut and shows diffuse paler grey subterminal band. Plains cultivation. Globally threatened (Vulnerable). HA: v, JK: v, MP: v, PU: nw, RA: v, UP: nw?

5

Common Wood Pigeon *Columba palumbus* 43 cm

a **b** ADULT White wing-patch and dark tail-band, buff neck-patch and deep vinous underparts. In flight, from below, shows greyish-white band across tail, blackish terminal band, and pale grey undertail-coverts and base of tail. *See* Appendix for differences from Ashy Wood Pigeon. Wooded hillsides. Breeds 1500–3500 m, winters down to 800 m. HA: nw, HP: nw, JK: nr, UR: nw.

6

Speckled Wood Pigeon *Columba hodgsonii* 38 cm

a MALE and **b** FEMALE Speckled underparts, and white spotting on wing-coverts. Male has maroon mantle and maroon on underparts, replaced by grey on female. In flight, from below, shows dark grey undertail-coverts and underside to tail. *See* Appendix for differences from Ashy Wood Pigeon. Mainly oak/rhododendron forest; 1100–4000 m. HP: nr, JK: v, UR: nr.

7

Green Imperial Pigeon *Ducula aenea* 43–47 cm

a **b** ADULT Large size, metallic-green upperparts and tail, pale grey head and underparts, and maroon undertail-coverts. Moist tropical broadleaved forest. UP: nr.

TAJ PALACE
2/22/14 DEHLI

1c 1a 1b
2a 2b
3b 3a 4a 4b
3c
6a 6b
5b 5a
7a
7b

1 **Oriental Turtle Dove** *Streptopelia orientalis* 33 cm

a **b** ADULT *S. o. meena*; **c** ADULT *S. o. agricola* Stocky dove with rufous-scaled scapulars and wing-coverts, vinaceous-pink underparts, and black and bluish-grey barring on neck sides. Has dusky-grey underwing. Eastern race *agricola* has grey (rather than white) sides and tip to tail. *See* Appendix for differences from European Turtle Dove. Open forest, especially near cultivation. Breeds from foothills up to 4000 m. DE: np, GU: nw, HA: np, HP: lcs, JK: lcs, MP: lcr, PU: nr, RA: nw, UP: lcw, UR: lcr.

2 **Laughing Dove** *Streptopelia senegalensis* 27 cm

a **b** ADULT Slim, small dove with fairly long tail. Brownish-pink head and underparts, uniform upperparts, and black stippling on upper breast. Dry cultivation and scrub-covered hills. DE: cr, GU: lcr, HA: cr, HP: nr, JK: nr, MP: lcr, PU: cr, RA: lcr, UP: cr, UR: lcr.

3 **Spotted Dove** *Streptopelia chinensis* 30 cm

a **b** ADULT Spotted upperparts, and black-and-white chequered patch on neck sides. Cultivation, habitation and open forest. DE: nr, GU: lcr, HA: lcr, HP: nr, JK: nr, MP: cr, PU: cr, RA: nr, UP: cr, UR: lcr.

4 **Red Collared Dove** *Streptopelia tranquebarica* 23 cm

a MALE and **b** FEMALE Small, stocky dove, with shorter tail than Eurasian Collared. Male has blue-grey head, pinkish-maroon upperparts and pink underparts. Female similar to Eurasian Collared, but is more compact, with darker buffish-grey underparts darker fawn-brown upperparts and greyer underwing-coverts. Light woodland and trees in open country. DE: lcr, GU: lcr, HA: cr, HP: ns, JK: ns, MP: nr, PU: cr, RA: lcr, UP: cr, UR: lcr.

5 **Eurasian Collared Dove** *Streptopelia decaocto* 32 cm

a **b** ADULT Sandy-brown with black half-collar. Larger and longer-tailed than Red Collared. Plumage similar to female Red Collared but with paler upperparts and underparts, and white underwing-coverts. Open dry country with cultivation and groves. DE: cr, GU: lcr, HA: cr, HP: lcr, JK: lcr, MP: cr, PU: cr, RA: lcr, UP: cr, UR: lcr.

6 **Barred Cuckoo Dove** *Macropygia unchall* 41 cm

a MALE and **b** FEMALE Long, graduated tail, slim body and small head. Upperparts and tail rufous, barred with dark brown. Male has unbarred head and neck, with extensive purple and green gloss. Female is heavily barred on head, neck and underparts. Dense broadleaved forest. HP: v, JK: v, UR: nr.

7 **Emerald Dove** *Chalcophaps indica* 27 cm

a MALE and **b** **c** FEMALE Stout and broad-winged dove, with very rapid flight. Upperparts green, with black-and-white banding on back. Male has grey crown and white shoulder-patch. Usually seen when flushed from forest road or forest floor, or in dashing flight through forest. Moist tropical and subtropical broadleaved forest. GU: nr, HA: nr, HP: nr, JK: nr, MP: nr, UP: lcr, UR: lcr.

1

Orange-breasted Green Pigeon *Treron bicincta*   29 cm

a MALE and **b** FEMALE Central tail feathers of both sexes are grey. Male has orange breast, bordered above by lilac band, grey hind-crown and nape, and green mantle. Female has yellow cast to breast and belly, and grey hind-crown and nape. Sal and riverine forest. From plains up to 1500 m. UP: nr, UR: nr.

2

Pompadour Green Pigeon *Treron pompadora*   28 cm

a MALE and **b** FEMALE Male has maroon mantle, female has green. Both sexes told from Thick-billed by thin blue-grey bill (without prominent red base) and lack of prominent greenish orbital skin. Also, male has orange patch on breast, yellow throat and chestnut undertail-coverts, and female has streaked rather than barred appearance to undertail-coverts. Grey cap, and tail shape or pattern, help separate it from female Orange-breasted and Wedge-tailed. Sal and riverine forest. UP: nr.

3

Thick-billed Green Pigeon *Treron curvirostra*   27 cm

a MALE and **b** FEMALE Male has maroon mantle, female has green. Both sexes distinguished from Pompadour by thick bill with red base and by prominent greenish orbital skin. Further, male lacks orange coloration to breast and has different undertail-covert pattern (inner undertail-coverts are barred with white, and outer undertail-coverts are pale cinnamon). In female, undertail-coverts appear barred rather than streaked as in female Pompadour. Sal and riverine forest. UR: v/nr?

4

Yellow-footed Green Pigeon *Treron phoenicoptera*   33 cm

ADULT Large size, broad olive-yellow collar, pale greyish-green upperparts, mauve shoulder-patch, and yellow legs and feet. Deciduous forest and fruiting trees around villages and cultivation. DE: cr, GU: lcr, HA: cr, HP: nr, MP: cr, PU: cr, RA: lcr, UP: lcr, UR: lcr.

5

Pin-tailed Green Pigeon *Treron apicauda*   42 cm

a MALE and **b** FEMALE Both sexes have pointed central tail feathers, grey tail, green mantle and lime-green rump. Male has pale orange wash to breast. Sal and riverine forest. Up to 1800 m. UP: lcr, UR: lcr.

6

Wedge-tailed Green Pigeon *Treron sphenura*   33 cm

a MALE and **b** FEMALE Both sexes have long, wedge-shaped tail, indistinct yellow edges to wing-coverts and tertials, and dark green rump and tail. Male has maroon patch on upperparts (less extensive than on Pompadour), and orange wash to crown and breast. Female has uniform green head (lacking grey crown of female Pompadour). Mixed broadleaved forest. Plains up to 2500 m. HA: nr, HP: lcr, JK: nr, MP: v, UP: nr?, UR: lcs.

1b

2b

1a

2a

5a

4 2/22/14 NEW DELHI

3b

6b

3a

6a

5a

6a

5b

1 Indian Bustard *Ardeotis nigriceps* 92–122 cm

a **b** MALE and **c** FEMALE Very large bustard. In all plumages, has greyish or white neck, black crown and crest, uniform brown upperparts and white-spotted black wing-coverts. Upperwing lacks extensive area of white. Male huge, with black breast-band, and with almost white neck only very finely vermiculated with dark grey. Female smaller; neck appears greyer owing to profuse dark grey vermiculations, and typically lacks black breast-band. Dry grassland with bushes. Globally threatened (Endangered). DE: v, GU: nr, HA: xr, MP: nr, RA: nr, UP: nr.

2 Macqueen's Bustard *Chlamydotis macqueeni* 55–65 cm

a **b** MALE Medium-sized bustard. In all plumages, shows dark vertical stripe down neck. In flight, extensive white patch visible on outer primaries. Sexes similar, but female is smaller and lacks whitish panel across greater coverts. Juvenile very similar to female, but lacks black-tipped crest, neck stripe is finer, and white on wing is washed with buff and less prominent. *See* Appendix for description of vagrant Little Bustard. Semi-desert with scattered shrubs and sandy grassland. DE: v, GU: nw, HA: v, JK: v, RA: nw, UP: v.

3 Bengal Florican *Houbaropsis bengalensis* 66 cm

a **b** MALE and **c** **d** FEMALE Larger and stockier than Lesser Florican, with broader head and thicker neck. Male has black head, neck and underparts, and in flight wings are entirely white except for black tips. Female and immature are buff-brown to sandy-rufous, and have buffish-white wing-coverts with fine dark barring. Mainly well concealed in tall grassland. Males in breeding season perform striking display by leaping high into the air. Tall grassland with scattered bushes; sometimes in cultivation. Globally threatened (Endangered). UP: nr.

4 Lesser Florican *Sypheotides indica* 46–51 cm

a **b** MALE BREEDING, **c** MALE NON-BREEDING and **d** **e** FEMALE Small, slim, long-necked bustard. Breeding male has spatulate-tipped head plumes, black head/neck and underparts, and white collar across upper mantle; white wing-coverts show as patch on closed wing, but has less white on wing than Bengal Florican. Non-breeding male similar to female, but has white wing-coverts. Female and immature are sandy or cinnamon-buff; separated from female/immature Bengal Florican by smaller size and slimmer appearance, heavily marked wing-coverts and rufous coloration to barred flight feathers. Grassland and cultivation. Globally threatened (Endangered). GU: nr, HA: v, MP: nr, RA: ns, UP: ns, UR: ns.

1

Siberian Crane *Grus leucogeranus* 120–140 cm

a **b** ADULT and **c** IMMATURE Adult is white, with bare red face, pinkish-red legs and noticeably down-curved reddish bill. Immature has brownish bill and fully feathered head at first, and is strongly marked with cinnamon-brown on head, neck, mantle and wings, with some white body feathers by first winter; by third winter, red mask is apparent and body feathers are mainly white. In flight, both adult and immature show black primaries that contrast with rest of wing. Freshwater marshes. Globally threatened (Critical). DE: v, GU: v, HA: v, JK: v, MP: v, RA: nw, UP: v.

2

Sarus Crane *Grus antigone* 156 cm

a **b** ADULT and **c** IMMATURE Adult is grey, with bare red head and upper neck, and bare ashy-green crown. In flight, black primaries contrast with rest of wing. Immature has rusty-buff feathering to head and neck, and upperparts are marked with brown; older immatures are similar to adult but have dull red head and upper neck, and lack greenish crown of adult. Cultivation in well-watered country. Globally threatened (Vulnerable). DE: nr, GU: nr, HA: nr, HP: nr, JK: nr, MP: nr, PU: nr, RA: nr, UP: nr, UR: nr.

3

Demoiselle Crane *Grus virgo* 90–100 cm

a **b** ADULT and **c** IMMATURE Small crane. Adult has black head and neck with white tuft behind eye, and grey crown; black neck feathers extend as a point beyond breast, and elongated tertials project as shallow arc beyond body, giving rise to distinctive shape. Immature similar to adult, but head and neck are dark grey, tuft behind eye is grey and less prominent, and has grey-brown cast to upperparts. In flight, Demoiselle is best separated at a distance from Common by black breast. Cultivation and large rivers. DE: np, GU: cw, HA: nw, JK: np, MP: nw, PU: nw, RA: lcw, UP: nw, UR: np.

4

Common Crane *Grus grus* 110–120 cm

a **b** ADULT and **c** IMMATURE Adult has mainly black head and fore-neck, with white stripe behind eye extending down side of neck. Immature has brown markings on upperparts, with buff or grey head and neck. Adult head pattern apparent on some by first winter, and as adult by second winter. Cultivation, large rivers and marshes. DE: np, GU: cw, HA: lcw, HP: np, MP: nw, PU: nw, RA: lcw, UP: nw, UR: np.

5

Black-necked Crane *Grus nigricollis* 139 cm

a **b** ADULT and **c** IMMATURE Adult is pale grey with contrasting black head, upper neck and bunched tertials; shows more contrast between black flight feathers and pale grey coverts than Common, and has black tail-band. Immature has buff or brownish head, neck, mantle and mottling to wing-coverts. As adult by second winter. Summers by high-altitude lakes, 4000–4800 m; winters in fallow cultivation and marshes Globally threatened (Vulnerable). JK: nr.

1

Slaty-legged Crake *Rallina eurizonoides*   25 cm

   a ADULT and **b** JUVENILE   Black-and-white barring on underparts. Has greenish or grey legs, uniform olive-brown mantle and wings contrasting with rufous neck and breast, and prominent white throat. Juvenile has head and breast concolorous with mantle. Marshes in well-wooded country. UR: nr.

2

Slaty-breasted Rail *Gallirallus striatus*   27 cm

   a ADULT MALE and **b** JUVENILE   Straightish, longish bill with red at base. Legs olive-grey. Adult has chestnut crown and nape, slate-grey fore-neck and breast, white barring and spotting on upperparts, and barred flanks and undertail-coverts. Juvenile is less strongly marked, with rufous-brown crown and nape. Marshes, mangroves and paddy-fields. DE: xr, GU: v, MP: nr, RA: nr, UP: v.

3

Water Rail *Rallus aquaticus*   23–28 cm

   a ADULT and **b** JUVENILE   Slightly down-curved bill with red at base. Legs pinkish. Adult has streaked upperparts, greyish underparts and barring on flanks. Juvenile has buff coloration to underparts. Marshes and wet fields. Breeds at 1500 m. HA: nw, HP: nw, JK: nr, MP: v, PU: nw, RA: nw, UP: v, UR: nw.

4

Brown Crake *Amaurornis akool*   28 cm

ADULT   Olive-brown upperparts, grey underparts, and olive-brown flanks and undertail-coverts; underparts lack barring. Has greenish bill and pinkish-brown to purple legs. Juvenile similar to adult. Marshes and vegetation bordering watercourses. DE: nr, GU: lcr, HA: nr, HP: nw, JK: v, MP: nr, PU: nw, RA: nr, UP: lcr, UR: nr.

5

White-breasted Waterhen *Amaurornis phoenicurus*   32 cm

   a ADULT and **b** JUVENILE   Adult has grey upperparts, and white face, fore-neck and breast; undertail-coverts rufous-cinnamon. Juvenile has greyish face, fore-neck and breast, and olive-brown upperparts. Marshes and thick cover close to pools, lakes and ditches. DE: cr, GU: lcr, HA: cr, HP: nr, JK: nr, MP: lcr, PU: cr, RA: lcr, UP: lcr, UR: lcr.

1

Baillon's Crake *Porzana pusilla* 17–19 cm

a ADULT and **b** JUVENILE Adult has rufous-brown upperparts, extensively marked with white. Flanks are barred. Bill and legs are green. Juvenile is similar but has buff underparts. *See* Appendix for comparison with Little Crake. Marshes, reedy lake edges and wet fields. Breeds up to 1800 m. DE: np, GU: nw, HA: nw, HP: np, JK: lcr?, MP: nw, PU: nw, RA: nw, UP: lcr?, UR: np.

2

Spotted Crake *Porzana porzana* 22–24 cm

a ADULT and **b** JUVENILE Profuse white spotting on head, neck and breast. Stout bill, barred flanks and unmarked buff undertail-coverts. Adult has yellowish bill with red at base, and grey head and breast. Juvenile has buffish-brown head and breast, and bill is brown. *See* Appendix for description of Corn Crake. Marshes and lakes. GU: nw, HA: nw, JK: np, MP: nw, PU: v, RA: nw, UP: nw.

3

Ruddy-breasted Crake *Porzana fusca* 22 cm

a ADULT and **b** JUVENILE Red legs, chestnut underparts, and black-and-white barring on rear flanks and undertail-coverts. Juvenile is dark olive-brown, with white-barred undertail-coverts and fine greyish-white mottling/barring on rest of underparts. Marshes and wet paddy-fields. Breeds up to 1830 m. DE: nr?, GU: nw, HA: nr, HP: nr, JK: lcr, PU: nw, RA: nw, UP: nr, UR: nr.

4

Watercock *Gallicrex cinerea* M 43 cm, F 36 cm

a MALE BREEDING, **b** JUVENILE MALE and **c** FEMALE Male is mainly greyish-black, with yellow-tipped red bill, and red shield and horn. Non-breeding male and female have buff underparts with fine barring, and buff fringes to dark brown upperparts. Juvenile has uniform rufous-buff underparts, and rufous-buff fringes to upperparts. Male is much larger than female. Marshes and flooded fields. DE: ns, GU: v, HA: ns, PU: ns, RA: ns, UP: ns.

5

Purple Swamphen *Porphyrio porphyrio* 45–50 cm

a ADULT and **b** JUVENILE Large size, purplish-blue coloration, and huge red bill and red frontal shield. Juvenile greyer, with duller bill. Reedbeds and marshes. DE: lcr, GU: lcr, HA: cr, HP: nr, JK: nr, MP: nr, PU: cr, RA: lcr, UP: lcr, UR: nr.

6

Common Moorhen *Gallinula chloropus* 32–35 cm

a ADULT and **b** JUVENILE White undertail-coverts and line along flanks. Adult has red bill with yellow tip and red shield. Juvenile has dull green bill, and is mainly brown. Marshes and reed-edged pools. DE: cr, GU: lcr, HA: cr, HP: nw, JK: lcr, MP: lcr, PU: cr, RA: lcr, UP: lcr, UR: lcr.

7

Common Coot *Fulica atra* 36–38 cm

a ADULT and **b** JUVENILE Blackish, with white bill and shield. Reed-edged lakes and pools. DE: cw, GU: lcr, HA: cw, HP: nw, JK: nr, MP: lcr, PU: cr, RA: lcr, UP: lcr, UR: nr.

1a

2a

2b

1b

3b

4a

3a

4c

4b

5a

6b

2 27 1 14
R ANTNAMDOR

6a

5b

7a

7b

1 Tibetan Sandgrouse *Syrrhaptes tibetanus* 48 cm
a **b** MALE and **c** FEMALE Large and pin-tailed. Black spotting on upperparts, finely barred breast and white belly. In flight, black flight feathers contrast with sandy coverts on upperwing, and underwing is mainly black except for white lesser coverts and trailing edge to primaries. Female has barred upperparts. *See* Appendix for comparison with Pallas's Sandgrouse. Semi-desert in Tibetan plateau country. 4200–5400 m. HP: nr, JK: nr, UR: v.

2 Pin-tailed Sandgrouse *Pterocles alchata* 31–39 cm
a **b** MALE BREEDING and **c** **d** FEMALE Pin-tailed. White belly, with two (male) or three (female) narrow black bands across neck and breast. Largely white underwing and pale grey upperside to primaries. Male in breeding plumage has greenish upperparts with yellowish spotting; buff and barred with black in non-breeding plumage. Desert and semi-desert. DE: v, GU: v, HA: nw, RA: nw.

3 Chestnut-bellied Sandgrouse *Pterocles exustus* 31–33 cm
a **b** MALE and **c** **d** FEMALE Pin-tailed, with dark underwing, blackish-chestnut belly and black breast-line. Female has buff banding across upperwing-coverts and lacks black gorget across throat, which are useful distinctions at rest from Black-bellied. Desert and sparse thorn scrub. DE: nr, GU: cr, HA: nr, HP: nr, JK: nr, MP: nr, PU: nr, RA: cr, UP: nr.

4 Spotted Sandgrouse *Pterocles senegallus* 30–35 cm
a **b** MALE and **c** FEMALE Pin-tailed. Rather pale upperwing with dark trailing edge, and whitish belly with black line down centre. Female is spotted on upperparts and breast. Sandy desert and arid foothills. GU: lcr, HA: v, RA: lcr.

5 Black-bellied Sandgrouse *Pterocles orientalis* 33–35 cm
a **b** MALE and **c** FEMALE Stocky and short-tailed. Both sexes have black belly, and white underwing-coverts contrast with black flight feathers. Male has black and chestnut throat, and grey neck and breast. Female is very heavily marked. Semi-desert. DE: v, GU: nw, HA: nw, MP: v, PU: nw, RA: lcw, UP: nw.

6 Painted Sandgrouse *Pterocles indicus* 28 cm
a **b** MALE and **c** FEMALE Small, stocky and heavily barred. Underwing dark grey. Male has chestnut, buff and black bands across breast, and unbarred orange-buff neck and inner wing-coverts. Female heavily barred all over, with yellowish face and throat. Arid low hills. DE: nr, GU: lcr, HA: nr?, JK: nr, MP: lcr, PU: nr, RA: lcr, UP: nr.

1a

1b

1c

2a

2c

2d

2b

3c

3b

3d

3a

4b

4a

4c

5b

5c

5a

6a 3/6/14
POONA
G. R.

6b

6c

1 Eurasian Woodcock *Scolopax rusticola* 33–35 cm

a **b** ADULT Bulky, with broad, rounded wings. Head banded black and buff; lacks sharply defined mantle and scapular stripes. Crepuscular and nocturnal. In breeding season, male has characteristic roding display flight at dawn and dusk, when it flies above the treetops with slow, deliberate wing beats, uttering *chiwich* call. Dense, moist forest. Breeds 1830–3900 m, winters 900–2100 m. DE: v, GU: v, HP: nr, JK: nr, PU: v, RA: v, UP: v, UR: nr.

2 Solitary Snipe *Gallinago solitaria* 29–31 cm

a **b** ADULT Large, dull-coloured snipe with long bill. Less rufous and less boldly marked than Wood, with less striking head pattern, white spotting on ginger-brown breast, and rufous barring on mantle and scapulars (with finer white mantle and scapular stripes). Wings longer and narrower than Wood. In aerial display utters a deep *chok-achok* call, combined with a mechanical bleating produced by outer tail feathers. Marshy edges and beds of mountain streams. Summers 2400–4600 m, winters from 1200 m to at least 3000 m. HP: nw, JK: nw, UP: v, UR: nr.

3 Wood Snipe *Gallinago nemoricola* 28–32 cm

a **b** ADULT Large snipe, with heavy and direct flight and broad wings. Bill relatively short and broad-based. More boldly marked than Solitary, with buff and blackish head-stripes, broad buff stripes on blackish mantle and scapulars, and warm buff neck and breast with brown streaking. Legs greenish. In aerial display, flying in a wide circle, it utters a nasal *che-dep, che-dep, che-dep, ip-ip-ip, ock, ock*. Breeds in alpine meadows and dwarf scrub at 3000–5000 m, winters in forest marshes. Globally threatened (Vulnerable). HP: nr?, MP: nw, UP: v, UR: nw.

4 Pintail Snipe *Gallinago stenura* 25–27 cm

a **b** **c** ADULT More rounded wings than Common, and slower and more direct flight. Lacks white trailing edge to secondaries, and has densely barred underwing-coverts and pale (buff-scaled) upperwing-covert panel (more pronounced than shown). Feet project noticeably beyond tail in flight. Flight call is a rasping *tetch*. Marshes and wet paddy-fields. DE: v, GU: v, HA: v, HP: np, JK: v, MP: v, RA: np, UP: v, UR: nw.

5 Common Snipe *Gallinago gallinago* 25–27 cm

a **b** **c** ADULT Compared with Pintail, wings are more pointed, and has faster and more erratic flight; shows prominent white trailing edge to wing and white banding on underwing-coverts. Flight call is a grating *scaaap*, higher-pitched and more anxious than Pintail. Marshes and wet paddy stubbles. Breeds 1600–4500 m. DE: lcw, GU: lcw, HA: cw, HP: lcw, JK: ns, MP: lcw, PU: nw, RA: lcw, UP: cw, UR: lcw.

6 Jack Snipe *Lymnocryptes minimus* 17–19 cm

a **b** **c** ADULT Small, with short bill. Rounded wing-tips, and flight weaker and slower than that of Common. Has divided supercilium but lacks pale crown-stripe. Mantle and scapular stripes very prominent. If flushed, flies off silently and without zigzagging flight. Marshes and wet paddy stubbles. DE: nw, GU: lcw, HA: nw, HP: nw, JK: np, MP: nw, PU: nw, RA: nw, UP: lcw, UR: nw.

7 Greater Painted-snipe *Rostratula benghalensis* 25 cm

a MALE, **b** FEMALE and **c** JUVENILE Rail-like wader, with broad, rounded wings and longish, down-curved bill. White or buff 'spectacles' and 'braces'. Adult female has maroon head and neck, and dark greenish wing-coverts. Adult male and juvenile are duller, and have buff spotting on wing-coverts. When flushed, rises heavily with legs trailing. Has a roding display flight. Marshes, vegetated pools and stream banks. Up to 1800 m. DE: lcs, GU: lcr, HA: lcs, HP: lcs, JK: lcs, MP: nr, PU: nw, RA: ns, UP: lcr, UR: ns.

1a

1b

2a

2b

3a

4b

4c

4a

3b

2 l28 l l4
5a RRUTHAMBOR

6c

6b

5b

5c

6a

7b

7c

7a

1   **Black-tailed Godwit** *Limosa limosa*   36–44 cm

    a MALE BREEDING, **b** NON-BREEDING, **c** JUVENILE and **d** FLIGHT White wing-bars and white tail-base with black tail-band. In breeding plumage, male has rufous-orange neck and breast, with blackish barring on underparts and white belly; breeding female is duller. In non-breeding plumage, is uniform grey on neck, upperparts and breast. Juvenile has cinnamon underparts and cinnamon fringes to dark-centred upperparts. Banks and shallow waters of lakes and rivers. DE: cw, GU: nw, HA: cw, HP: np, JK: v, MP: v, PU: nwp, RA: lcw, UP: lcw, UR: np.

2   **Bar-tailed Godwit** *Limosa lapponica*   37–41 cm

    a MALE BREEDING, **b** NON-BREEDING, **c** JUVENILE and **d** FLIGHT Lacks wing-bar, has barred tail and white V on back. Breeding male has chestnut-red underparts. Breeding female has pale chestnut or cinnamon underparts, although many as non-breeding. Non-breeding has dark streaking on breast and streaked appearance to upperparts. Juvenile similar to non-breeding, but with buff wash to underparts and buff edges to mantle/scapulars. *See* Appendix for comparison with Asian and Long-billed dowitchers. Estuaries and lagoons. GU: nw, PU: v, RA: v.

3   **Whimbrel** *Numenius phaeopus*   40–46 cm

    a **b** ADULT Smaller than Eurasian Curlew, with shorter bill. Distinctive head pattern, with whitish supercilium and crown-stripe, dark eye-stripe and dark sides of crown. Flight call distinctive *he-he-he-he-he-he-he*. Banks of rivers and lakes, grassy areas. GU: lcw, JK: v, MP: v, PU: v, UP: v.

4   **Eurasian Curlew** *Numenius arquata*   50–60 cm

    a **b** ADULT Large size and long, curved bill. Rather plain head. Has distinctive mournful *cur-lew* call. Banks of rivers and lakes, grassy areas. DE: nw, GU: lcw, HA: nw, HP: np, JK: v, MP: nw, PU: nw, RA: nw, UP: lcw, UR: v.

5   **Spotted Redshank** *Tringa erythropus*   29–32 cm

    a ADULT BREEDING, **b** **c** ADULT NON-BREEDING and **d** JUVENILE Red at base of bill, and red legs. Longer bill and legs than Common Redshank, and upperwing uniform. Non-breeding plumage is paler grey above and whiter below than Common. Underparts mainly black in breeding plumage. Juvenile has grey barring on underparts. Has distinctive *tu-ick* flight call. Banks and shallow waters of rivers and lakes. DE: lcw, GU: v, HA: cw, HP: np, JK: v, MP: nw, PU: nw, RA: nw, UP: nw, UR: nw.

6   **Common Redshank** *Tringa totanus*   27–29 cm

    a ADULT BREEDING, **b** **c** ADULT NON-BREEDING and **d** JUVENILE Orange-red at base of bill and orange-red legs. Shorter bill and legs than Spotted Redshank, and with broad white trailing edge to wing. Non-breeding plumage is grey-brown above, with grey breast. Neck and underparts heavily streaked in breeding plumage. Juvenile has brown upperparts with buff spotting. Call is an anxious *teu-hu-hu*. Banks of rivers and lakes, marshes. Breeds 3500–5000 m. DE: cw, GU: cw, HA: cw, HP: np, JK: ns, MP: nw, PU: nw, RA: lcw, UP: lcw, UR: lcw.

7   **Marsh Sandpiper** *Tringa stagnatilis*   22–25 cm

    a ADULT BREEDING and **b** **c** ADULT NON-BREEDING Smaller and daintier than Common Greenshank, with proportionately longer legs and finer bill. Legs greenish or yellowish. Upperparts grey and fore-neck and underparts white in non-breeding plumage. In breeding plumage, fore-neck and breast streaked and upperparts blotched and barred. Juvenile has dark-streaked upperparts with buff fringes. Has an abrupt dull *yup* flight call. Banks of rivers and lakes, marshes. DE: cw, GU: cw, HA: nw, HP: v, JK: v, MP: nw, PU: nw, RA: nw, UP: lcw, UR: lcw.

8   **Common Greenshank** *Tringa nebularia*   30–34 cm

    a ADULT BREEDING and **b** **c** NON-BREEDING Stocky, with long, stout bill and long, stout greenish legs. Upperparts grey and fore-neck and underparts white in non-breeding plumage. In breeding plumage, fore-neck and breast streaked and upperparts untidily streaked. Juvenile has dark-streaked upperparts with fine buff or whitish fringes. Call is a loud, ringing and very distinctive *tu-tu-tu*. Wetlands. DE: cw, GU: cw, HA: cw, HP: lcw, JK: np, MP: nw, PU: nw, RA: nw, UP: lcw, UR: nw.

1

Green Sandpiper *Tringa ochropus* 21–24 cm
a **b** **c** ADULT NON-BREEDING Greenish legs. White rump, dark upperwing and under-wing. Compared with Wood, has indistinct (or non-existent) supercilium behind eye and dark-er upperparts. *Tluee-tueet* flight call. Wetlands. DE: cw, GU: cw, HA: cw, HP: lcw, JK: np, MP: cw, PU: nw, RA: nw, UP: lcw, UR: nw.

2

Wood Sandpiper *Tringa glareola* 18–21 cm
a **b** **c** ADULT NON-BREEDING and **d** JUVENILE Yellowish legs. White rump, and upper-wing lacks wing-bar. Compared with Green, shows prominent supercilium, more heavily spot-ted upperparts, and paler underwing. Flight call is a soft *chiff-if-if*. Banks of rivers and lakes, marshes. DE: cw, GU: cw, HA: cw, HP: v, JK: np, MP: lcw, PU: nw, RA: nw, UP: lcw, UR: np.

3

Terek Sandpiper *Xenus cinereus* 22–25 cm
a **b** ADULT BREEDING, **c** ADULT NON-BREEDING and **d** JUVENILE Longish, upturned bill and short yellowish legs. In flight, shows prominent white trailing edge to secondaries, and grey rump and tail. Adult breeding has blackish scapular lines. Flight call is a pleasant *hu-hu-hu*. Mainly coastal wetlands. DE: v, GU: lcw, HA: nw, JK: v, MP: v, PU: v, RA: v.

4

Common Sandpiper *Actitis hypoleucos* 19–21 cm
a **b** ADULT and **c** JUVENILE Horizontal stance and constant bobbing action. In flight, rapid, shallow wing-beats are interspersed with short glides. Juvenile has buff fringes to upper-parts. Flight call is an anxious *wee-wee-wee*. Wetlands. Breeds 1800–3200 m. DE: lcw, GU: cw, HA: cw, HP: nw, JK: ns, MP: cw, PU: nw, RA: nw, UP: cw, UR: nr cw.

5

Sanderling *Calidris alba* 20 cm
a ADULT BREEDING, **b** **c** ADULT NON-BREEDING and **d** JUVENILE Stocky, with short bill. Very broad, white wing-bar. Adult breeding usually shows some rufous on sides of head, breast and upperparts. Non-breeding is pale grey above and very white below. Juvenile chequered black-and-white above. Sandy beaches. GU: lcw, JK: v.

6

Little Stint *Calidris minuta* 13–15 cm
a ADULT BREEDING, **b** **c** ADULT NON-BREEDING and **d** **e** JUVENILE More rotund than Temminck's, with dark legs. Grey sides to tail; has weak *pi-pi-pi* flight call. Adult breeding has pale mantle V, rufous wash to face, neck sides and breast, and rufous fringes to upperpart feath-ers. Non-breeding has untidy, mottled/streaked appearance, with grey breast sides. Juvenile has whitish mantle V, greyish nape and rufous fringes to upperparts. *See* Appendix for comparison with Red-necked and Long-toed stints. Muddy edges of lakes, streams and rivers. DE: cw, GU: cw, HA: cw, HP: np, JK: v, MP: nw, PU: nw, RA: lcw, UP: lcw, UR: lcw.

7

Temminck's Stint *Calidris temminckii* 13–15 cm
a ADULT BREEDING, **b** ADULT NON-BREEDING and **c** **d** JUVENILE More elongated and horizontal than Little. White sides to tail in flight; flight call a purring trill. Legs yellowish. In all plumages, lacks mantle V and is usually rather uniform, with complete breast-band and indis-tinct supercilium. *See* Appendix for description of Long-toed Stint. Wetlands. DE: cw, GU: cw, HA: cw, HP: np, JK: np, MP: nw, PU: nw, RA: lcw, UP: lcw, UR: lcw.

1c

1a

1b

2a

2b

2c

3a

3b

3c

5b

4a

4b

5a

7b

6a

7a

6c

6b

8c

7c

8b

8a 2/22/24
DELHI

9b

9a

1 Pacific Golden Plover *Pluvialis fulva* 23–26 cm

a **b** ADULT BREEDING and **c** **d** ADULT NON-BREEDING In all plumages, has golden-yellow markings on upperparts, and dusky grey underwing-coverts and axillaries. In flight, shows narrower white wing-bar and dark rump. In non-breeding plumage, usually shows prominent pale supercilium and dark patch at rear of ear-coverts (not depicted well in plate). Black underparts with white border in breeding plumage. *See* Appendix for comparison with European Golden Plover. Call is a plaintive *tu-weep*. Mudbanks of wetlands, ploughed fields and grassland. DE: np, GU: np, HA: np, JK: v, MP: nw, PU: np, RA: np, UP: nw.

2 Grey Plover *Pluvialis squatarola* 27–30 cm

a ADULT BREEDING and **b** **c** **d** ADULT NON-BREEDING White underwing and black axillaries. Stockier, with stouter bill and shorter legs, than Pacific Golden. Whitish rump and prominent white wing-bar. Has extensive white spangling to upperparts in breeding plumage; upperparts mainly grey in non-breeding (in all plumages lacks golden spangling of Pacific Golden). Call is a mournful *chee-woo-ee*. Sandy shores, mudflats and tidal creeks. DE: np, GU: lcw, JK: v, MP: v, PU: nw, RA: v, UP: v.

3 Common Ringed Plover *Charadrius hiaticula* 18–20 cm

a ADULT BREEDING and **b** **c** ADULT NON-BREEDING Prominent breast-band and white hindcollar. Prominent wing-bar. Adult breeding has orange legs and bill-base (duller in non-breeding; more olive-yellow in juvenile). Non-breeding and juvenile have prominent whitish supercilium and forehead compared with Little Ringed. Call is a soft *too-li*, or *too weep* when alarmed. Mudbanks of freshwater and coastal wetlands. DE: np, GU: v, HA: np, JK: v, MP: v, PU: np, RA: v.

4 Long-billed Plover *Charadrius placidus* 19–21 cm

a ADULT BREEDING and **b** **c** ADULT NON-BREEDING Like a large Little Ringed, but has longer tail with clearer dark subterminal bar, and more prominent white wing-bar (although wing-bar is still narrow). In breeding plumage, shows a combination of black band across forecrown, brownish ear-coverts (ear-coverts black in breeding Little Ringed) and black breast-band, and has less distinct eye-ring than Little Ringed. Compared with Little Ringed, white forehead and supercilium more prominent in non-breeding plumage. Flight call is a clear *piwee*. Shingle banks of large rivers. DE: v, UP: v, UR: np.

5 Little Ringed Plover *Charadrius dubius* 14–17 cm

a ADULT BREEDING and **b** **c** ADULT NON-BREEDING Small size, elongated and small-headed appearance, and uniform upperwing with only a narrow wing-bar. Legs yellowish or pinkish. Adult breeding has striking yellow eye-ring. Adult non-breeding and juvenile have less distinct head pattern. Flight call is a clear *peeu*. Shingle and mudbanks of rivers, pools and lakes. DE: cr, GU: cr, HA: cr, HP: nr, JK: lcs, MP: lcr, PU: nw, RA: lcr, UP: lcr, UR: lcr.

6 Kentish Plover *Charadrius alexandrinus* 15–17 cm

a ADULT MALE BREEDING and **b** **c** ADULT NON-BREEDING Small size and stocky appearance. White hind-collar and usually small, well-defined patches on sides of breast. Male has rufous cap. Flight call is a soft *pi...pi...pi*, or a rattling trill. Banks of rivers and lakes. DE: lcw, GU: lcr, HA: cw, HP: np, JK: v, MP: nw, PU: nw, RA: nw, UP: lcr, UR: nr.

7 Lesser Sand Plover *Charadrius mongolus* 19–21 cm

a MALE BREEDING, **b** FEMALE BREEDING and **c** **d** ADULT NON-BREEDING Larger and longer-legged than Kentish, lacking white hind-collar. Very difficult to identify from Greater Sand Plover, although is smaller and has stouter bill (with blunt tip), and shorter dark grey or dark greenish legs. In flight, feet do not usually extend beyond tail and white wing-bar is narrower across primaries. Breeding male typically shows full black mask and forehead, and more extensive rufous on breast compared with Greater Sand (although variation exists in these characters). Flight call is a hard *chitik* or *chi-chi-chi*. Banks of rivers and lakes. Breeds at 3900–5300 m. in Ladakh. DE: np, GU: cw, HA: np, HP: ns, JK: ns, MP: v, PU: np, RA: np, UP: v, UR: v.

8 Greater Sand Plover *Charadrius leschenaultii* 22–25 cm

a MALE BREEDING, **b** FEMALE BREEDING and **c** **d** ADULT NON-BREEDING Larger and lankier than Lesser Sand, with longer and larger bill, usually with pronounced gonys and more pointed tip. Longer legs are paler, with distinct yellowish or greenish tinge. In flight, feet project beyond tail and has broader white wing-bar across primaries. *See* Appendix for information on Caspian Plover. Flight call is a trilling *prrrirt*, softer than that of Lesser. Coastal wetlands. DE: v, GU: cw, HA: v, HP: v, JK: v, PU: np, RA: np, UR: v.

1
Northern Lapwing *Vanellus vanellus* 28–31 cm
a **b** ADULT NON-BREEDING Black crest, white (or buff) and black face pattern, black breast-band, and dark green upperparts. Shows all-dark upperwing, and whitish rump and blackish tail-band in flight. Has very broad, rounded wing-tips. Distinctive slow-flapping flight with rather erratic wing beats. Wet grassland, marshes, fallow fields and wetland edges. DE: nw, HA: nw, HP: nw, JK: nw, MP: v, PU: nw, RA: nw, UP: nw, UR: nw.

2
Yellow-wattled Lapwing *Vanellus malarbaricus* 26–28 cm
a **b** ADULT Yellow wattles and legs. White supercilium, dark cap and brown breast-band. Wing and tail pattern much as Red-wattled. Call is a strident *chee-eet* and a hard *tit-tit-tit*. Dry river beds and open dry country. DE: nr, GU: lcr, HA: lcr, MP: nr, PU: nr, RA: nr, UP: nr, UR: nr.

3
River Lapwing *Vanellus duvaucelii* 29–32 cm
a **b** ADULT Black cap and throat, grey sides to neck, and black bill and legs. Black patch on belly. Call is a high-pitched *did, did, did*. Sand and shingle banks of rivers. DE: cr, HA: cr, HP: np, MP: lcr, PU: nr, RA: nr, UP: lcr, UR: lcr.

4
Grey-headed Lapwing *Vanellus cinereus* 34–37 cm
a **b** ADULT NON-BREEDING and **c** JUVENILE Yellow bill with black tip, and yellow legs. Grey head, neck and breast, latter with diffuse black border, and black tail-band. In flight, sec-ondaries are all-white. Call is a plaintive *chee-it, chee-it*. River banks, marshes and wet fields. DE: v, HA: v, JK: v, MP: v, RA: v, UP: nw, UR: nw.

5
Red-wattled Lapwing *Vanellus indicus* 32–35 cm
a ADULT and **b** JUVENILE Black cap and breast, red bill with black tip, and yellow legs. Wing and tail pattern much as Yellow-wattled. Call is an agitated *did he do it, did he do it*. Open flat ground near water. Up to 1800 m. DE: cr, GU: cr, HA: cr, HP: lcr, JK: lcr, MP: cr, PU: cr, RA: lcr, UP: cr, UR: lcr.

6
Sociable Lapwing *Vanellus gregarius* 27–30 cm
a **b** ADULT BREEDING and **c** ADULT NON-BREEDING Dark cap, with white supercilia that join at nape. Adult breeding has yellow wash to sides of head, and black-and-maroon patch on belly. Non-breeding and immature have duller head pattern, white belly and streaked breast. Dry fallow fields and scrub desert. Globally threatened (Vulnerable). DE: v, GU: nw, HA: v, HP: v, JK: v, MP: v, PU: v, RA: nw, UP: nw, UR: v.

7
White-tailed Lapwing *Vanellus leucurus* 26–29 cm
a **b** ADULT and **c** JUVENILE Blackish bill, and very long yellow legs. Plain head. Tail all white, lacking black band of other *Vanellus* plovers. Freshwater marshes and marshy lake edges. DE: lcw, GU: nw, HA: cw, MP: nw, PU: nw, RA: lcw, UP: lcw, UR: nw.

2/24/14
NEGUARA

1

Cream-coloured Courser *Cursorius cursor* 21–24 cm
  a b ADULT and **c** JUVENILE Pale sandy upperparts and underparts. Adult has sandy-rufous forehead, grey nape and pale lores. Juvenile has buffish crown and dark scaling on upperparts. Sand dunes and stony desert. GU: nw, HA: v, PU: v, RA: nr.

2

Indian Courser *Cursorius coromandelicus* 23 cm
  a b ADULT Grey-brown upperparts and orange underparts, with dark belly. Has chestnut crown, prominent white supercilium, and dark eye-stripe. In flight, shows white band across uppertail-coverts; underwing very dark, and wings broad with rounded wing-tips. Juvenile has brown barring on chestnut-brown underparts. Open dry country and dry river beds. DE: v, GU: lcr, HA: nr, MP: nr, PU: nr, RA: nr, UP: nr, UR: nr.

3

Oriental Pratincole *Glareola maldivarum* 23–24 cm
  a b c ADULT BREEDING, **d** ADULT NON-BREEDING and **e** JUVENILE Adult breeding has black-bordered creamy-yellow throat and peachy-orange wash to underparts (patterning much reduced in non-breeding plumage). Shows red underwing-coverts in flight. Very graceful, feeding mainly by hawking insects on the wing in tern-like manner. *See* Appendix for comparison with Collared Pratincole. Dry bare ground near wetlands. DE: lcs, GU: np, HA: lcs, MP: nr, PU: np, RA: np, UP: v.

4

Small Pratincole *Glareola lactea* 16–19 cm
  a b c ADULT BREEDING and **d** ADULT NON-BREEDING Small size, with sandy-grey coloration, and shallow fork to tail. In flight, shows white panel across secondaries, blackish underwing-coverts and black tail-band. Also hawks insects on the wing, often in large groups. Large rivers and lakes with sand or shingle banks. DE: lcs, GU: nr, HA: lcs, HP: nr, JK: nr, MP: lcr, PU: nr, RA: nr, UP: lcr, UR: ns.

5

Indian Skimmer *Rynchops albicollis* 40 cm
  a ADULT and **b** JUVENILE Large, drooping, orange-red bill. Juvenile has whitish fringes to upperparts. Large rivers. Flies close to the surface of the water, skimming it with bill open. Globally threatened (Vulnerable). DE: xr, GU: nr, HA: xr, MP: nr, PU: nr, RA: nr, UP: nr, UR: nr.

1a

1c

1b

2a

3b

3a

2b

3c

3e

4a

4b

4c

4d

3d

5b

5a

1 Heuglin's Gull *Larus heuglini* 58–65 cm
a ADULT NON-BREEDING, **b** 1ST-WINTER and **c** 2ND-WINTER Darkest large gull of region. Adult has darker grey upperparts than Caspian. First-winter differentiated from Yellow-legged by dark inner primaries and darker underwing-coverts, and usually broader dark tail-band. Second-year has darker grey mantle and darker upperwing and underwing than second-year Yellow-legged. Lakes and large rivers. DE: np, GU: nw, HA: np, PU: nwp.

2 Caspian Gull *Larus cachinnans* 55–65 cm
a ADULT NON-BREEDING, **b** 1ST-WINTER and **c** 2ND-WINTER Much larger and broader-winged than Mew Gull (*see* Appendix). Adult has paler grey upperparts than Heuglin's. Adult may show faint streaking on head in non-breeding plumage, but head is generally less heavily marked than in non-breeding Heuglin's. First-winter differentiated from Heuglin's by paler inner primaries, and much paler underwing-coverts with dark barring; brown mottling on mantle best distinction from first-winter Pallas's. Second-year has paler grey mantle than second-year Heuglin's; diffusely barred tail, dark greater-covert bar, and lack of distinct mask help separate it from first-year Pallas's. Lakes and large rivers. DE: lcw, GU: nw, HA: lcw, HP: np, JK: np, MP: nw, PU: lcw, RA: np, UP: nw, UR: nw.

3 Pallas's Gull *Larus ichthyaetus* 69 cm
a ADULT BREEDING, **b** ADULT NON-BREEDING, **c** 1ST-WINTER and **d** 2ND-WINTER Angular head with gently sloping forehead, crown peaking behind eye. Bill large, 'dark-tipped', with bulging gonys. Adult breeding has black hood with bold white eye-crescents, and distinctive wing pattern. Adult non-breeding has largely white head with variable black mask. First-winter has grey mantle and scapulars; told from second-winter Yellow-legged by head pattern (as adult non-breeding), absence of dark greater-covert bar, and more pronounced dark tail-band. Second-winter has largely grey upperwing, with dark lesser-covert bar and extensive black on primaries and primary coverts. Lakes and large rivers. DE: lcw, GU: nw, HA: lcw, HP: nw, JK: np, MP: v, PU: lcw, RA: np, UP: nw, UR: lcw.

4 Brown-headed Gull *Larus brunnicephalus* 42 cm
a ADULT BREEDING, **b** ADULT NON-BREEDING and **c** 1ST-WINTER Larger than Black-headed, with more rounded wing-tips and broader bill. Adult has broad black wing-tips (broken by white 'mirrors') and white patch on outer wing; underside to primaries largely black; iris pale yellow (rather than brown as in adult Black-headed). In breeding plumage, hood paler brown than Black-headed's. First-winter has broad black wing-tips. Lakes and rivers. Breeds in Ladakh at 3000–4500 m. DE: cw, GU: cw, HA: lcw, HP: np, JK: ns, MP: nw, PU: lcw, RA: nw, UP: nw, UR: nw.

5 Black-headed Gull *Larus ridibundus* 38 cm
a ADULT BREEDING, **b** ADULT NON-BREEDING and **c** 1ST-WINTER White 'flash' on primaries of upperwing. In non-breeding and first-winter, bill is tipped black and head is largely white with dark ear-covert patch. *See* Appendix for description of Little Gull, which is a vagrant to the region. Lakes and rivers. DE: cw, GU: nw, HA: lcw, HP: nw, JK: np, MP: nw, PU: lcw, RA: nw, UP: lcw, UR: nw.

6 Slender-billed Gull *Larus genei* 43 cm
a ADULT BREEDING, **b** ADULT NON-BREEDING and **c** 1ST-WINTER Head white throughout year, although may show grey ear-covert spot in winter. Gently sloping forehead and longish neck. Iris pale, except in juvenile. Adult has variable pink flush on underparts. Large rivers. DE: v, GU: nw, PU: v.

1 Gull-billed Tern *Gelochelidon nilotica* 35–38 cm

a **b** ADULT BREEDING and **c** ADULT NON-BREEDING Stout, gull-like black bill and gull-like appearance. Grey rump and tail concolorous with back. Black half-mask in non-breeding and immature plumages. Lakes and large rivers. DE: lcr, GU: cw, HA: lcr, HP: np, JK: v, MP: np, PU: np, RA: np, UP: lcw, UR: nw.

2 Caspian Tern *Sterna caspia* 47–54 cm

a ADULT BREEDING, **b** ADULT NON-BREEDING and **c** JUVENILE Large size with huge red bill. Lakes and large rivers. DE: v, GU: nr, PU: np.

3 River Tern *Sterna aurantia* 38–46 cm

a **b** ADULT BREEDING, **c** ADULT NON-BREEDING and **d** JUVENILE Adult breeding has orange-yellow bill, black cap, greyish-white underparts and long tail. Large size, stocky appearance and stout yellow bill (with dark tip) help separate adult non-breeding and immature from Black-bellied. Marshes, streams and rivers. DE: lcr, GU: lcr, HA: cr, HP: nr, JK: nr, MP: lcr, PU: nr, RA: lcr, UP: lcr, UR: lcr.

4 Lesser Crested Tern *Sterna bengalensis* 35–37 cm

a **b** ADULT BREEDING, **c** ADULT NON-BREEDING, **d** 1ST-WINTER and **e** JUVENILE Orange to orange-yellow bill, smaller and slimmer than Great Crested's, with paler grey upperparts (adult) and usually less boldly patterned upperwing (immatures). Mainly offshore waters; also tidal creeks and harbours. GU: nwp.

5 Great Crested Tern *Sterna bergii* 46–49 cm

a **b** ADULT BREEDING, **c** ADULT NON-BREEDING, **d** 1ST-WINTER and **e** JUVENILE Lime-green to cold yellow bill. Larger and stockier than Lesser Crested, with darker grey upperparts (adult) or darker and usually more strongly patterned upperwing (immatures). Mainly offshore waters; also tidal channels. GU: nr.

6 Sandwich Tern *Sterna sandvicensis* 36–41 cm

a **b** ADULT BREEDING, **c** ADULT NON-BREEDING and **d** 1ST-WINTER Slim black bill with yellow tip, and more rakish appearance than Gull-billed. White rump and tail contrast with greyer back. U-shaped black crest in non-breeding and first-winter/first-summer plumages. Coasts, tidal creeks and open sea. GU: nw, PU: v.

1   Common Tern *Sterna hirundo*   31–35 cm

a **b** ADULT BREEDING, **c** ADULT NON-BREEDING and **d** JUVENILE In breeding plumage, has orange-red bill with black tip, pale grey wash to underparts, and long tail streamers. Has dark bill, whitish forehead and dark lesser-covert bar in non-breeding plumage. *See* Appendix for comparison with Arctic Tern. Lakes and large rivers. DE: v, GU: nw, HA: v, HP: np, JK: ns, PU: v, RA: v, UR: v.

2   Little Tern *Sterna albifrons*   22–24 cm

a **b** ADULT BREEDING, **c** ADULT NON-BREEDING and **d** JUVENILE Fast flight with rapid wing beats, and narrow-based wings. Adult breeding has white forehead and black-tipped yellow bill. Adult non-breeding has blackish bill, black mask and nape-band, and dark lesser-covert bar. Lakes and rivers. DE: np, GU: nr, HA: nr, JK: v, MP: nr, PU: ns, RA: nr, UP: nr, UR: nr.

3   Saunders's Tern *Sterna saundersi*   23 cm

a **b** ADULT BREEDING and **c** 1ST-WINTER Adult breeding as Little Tern, but more rounded white forehead-patch (lacking short white supercilium), shorter reddish-brown to brown legs (orange on Little), broader black outer edge to primaries, and grey rump and centre of tail. There are no sure features for separating other plumages, although darker grey upperparts, including rump and dark bar on secondaries, may be useful. Coastal waters. GU: nr.

4   Black-bellied Tern *Sterna acuticauda*   33 cm

a **b** ADULT BREEDING, **c** ADULT NON-BREEDING and **d** JUVENILE Much smaller than River Tern, with orange bill (with variable black tip) in all plumages. Adult breeding has black belly and vent. Adult non-breeding and juvenile have white underparts, and black mask and streaking on crown. Marshes, lakes and rivers. DE: np, GU: nr, HA: nr, HP: nr, MP: nr, PU: nr, RA: nr, UP: nr, UR: nr.

5   Whiskered Tern *Chlidonias hybridus*   23–25 cm

a **b** ADULT BREEDING, **c** **d** ADULT NON-BREEDING and **e** JUVENILE In breeding plumage, white cheeks contrast with grey underparts; lacks greatly elongated outer tail feathers shown by *Sterna* terns. In non-breeding and juvenile, distinguished from White-winged by larger bill, grey rump concolorous with back and tail, and different patterning of black on head. Marshes, lakes and rivers. DE: cr, GU: cw, HA: cw, HP: np, JK: lcs, MP: lcr, PU: nw, RA: nw, UP: lcw, UR: ns.

6   White-winged Tern *Chlidonias leucopterus*   20–23 cm

a ADULT BREEDING, **b** **c** ADULT NON-BREEDING and **d** JUVENILE In breeding plumage, black head and body contrast with pale upperwing-coverts, and has black underwing-coverts. In non-breeding and juvenile, smaller bill, whitish rump contrasting with grey tail, and different patterning of black on head are distinctions from Whiskered. *See* Appendix for differences from Black Tern. Marshes, lakes and rivers. DE: v, GU: nw, JK: v, MP: v, PU: np, RA: v.

1 Osprey *Pandion haliaetus* 55–58 cm

a **b** ADULT Long wings, typically angled at carpals, and short tail. Has whitish head with black stripe through eye, white underbody and underwing-coverts, and black carpal patches. Frequently hovers over water when fishing. Lakes and rivers. Breeds 2000–3000 m, widespread in winter. DE: np, GU: cw, HA: nw, HP: np, JK: ns, MP: nw, PU: nw, RA: nw, UP: lcw, UR: nr.

2 Black Baza *Aviceda leuphotes* 33 cm

a **b** **c** ADULT Largely black, with long crest, white breast-band and greyish underside to primaries contrasting with black underwing-coverts. Broadleaved evergreen forest. UR: np.

3 Black-shouldered Kite *Elanus caeruleus* 31–35 cm

a **b** **c** ADULT and **d** JUVENILE Small size. Grey and white with black 'shoulders'. Flight buoyant, with much hovering. Juvenile has brownish-grey upperparts with pale fringes, and less distinct shoulder-patch. Grassland with cultivation and open scrub. Up to 1600 m. DE: lcr, GU: cr, HA: cr, HP: nr, JK: nr, MP: nr, PU: nr, RA: lcr, UP: lcr, UR: nr.

4 Black Kite *Milvus migrans* 55–68.5 cm

a **b** **c** ADULT and **d** **e** JUVENILE Shallow tail-fork. Much manoeuvring of arched wings and twisting of tail in flight. Dark rufous-brown, with variable whitish crescent at primary bases on underwing, and pale band across median coverts on upperwing. Juvenile has broad whitish or buffish streaking on head and underparts. *See* Appendix for comparison with Red Kite. Mainly around habitation, also mountains. Breeds up to 3000 m. DE: cr/cw, GU: cr, HA: cr/cw, HP: lcr, JK: lcr, MP: lcr, PU: cr, RA: lcr, UP: cr, UR: lcr.

5 Brahminy Kite *Haliastur indus* 48 cm

a **b** ADULT and **c** **d** JUVENILE Small size and kite-like flight. Wings usually angled at carpals. Tail rounded. Adult mainly chestnut, with white head, neck and breast. Juvenile mainly brown, with pale streaking on head, mantle and breast, large pale patches at bases of primaries on underwing, and cinnamon-brown tail. Wetlands in the plains and lower hills. DE: xr, GU: cr, HA: nr, HP: ns, MP: nr, PU: nr, RA: nr, UP: nr, UR: nr.

RANTHANBOR
2/28/14

1a
1b

2a
2b
2c

3a
3b
3c
3d

2/22/14
TA2
PALACE
DEHLI
4b
4c

4a
4d
4e

5a
5c
5b
5d

1 **White-bellied Sea Eagle** *Haliaeetus leucogaster* 66–71 cm

a b ADULT and c d JUVENILE Soars and glides with wings pressed forward and in pronounced V. Distinctive shape, with slim head, bulging secondaries, and short wedge-shaped tail. Adult has white head and underparts, grey upperparts, white underwing-coverts contrasting with black remiges, and mainly white tail. Juvenile has pale head, whitish tail with brownish subterminal band, and pale wedge on inner primaries. Immatures show mixture of juvenile and adult features. Mainly coastal habitats. GU: nr, RA: v.

2 **Pallas's Fish Eagle** *Haliaeetus leucoryphus* 76–84 cm

a b ADULT and c d JUVENILE Soars and glides with wings flat. Long, broad wings and protruding head and neck. Adult has pale head and neck, dark brown upperwing and underwing, and mainly white tail with broad black terminal band. Juvenile less bulky, looks slimmer-winged, longer-tailed and smaller-billed than juvenile White-tailed; has dark mask, pale band across underwing-coverts, pale patch on underside of inner primaries, all-dark tail, and pale crescent on uppertail-coverts. Large rivers and lakes. Globally threatened (Vulnerable). DE: xr, GU: np, HA: xr, HP: nr, JK: nr, MP: nr, PU: nr, RA: nr, UP: nr, UR: nr.

3 **White-tailed Eagle** *Haliaeetus albicilla* 70–90 cm

a b ADULT and c d JUVENILE Huge, with broad parallel-edged wings, short wedge-shaped tail, and protruding head and neck. Soars and glides with wings level. Adult has large yellow bill, pale head and white tail. Juvenile has whitish centres to tail feathers, pale patch on axillaries and variable pale band across underwing-coverts. Catches fish and waterfowl by flying low over the water surface. Large rivers and lakes. GU: v, HA: v, HP: v, JK: v, MP: v, RA: nw, UP: nw, UR: nw.

4 **Lesser Fish Eagle** *Ichthyophaga humilis* 64 cm

a b ADULT and c d JUVENILE Adult differs from Grey-headed in smaller size, greyish tail, paler grey upperparts, white patch at base of outer primaries on underwing, and greyer underparts. Juvenile browner than adult, with paler underwing and paler base to tail; lacks prominent streaking of juvenile Grey-headed, and has clear-cut white belly and different tail pattern. As Grey-headed, usually seen perched above water, and rarely soars above the tree canopy. Forested streams and lakes. From foothills up to 1300 m. HA: xr, HP: nr, JK: xr, MP: nr, UP: nr, UR: nr.

5 **Grey-headed Fish Eagle** *Ichthyophaga ichthyaetus* 69–74 cm

a b ADULT and c d JUVENILE Adult told from Lesser Fish Eagle by largely white tail with broad black subterminal band, darker and browner upperparts, and rufous-brown breast. Juvenile has pale supercilium, boldly streaked head and underparts, diffuse brown tail-barring, and whitish underwing with pronounced dark trailing edge. Spends most of the day perched in regularly used trees above the water. Very noisy during the breeding season; the call is a far-carrying *tiu-weeeu*. Slow-running waters and lakes in wooded country. DE: v, GU: np, HA: nw?, HP: nr, MP: v, RA: v, UP: nr, UR: nr.

1. Lammergeier *Gypaetus barbatus* 100–115 cm

a **b** ADULT and **c** **d** IMMATURE Huge size, long and narrow pointed wings, and large wedge-shaped tail. Adult has blackish upperparts, wings and tail, and cream or rufous-orange underparts contrasting with black underwing-coverts. Immature has blackish head and neck, and grey-brown underparts. Has a unique habit of splitting bones for the marrow by dropping them from a great height. Open country in mountains. Above 1500 m, most frequent at high altitudes. HP: cr, JK: nr, UR: nr.

2. Egyptian Vulture *Neophron percnopterus* 60–70 cm

a **b** **c** ADULT, **d** **e** IMMATURE and **f** JUVENILE Small vulture with long, pointed wings, small and pointed head, and wedge-shaped tail. Adult mainly dirty white, with bare yellowish face and black flight feathers. Juvenile blackish-brown with bare grey face. With maturity, tail, body and wing-coverts become whiter and face yellower. Open country around habitation. Up to 2500 m in Himalayas. DE: nr, GU: cr, HA: nr, HP: lcr, JK: nr, MP: cr, PU: nr, RA: cr, UP: cr, UR: lcr.

3. White-rumped Vulture *Gyps bengalensis* 75–85 cm

a **b** **c** ADULT and **d** **e** **f** JUVENILE Smallest of the *Gyps* vultures. Adult mainly blackish, with white rump and back, and white underwing-coverts. Key features of juvenile are dark brown coloration, streaking on underparts and upperwing-coverts are dark rump and back, whitish head and neck, and all-dark bill. In flight, underbody and underwing-coverts are distinctly darker than on Indian and Slender-billed. Juvenile is similar in coloration to juvenile Himalayan, but much smaller and less heavily built, with narrower-looking wings and shorter tail. Its underparts are also less heavily streaked, and it lacks prominent streaking on mantle and scapulars. Around habitation. Plains and hills up to 2500 m. Globally threatened (Critical). DE: nr, GU: nr, HA: nr, HP: nr, JK: nr, MP: nr, PU: nr, RA: nr, UP: nr, UR: nr.

4. Indian Vulture *Gyps indicus* 80–95 cm

a **b** ADULT and **c** JUVENILE 'Long-billed Vulture' was previously recognised as two distinct subspecies *indicus* and *tenuirostris*, but recent studies have demonstrated that they are better treated as separate species, Indian and Slender-billed. Adult Indian has sandy-brown body and upperwing-coverts, blackish head and neck with sparse white down on hind neck, white downy ruff, and yellowish bill and cere, and lacks pale streaking on underparts; in flight, lacks broad whitish band across median underwing-coverts shown by Eurasian Griffon, and has whiter rump and back. *See* account for Slender-billed for differences from that species. Much smaller and less heavily built than Himalayan Griffon, with darker head and neck, white ruff, and dark legs and feet. Juvenile has feathery buff neck-ruff, dark bill and cere with a pale culmen, and the head and neck have whitish down; distinguished from juvenile Eurasian Griffon by pale culmen, darker brown upperparts with more pronounced pale streaking, and paler and less rufescent coloration to streaked underparts. Best distinctions of juvenile Indian from juvenile White-rumped are paler and less clearly streaked underparts, paler upper- and underwing-coverts, and whitish rump and back. Around habitation and open forests. Globally threatened (Critical). DE: xr, GU: nr, HA: nr, MP: nr, RA: nr.

5. Slender-billed Vulture *Gyps tenuirostris* 80–95 cm

a **b** ADULT and **c** JUVENILE Bill, head and neck are more slender than in Indian Vulture, and has angular crown (and prominent ear canals). Darker and colder brown in coloration than Indian, and body appears more slender, with prominent white thigh-patches (especially prominent in flight). In flight, the trailing edges of the wings appear rounded and pinched in at the body, and the outer primaries appear noticeably longer than the inner primaries. The underside of the flight feathers are uniformly dark (these feathers have a pale cast and dark tips in Indian). The undertail-coverts appear dark (pale in Indian) and in flight the feet reach the tip of tail (falling short of tail-tip in Indian). Adult has dark bill and cere with pale culmen, lacks any down on head and neck, has dirty white ruff that is rather small and ragged, and dark claws (yellowish in Indian). Juvenile has mainly dark bill, some white down on head and neck, and pale streaking on underparts. Open forests. Up to 1500 m. Globally threatened (Critical). HA: nr, HP: nr, JK: nr, PU: nr, UP: nr, UR: nr.

1a 1b 1c 1d

2a 2b 2c 2d 2e 2f

3a 3b 3c 3d 3e 3f

4a 4b 4c

5a 5b 5c

3/3/14
TAJ
MAHAL

1

Himalayan Griffon *Gyps himalayensis* 115–125 cm

a **b** **c** ADULT and **d** **e** **f** JUVENILE Larger than Eurasian Griffon, with broader body and slightly longer tail. Wing-coverts and body pale buffish-white, contrasting strongly with dark flight feathers and tail, and ruff is buffish. Underparts lack pronounced streaking. Legs and feet pinkish with dark claws, and has yellowish bill and cere. Juvenile has brown feathered ruff, with bill and cere initially black, dark brown body and upperwing-coverts boldly and prominently streaked with buff (wing-coverts almost concolorous with flight feathers), and back and rump also dark brown. Streaked upperparts and underparts and pronounced white banding across underwing-coverts are best distinctions of juvenile from Cinereous Vulture; very similar in plumage to juvenile White-rumped Vulture, but much larger and more heavily built, with broader wings and longer tail, underparts more heavily streaked, and streaking on mantle and scapulars. Open country in mountains. Above 600 m, foraging to over 5000 m, winters down to plains. GU: v, HA: v, HP: nr, JK: nr, PU: nw, RA: nw, UP: v, UR: nr.

2

Eurasian Griffon *Gyps fulvus* 95–105 cm

a **b** **c** ADULT and **d** **e** **f** JUVENILE Larger than Indian Vulture, with stouter bill. Key features of adult are yellowish bill with blackish cere, whitish head and neck, fluffy white ruff, rufescent-buff upperparts, rufous-brown underparts and thighs with prominent pale streaking, and dark grey legs and feet. Rufous-brown underwing-coverts usually show prominent whitish banding, especially across medians (*see* accounts for Indian Vulture and Himalayan Griffon for comparison). Immature is richer rufous-brown on upperparts and upperwing-coverts (with prominent pale streaking) than adult; has rufous-brown feathered neck-ruff, more whitish down covering grey head and neck, blackish bill, and dark iris (pale yellowish-brown in adult). Open country. Mainly below 910 m, summers up to 3000 m. DE: v, GU: nr, HA: nw?, HP: nr, JK: nr, MP: nr, PU: nr, RA: nr, UP: nr, UR: nr.

3

Cinereous Vulture *Aegypius monachus* 100–110 cm

a **b** ADULT and **c** JUVENILE Very large vulture with broad, parallel-edged wings. Soars with wings flat (wings usually held in shallow V in *Gyps* species). At a distance appears typically uniformly dark, except for pale areas on head and bill. Adult blackish-brown with paler brown ruff; may show paler band across greater underwing-coverts, but underwing darker and more uniform than on *Gyps* species. Juvenile blacker and more uniform than adult. Open country. Below 3000 m. DE: v, GU: nw, HA: nw, HP: nw, JK: nw, MP: nw, PU: v, RA: nw, UP: v, UR: lcw.

4

Red-headed Vulture *Sarcogyps calvus* 85 cm

a **b** **c** ADULT and **d** **e** **f** JUVENILE Comparatively slim and pointed wings. Adult has bare reddish head and cere, white patches at base of neck and upper thighs, and reddish legs and feet; in flight, greyish-white bases to secondaries show as broad panel. Juvenile has white down on head; pinkish coloration to head and feet, white patch on upper thighs, and whitish undertail-coverts are best features. Open country near habitation, and well-wooded hills. Up to 2500 m in Himalayas. DE: xr, GU: nr, HA: nr, HP: nr, MP: nr, PU: nr, RA: nr, UP: nr, UR: nr.

1   Short-toed Snake Eagle *Circaetus gallicus*   62–67 cm

a **b** **c** PALE PHASE and **d** DARK PHASE   Long and broad wings, pinched in at base, and rather long tail. Head broad and rounded. Soars with wings flat or slightly raised; frequently hovers. Pattern variable, often with dark head and breast, barred underbody, dark trailing edge to underwing, and broad subterminal tail-band; can be very pale on underbody and underwing. Open dry country. Plains and hills up to 2300 m. DE: nw, GU: lcr, HA: lcw, HP: nr, JK: v, MP: nr, PU: nr, RA: nr, UP: lcr, UR: nr.

2   Crested Serpent Eagle *Spilornis cheela*   56–74 cm

a **b** ADULT and **c** **d** JUVENILE   Broad, rounded wings. Soars with wings held forward and in pronounced V. Adult has broad white bands across wings and tail; hooded appearance at rest, with yellow cere and lores, and white spotting on brown underparts. Juvenile has blackish ear-coverts, yellow cere and lores, whitish head and underparts, narrower barring on tail (compared to adult), and largely white underwing with fine dark barring and dark trailing edge. Frequently soars above forest, often in pairs, uttering loud whistling cry. Forest and well-wooded country. Up to 2130 m in Himalayas. DE: v, GU: lcr, HA: nw?, HP: nr, JK: v, MP: lcr, PU: nr, RA: nr, UP: lcr, UR: lcr.

3   Black Eagle *Ictinaetus malayensis*   69–81 cm

a **b** ADULT and **c** **d** JUVENILE   In flight has distinctive wing shape and long tail. Flies with wings raised in V, and with primaries upturned. At rest, long wings extend to tip of tail. Adult dark brownish-black, with striking yellow cere and feet; in flight, shows whitish barring on uppertail-coverts, and faint greyish barring on tail and underside of remiges (*compare with* dark morph of Changeable Hawk Eagle, Plate 56). Juvenile has dark-streaked buffish head, underparts and underwing-coverts. Hunts by sailing buoyantly and slowly over the canopy, sometimes weaving in and out of tree-tops. Broadleaved forest in hills and mountains. Up to 2700 m. DE: v, GU: nr, HA: nr, HP: nr, MP: v, PU: v, RA: v, UR: nr.

4   Eurasian Marsh Harrier *Circus aeruginosus*   48–58 cm

a **b** **c** MALE, **d** **e** **f** FEMALE and **g** JUVENILE   Broad-winged and stocky. As with other harriers glides and soars with wings in noticeable V, quartering the ground a few metres above it, occasionally dropping to catch prey. Male has brown mantle and upperwing-coverts contrasting with grey secondaries/inner primaries. Female mainly dark brown, except for cream on head and on leading edge of wing. Juvenile may be entirely dark. Marshes, lakes and grasslands. Up to 2000 m. DE: cw, GU: cw, HA: cw, HP: np, JK: v, MP: lcw, PU: lcw, RA: lcw, UP: lcw, UR: lcw.

1a 1b 1c 1d

2c 2a 2b 2d

3c 3a 3d 3b

4b 4c

4a 4e

4d 4f 4g

1

Pied Harrier *Circus melanoleucos* 41–46.5 cm

a **b** **c** MALE, **d** **e** **f** FEMALE and **g** **h** **i** JUVENILE Male has black head, upperparts and breast, white underbody and forewing, and black median-covert bar. Female has white uppertail-covert patch, dark-barred greyish remiges and rectrices, pale leading edge to wing, pale underwing, and whitish belly. Juvenile has pale markings on head, rufous-brown underbody, white uppertail-covert patch, and dark underwing with pale patch on primaries. Open grassland and cultivation. Mainly below 300 m. MP: nw, PU: v, RA: v, UP: nw, UR: v.

2

Hen Harrier *Circus cyaneus* 44–52 cm

a **b** **c** MALE and **d** **e** **f** FEMALE Comparatively broad-winged and stocky. Male has dark grey upperparts and extensive black wing-tips, and lacks black secondary bars. Female has broad white band across uppertail-coverts and rather plain head pattern (usually lacking dark ear-covert patch). Juvenile has streaked underparts as female, but with rufous-brown coloration. Open country. Plains and hills up to 2500 m. DE: np, GU: nw, HA: nw, HP: np, JK: np, MP: v, PU: nw, RA: v, UP: nw, UR: lcw.

3

Pallid Harrier *Circus macrourus* 40–48 cm

a **b** **c** MALE, **d** **e** **f** FEMALE and **g** **h** JUVENILE Slim-winged and fine-bodied, with buoyant flight. As with other harriers, glides and soars with wings in noticeable V, quartering the ground a few metres above it, occasionally dropping to catch prey. Folded wings fall short of tail-tip, and legs longer than on Montagu's. Male has pale grey upperparts, dark wedge on primaries, very pale grey head and underbody, and lacks black secondary bars. Female has distinctive underwing pattern: pale primaries, irregularly barred and lacking dark trailing edge, contrast with darker secondaries, which have pale bands narrower than on female Montagu's and tapering towards body (although first-summer Montagu's more similar in this respect); also lacks prominent barring on axillaries. Typically, female has stronger head pattern than Montagu's, with more pronounced pale collar, dark ear-coverts and dark eye-stripe, and upperside of flight feathers darker and lacking banding; told from female Hen by narrower wings with more pointed hand, stronger head pattern, and patterning of underside of primaries. Juvenile has evenly barred primaries (lacking pronounced dark fingers), without dark trailing edge, and usually with pale crescent at base; head pattern more pronounced than Montagu's, with narrower white supercilium, more extensive dark ear-covert patch, and broader pale collar contrasting strongly with dark neck sides. Open country. Plains and hills up to 3000 m. DE: np, GU: cw, HA: nw, HP: nw, JK: np, MP: nw, PU: nw, RA: lcw, UP: lcw, UR: lcw.

4

Montagu's Harrier *Circus pygargus* 43–47 cm

a **b** **c** MALE, **d** **e** **f** FEMALE and **g** **h** JUVENILE Folded wings reach tail-tip, and legs shorter than on Pallid. Male has black band across secondaries, extensive black on underside of primaries, and rufous streaking on belly and underwing-coverts. Female differs from female Pallid in distinctly and evenly barred underside to primaries with dark trailing edge, broader and more pronounced pale bands across secondaries, barring on axillaries, less pronounced head pattern, and distinct dark banding on upperside of remiges. Juvenile has unstreaked rufous underparts and underwing-coverts, and darker secondaries than female; differs from juvenile Pallid in having broad dark fingers and dark trailing edge to hand on underwing, and paler face with smaller dark ear-covert patch and less distinct collar. Open country. Mainly below 250 m. DE: np, GU: lcw, HA: np, HP: np, JK: np, MP: nw, PU: np, RA: nw, UP: nw, UR: nw.

1 Crested Goshawk *Accipiter trivirgatus* 30–46 cm

a b MALE and **c** JUVENILE Larger size and crest are best distinctions from Besra. In flight, short and broad wings, pinched in at base. Wing-tips barely extend beyond tail-base at rest. Male has dark grey crown and paler grey ear-coverts, black submoustachial and gular stripes, rufous-brown streaking on breast, and barring on belly and flanks. Female has browner crown and ear-coverts, and browner streaking and barring on underparts. Juvenile has rufous or buffish fringes to crown, crest and nape feathers, streaked ear-coverts, and buff/rufous wash to streaked underparts (barring restricted to lower flanks and thighs). Mainly forest. Up to 2000 m. HP: nr, MP: nr, UP: nr, UR: nr.

2 Shikra *Accipiter badius* 30–36 cm

a b MALE, **c** FEMALE and **d e** JUVENILE Adults paler than Besra and Eurasian Sparrowhawk. Underwing pale, with fine barring on remiges, and slightly darker wing-tips. Male has pale blue-grey upperparts, indistinct grey gular stripe, fine brownish-orange barring on underparts, unbarred white thighs, and unbarred or only lightly barred central tail feathers. Upperparts of female are more brownish-grey. Juvenile has pale brown upperparts, more prominent gular stripe, and streaked underparts; distinguished from juvenile Besra by paler upperparts and narrower tail barring, and from Eurasian Sparrowhawk by streaked underparts. Open woods and groves. Up to 1500 m. DE: cr, GU: cr, HA: cr, HP: lcr, JK: nr, MP: cr, PU: cr, RA: lcr, UP: cr, UR: lcr.

3 Besra *Accipiter virgatus* 29–36 cm

a MALE, **b c** FEMALE and **d e** JUVENILE Small. Upperparts darker than Shikra, and prominent gular stripe and streaked breast should separate it from Eurasian Sparrowhawk; underwing strongly barred compared with Shikra. In all plumages, resembles Crested Goshawk, but considerably smaller, lacks crest, and has longer and finer legs. Male has dark slate-grey upperparts, broad blackish gular stripe, and bold rufous streaking on breast and barring on belly. Female browner on upperparts, with blackish crown and nape. Juvenile told from juvenile Shikra by darker, richer brown upperparts, broader gular stripe, and broader tail barring. Breeds in dense broadleaved forest up to 3000 m; also found in open country in foothills and plains in winter. GU: nw, HA: nw, HP: nr, JK: nr, MP: v, RA: nw, UP: nw, UR: nr.

4 Eurasian Sparrowhawk *Accipiter nisus* 31–36 cm

a b MALE, **c d** FEMALE and **e** JUVENILE Upperparts of adult darker than Shikra, with prominent tail barring, and strongly barred underwing. Uniform barring on underparts and absence of prominent gular stripe should separate it from Besra. Male has dark slate-grey upperparts and reddish-orange barring on underparts. Female is dark brown on upperparts, with dark brown barring on underparts. Juvenile has dark brown upperparts and barred underparts. Well-wooded country and open forest. Breeds 1400–3500 m, winters in foothills and plains. DE: nw, GU: nw, HA: nw, HP: nr, JK: lcr, MP: nw, PU: nw, RA: nw, UP: lcw, UR: nw.

5 Northern Goshawk *Accipiter gentilis* 50–61 cm

a b FEMALE and **c** JUVENILE Very large, with heavy, deep-chested appearance. Wings comparatively long, with bulging secondaries. Male has grey upperparts (greyer than female Eurasian Sparrowhawk), white supercilium and finely barred underparts. Female considerably larger, with browner upperparts. Juvenile has heavy streaking on buff-coloured underparts. Forest. Mainly above 1500 m. GU: v, HA: v, HP: nw, JK: nr?, MP: nw, RA: v, UR: nr?.

1a

1c

1b

2b

2e

2d

3a

3b

2a

2c

3c

3e

3d

4d

4a

5b

4c

5c

4b

4e

5a

1

Oriental Honey-buzzard *Pernis ptilorhyncus* 57–60 cm

a b c MALE and **d** FEMALE Long and broad wings and tail, narrow neck and small head with small crest. Soars with wings flat. Very variable in plumage; often shows dark moustachial stripe and gular stripe, and gorget of streaking across lower throat. Lacks dark carpal patch. Male has grey face, greyish-brown upperparts, two black tail-bands, usually three black bands across underside of remiges, and dark brown iris. Female has browner face and upperparts, three black tail-bands, four narrower black bands across remiges, and yellow iris. Well-wooded country, usually of broadleaves. Up to 1800 m. DE: cr, GU: cr, HA: cr, HP: ns, JK: ns, MP: lcr, PU: lcr, RA: nr, UP: lcr, UR: lcr.

2

White-eyed Buzzard *Butastur teesa* 43 cm

a b c ADULT and **d e** JUVENILE Longish, rather slim wings, long tail and buzzard-like head. Pale median-covert panel. Flight *Accipiter*-like. Adult has black gular stripe, white nape-patch, barred underparts, dark wing-tips and rufous tail; iris yellow. Juvenile has buffish head and breast streaked with dark brown, with moustachial and throat stripes indistinct or absent; rufous uppertail more strongly barred; iris brown. Dry open country, scrub and open dry forest. Up to 1200 m. DE: np, GU: cr, HA: ns, HP: nr, MP: cr, PU: cr, RA: nr, UP: cr, UR: lcr.

3

Common Buzzard *Buteo buteo* 51–56 cm

a b c d ADULT *B. b. japonicus* and **e f** ADULT *B. b. refectus* Stocky, with broad wings and moderate-length tail. Soars with wings held in V shape. Variable; some very similar to Long-legged and Upland. *B. b. japonicus* typically has rather pale head and underparts, with variable dark streaking on breast and brown patch on belly/thighs; tail dark-barred grey-brown. *B. b. refectus* is dark brown to rufous-brown, with variable amounts of white on underparts; tail dull brown with some dark barring, or uniform sandy-brown. *B. b. vulpinus* (not illustrated) is extremely variable, and usually has rufous tail (and is similar to Long-legged; *see* that species). Open country. Breeds 3000–4000 m, widespread in winter. DE: nw, GU: nw, HA: nw, HP: nr, JK: nr, MP: v, PU: nw, RA: nw, UP: nw, UR: nw.

4

Long-legged Buzzard *Buteo rufinus* 61 cm

a b c d ADULT Larger and longer-necked than Common, with longer wings and tail (appears more eagle-like); soars with wings in deeper V. Variable in plumage. Most differ from Common in having combination of paler head and upper breast, rufous-brown lower breast and belly, more uniform rufous underwing-coverts, more extensive black carpal patches, larger pale primary patch on upperwing, and unbarred pale orange uppertail. Rufous and black morphs are similar to some plumages of Common. Open country. Breeds 1830–3900 m, winters in lower hills and northern plains. DE: nw, GU: cw, HA: lcw, HP: cw, JK: nr, MP: v, PU: nw, RA: nw, UP: nw, UR: nw.

5

Upland Buzzard *Buteo hemilasius* 71 cm

a b c d ADULT Larger, longer-winged and longer-tailed than Common (appearing more eagle-like); soars with wings in deeper V. Tarsus always at least three-quarters feathered, often entirely feathered (half-feathered or less on Common and Long-legged). Plumage variable. Pale morph has combination of large white primary patch on upperwing, greyish-white tail (with fine bars towards tip), whitish head, underparts with dark brown streaking, brown thighs forming dark U-shape on underparts, and extensive black carpal patches (*japonicus* race of Common can be very similar); never has rufous tail or rufous thighs as Long-legged. Dark morph probably not distinguishable on plumage from dark morph Common and Long-legged. Open country. Breeds at 4500 m, winters down to foothills. DE: v, GU: v, HP: nw, JK: nr, PU: v, UR: nw.

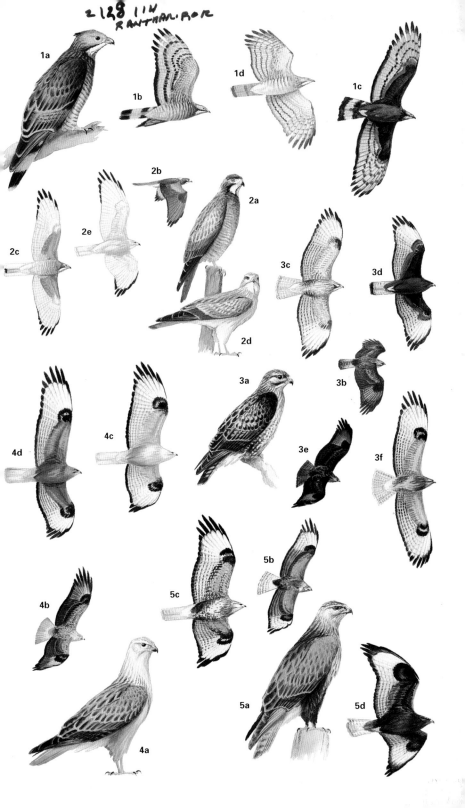

2128 11H
RANTHAMBOR

1a
1b
1d
1c

2b
2e
2c
2a
2d
3c
3d

4d
4c
3a
3b
3e
3f

4b
5c
5b
5a
5d
4a

1 Indian Spotted Eagle *Aquila hastata* 60–65 cm

a **b** **c** ADULT and **d** **e** **f** JUVENILE Now recognised, once again, as a distinct species from Lesser Spotted Eagle *Aquila pomarina* (which is now best considered extralimital). As Greater Spotted, Indian Spotted is a stocky, medium-sized eagle with rather short and broad wings, buzzard-like head with comparatively fine bill, and a rather short tail. The wings are angled down at carpals when gliding and soaring. Adult is similar in overall appearance to Greater Spotted, and field characters are poorly understood. Has a wider gape than Greater Spotted, with thick 'lips', with gape-line extending well behind eye (reaching to below centre of eye in Spotted). A possible additional feature of the adult in the field is the paler brown lesser underwing-coverts, which contrast with rest of underwing (Greater Spotted typically has uniform dark underwing-coverts). Juvenile is more distinct from juvenile Greater Spotted. Spotting on upperwing coverts is less prominent, tertials are pale brown with diffuse white tips (dark with bold white tips in Greater Spotted), uppertail coverts are pale brown with white barring (white in Greater Spotted), and underparts are paler light yellowish brown with dark streaking. In some plumages can resemble Steppe Eagle – differences mentioned below for Greater Spotted are likely to be helpful for separation (although gape-line is also long in Steppe). Wooded areas in plains to the edge of the hills. DE: nr?, GU: nr?, HA: nr?, MP: v, PU: nr, RA: nr, UP: nr, UR: nr.

2 Greater Spotted Eagle *Aquila clanga* 65–72 cm

a **b** **c** ADULT and **d** **e** **f** JUVENILE; **g** **h** JUVENILE '*fulvescens*' Medium-sized eagle with rather short and broad wings, stocky head, and short tail. Wings distinctly angled down at carpals when gliding, almost flat when soaring. See account for Indian Spotted for differences from that species. Compared with Steppe Eagle, has less protruding head in flight, with shorter wings and less deep-fingered wing-tips; at rest, trousers less baggy, and bill smaller with rounded (rather than elongated) nostril and shorter gape; lacks adult Steppe's barring on underside of flight and tail feathers, and dark trailing edge to wing, and has a dark chin. Pale variant '*fulvescens*' distinguished from juvenile Imperial Eagle by structural differences, lack of prominent pale wedge on inner primaries on underwing, and unstreaked underparts. Juvenile has bold whitish tips to dark brown coverts. Large rivers and lakes; prefers wooded areas near water. Globally threatened (Vulnerable). DE: lcp, GU: nr, HA: cw, HP: np, JK: np, MP: nw, PU: nw, RA: nr, UP: nw, UR: nw.

3 Golden Eagle *Aquila chrysaetos* 75–88 cm

a **b** **c** ADULT and **d** **e** JUVENILE Large eagle, with long and broad wings (with pronounced curve to trailing edge), long tail, and distinctly protruding head and neck. Wings clearly pressed forward and raised (with upturned fingers) in pronounced V when soaring. Adult has pale panel across upperwing-coverts, gold crown and nape, and two-toned tail. Juvenile has white base to tail and white patch at base of flight feathers. Rugged mountains above treeline. Mainly 2745–4570 m. HP: nr, JK: nr, PU: v, RA: v, UR: nr.

POKHA G.R.
3/6/14

1a

1e

1b

1c

1f

1d

2a

2h

2b

2f

2d

2g

2e

2c

3a

3c

3b

3e

3d

Tawny Eagle *Aquila rapax* 63–71 cm

a **b** **c** **d** **e** ADULT, **f** **g** JUVENILE and **h** SUB-ADULT Compared with Steppe, hand of wing does not appear as long and broad, tail slightly shorter, and looks smaller and weaker at rest; gape-line ends level with centre of eye (extends to rear of eye in Steppe), and adult has yellowish iris. Differs from the spotted eagles in more protruding head and neck in flight, baggy trousers, yellow iris and oval nostril. Adult extremely variable, from dark brown through rufous to pale cream, and unstreaked or streaked with rufous or dark brown. Dark morph very similar to adult Steppe (which shows much less variation); distinctions include less-pronounced barring and dark trailing edge on underwing, dark nape and dark chin. Rufous to pale cream Tawny is uniformly pale from uppertail-coverts to back, with undertail-coverts same colour as belly (contrast often apparent on similar species). Pale adults also lack prominent whitish trailing edge to wing, tip to tail and greater-covert bar (present on immatures of similar species). Characteristic, if present, is distinct pale inner-primary wedge on underwing. Juvenile also variable, with narrow white tips to unbarred secondaries; otherwise as similar-plumaged adult. Many (possibly all) non-dark Tawnys have distinctive immature/sub-adult plumage: dark throat and breast contrasting with pale belly, and can show dark banding across underwing-coverts; whole head and breast may be dark. Cultivation and open wooded country. DE: xr, GU: cr, HA: nw, HP: nr, MP: lcr, PU: nr, RA: nr, UP: lcr, UR: nw.

Steppe Eagle *Aquila nipalensis* 76–80 cm

a **b** **c** ADULT, **d** **e** **f** JUVENILE and **g** **h** IMMATURE Broader and longer wings than Greater and Indian Spotted with more pronounced and spread fingers, and more protruding head and neck; wings flatter when soaring, and less distinctly angled down at carpals when gliding. When perched, clearly bigger and heavier, with heavier bill and baggy trousers. Adult separated from adult spotted eagles by underwing pattern (dark trailing edge, distinct barring on remiges, pale rufous nape-patch and pale chin). Juvenile has broad white bar across underwing, double white bar on upperwing, and white crescent across uppertail-coverts; prominence of bars on upperwing and underwing much reduced on older immatures. Wooded hills, open country and lakes. DE: lcw, GU: cw, HA: cw, HP: nw, JK: np, MP: nw, PU: nw, RA: lcw, UP: nw, UR: lcw.

Imperial Eagle *Aquila heliaca* 72–83 cm

a **b** **c** ADULT and **d** **e** **f** JUVENILE Large, stout-bodied eagle with long and broad wings, longish tail, and distinctly protruding head and neck. Wings flat when soaring and gliding. Adult has almost uniform upperwing, small white scapular patches, golden-buff crown and nape, and two-toned tail. Juvenile has pronounced curve to trailing edge of wing, pale wedge on inner primaries, streaked buffish body and wing-coverts, uniform pale rump and back (lacking distinct pale crescent shown by other species except Tawny), and white tips to median coverts and greater upperwing-coverts. Large rivers and lakes, open country. Globally threatened. DE: np, GU: nw, HA: lcw, HP: nw, MP: v, PU: nw, RA: nw, UP: nw, UR: nw.

1a

1c

1d

1h

1e

1b

1g

1f

2b

2a

2d

2e

2c

2f

27
21/1/14
RANTHAMBOR

2g

3c

2h

3e

3a

3b

3d

3f

Bonelli's Eagle *Hieraaetus fasciatus* 65–72 cm

a b c ADULT and **d e f** JUVENILE Medium-sized eagle with long and broad wings, distinctly protruding head and long, square-ended tail. Soars with wings flat. Adult has pale underbody and forewing, blackish band along underwing-coverts, whitish patch on mantle, and pale greyish tail with broad dark terminal band. Juvenile has ginger-buff to reddish-brown underbody and underwing-coverts (with variable dark band along greater underwing-coverts), uniform upperwing, pale crescent on uppertail-coverts and patch on back. Well-wooded country. Plains and hills up to 2400 m. DE: nw, GU: lcr, HA: lcw, HP: nr, JK: nr, MP: nr, PU: nw, RA: nr, UP: nr, UR: nr.

Booted Eagle *Hieraaetus pennatus* 45–53 cm

a b c PALE MORPH and **d e** DARK MORPH Smallish eagle with long wings and long square-ended tail. Glides and soars with wings flat or slightly angled down at carpal. Always shows white shoulder patches, pale median-covert panel, pale wedge on inner primaries, white crescent on uppertail-coverts, and greyish undertail with darker centre and tip. Head, body and wing-coverts whitish, brown or rufous respectively in pale, dark and rufous morphs. Well-wooded country. Breeds in Himalayas at 1500–3000 m, widespread in plains and hills in winter. DE: nw, GU: nw, HA: nw?, HP: ns, JK: ns, MP: v, PU: np, RA: nw, UP: nr, UR: nr.

Rufous-bellied Eagle *Hieraaetus kienerii* 53–61 cm

a b ADULT and **c d** JUVENILE Smallish, with buzzard-shaped wings and tail. At rest, wing-tips extend well down tail. Glides and soars with wings flat. Adult has blackish hood and upperparts, white throat and breast, and (black-streaked) rufous rest of underparts. Juvenile has white underparts and underwing-coverts, dark mask and white supercilium, and dark patches on breast and flanks. Moist broadleaved forest. Up to 1000 m in Himalayas. MP: nr, UR: nr.

Changeable Hawk Eagle *Spizaetus cirrhatus* 61–72 cm

a b PALE MORPH, **c d** DARK MORPH, **e f** JUVENILE *S. c. limnaetus*; **g h** ADULT *S. c. cirrhatus* Narrower, more parallel-edged wings than Mountain Hawk Eagle. Soars with wings flat (except in display, when both wings and tail raised). Adult *limnaetus* lacks prominent crest, and has boldly streaked underparts and narrower tail-barring compared with Mountain; dark morph told from Black Eagle by structural differences, greyish undertail with diffuse dark terminal band, and extensive greyish bases to underside of remiges. Juvenile generally whiter on head than juvenile Mountain. Nominate *cirrhatus*, with prominent crest and brown thighs, occurs in south of region. Broadleaved forest and well-wooded country. Up to 1900 m in Himalayas. DE: v, GU: lcr, HP: v, MP: lcr, RA: nr, UP: nr, UR: lcr.

Mountain Hawk Eagle *Spizaetus nipalensis* 70–72 cm

a b ADULT and **c d** JUVENILE Prominent crest. Wings broader than on Changeable, with more pronounced curve to trailing edge. Soars with wings in shallow V. Distinguished from Changeable by extensive barring on underparts, whitish-barred rump, and stronger dark barring on tail. Juvenile told from juvenile Changeable by more extensive dark streaking on crown and sides of head, white-tipped black crest, buff-barred rump, and fewer, more prominent tail-bars. Forested hills and mountains. From 120–2400 m. HP: nr, JK: nr, MP: v, UP: v, UR: lcr.

1b

1a

2c

2b

2a

3b

3a

4d

4b

3c

4a

4c

6a

6b

2/28/14
RANTHAMBOR

5b

5a

2/25/14
JAIPUR

7a

7c

7b

Indian Pond Heron *Ardeola grayii* 42–45 cm
a **b** ADULT BREEDING and **c** ADULT NON-BREEDING Whitish wings contrast with dark saddle. Adult breeding plumage has yellowish-buff head and neck, white nape-plumes and maroon-brown mantle/scapulars. Head, neck and breast streaked in non-breeding plumage. Wetlands. Up to 1500 m in Himalayas. DE: cr, GU: cr, HA: cr, HP: nr, JK: nr, MP: cr, PU: cr, RA: lcr, UP: cr, UR: lcr.

Little Heron *Butorides striatus* 40–48 cm
a **b** ADULT and **c** JUVENILE Small, stocky and short-legged heron. Adult has black crown and long crest, dark greenish upperparts, and greyish underparts. Juvenile has buff streaking on upperparts, and dark-streaked underparts. Wetlands with dense shrub cover. DE: xr, GU: nr, HA: nr, HP: nr, MP: nr, PU: nr, RA: nr, UP: nr, UR: nr.

Black-crowned Night Heron *Nycticorax nycticorax* 58–65 cm
a **b** ADULT and **c** JUVENILE Stocky heron, with thick neck. Adult has black crown and mantle contrasting with grey wings and whitish underparts. Breeding plumage has elongated white nape-plumes. Juvenile is boldly streaked and spotted. Immature resembles juvenile but has unstreaked brown mantle/scapulars. Wetlands, often with reedbeds. DE: lcr, GU: cr, HA: lcr, HP: nr, JK: nr, MP: nr, PU: cr, RA: lcr, UP: lcr, UR: lcr.

Little Bittern *Ixobrychus minutus* 33–38 cm
a **b** MALE, **c** FEMALE and **d** JUVENILE Small size. Buffish wing-coverts contrast with dark flight feathers in all plumages. Male has black crown and mantle/scapulars, and buff neck. Female has brown mantle/scapulars, with brownish-buff streaking on fore-neck. Juvenile has warm buff upperparts streaked with dark brown, and brown streaking on underparts; very similar to juvenile Yellow, but streaking on fore-neck and breast of Yellow is generally more rufous-orange. Reedbeds. Up to 1800 m in Kashmir. DE: xr, GU: v, HA: v, JK: lcs, RA: v, UP: nw, UR: nw.

Yellow Bittern *Ixobrychus sinensis* 38 cm
a **b** ADULT MALE and **c** JUVENILE Small size. Yellowish-buff wing-coverts contrast with dark brown flight feathers. Male has pinkish-brown mantle/scapulars, and face and sides of neck are vinaceous. Female is similar to male but with rufous streaking on black crown, rufous-orange streaking on fore-neck and breast, and diffuse buff edges to rufous-brown mantle/scapulars. Juvenile appears buff, with bold dark streaking to upperparts including wing-coverts; foreneck and breast are heavily streaked. Reedbeds and marshes. DE: lcs, GU: ns, HA: lcs, PU: ns, RA: nr, UP: nr, UR: ns.

Cinnamon Bittern *Ixobrychus cinnamomeus* 38 cm
a **b** MALE, **c** FEMALE and **d** JUVENILE Small size. Uniform-looking cinnamon-rufous flight feathers and tail in all plumages. Male has cinnamon-rufous crown, hind-neck and mantle/scapulars. Female has dark brown crown and mantle, and dark brown streaking on fore-neck and breast. Juvenile has buff mottling on dark brown upperparts, and is heavily streaked with dark brown on underparts. DE: lcs, GU: ns, HA: lcs, HP: np, MP: ns?, PU: ns, RA: ns, UP: lcr, UR: ns.

Black Bittern *Dupetor flavicollis* 58 cm
a **b** ADULT and **c** JUVENILE Blackish upperparts including wings, with orange-buff patch on side of neck. Juvenile has rufous fringes to upperparts. Forest pools, marshes and reed-edged lakes. DE: lcs, GU: ns, HA: lcs, MP: nr, PU: nr, RA: ns, UP: lcr.

Great Bittern *Botaurus stellaris* 70–80 cm
a **b** ADULT Stocky. Large size. Cryptically patterned with golden-brown, blackish and buff. Wet reedbeds. DE: nw, GU: nr, HA: nw, JK: nw, MP: nw, PU: v, RA: nw, UP: nw.

Greater Flamingo *Phoenicopterus ruber* 125–145 cm

a **b** ADULT, **c** IMMATURE and **d** JUVENILE Larger than Lesser, with longer and thinner neck. Bill larger and less prominently kinked. Adult has pale pink bill with prominent dark tip, and variable amount of pinkish-white on head, neck and body; in flight, crimson-pink upper-wing-coverts contrast with whitish body. Immature has greyish-white head and neck, and white body lacking any pink; pink on bill develops with increasing age. Juvenile brownish grey, with white on coverts; bill grey, tipped with black, and legs grey. Shallow brackish lakes, mudflats and saltpans. DE: cr, GU: lcr, HA: lcw, MP: v, PU: np, RA: nr, UP: nw.

Lesser Flamingo *Phoenicopterus minor* 80–90 cm

a **b** ADULT, **c** IMMATURE and **d** JUVENILE Smaller than Greater Flamingo; neck appears shorter, and bill is smaller and more prominently kinked. Adult has black-tipped dark red bill, dark red iris and facial skin, and deep rose-pink on head, neck and body; blood-red centres to lesser and median upperwing-coverts contrast with paler pink of rest of coverts in flight. Immature has greyish-brown head and neck, pale pink body, and mainly pink coverts; bill coloration develops with increasing age. Juvenile mainly grey-brown, with dark-tipped purplish-brown bill and grey legs. Salt and brackish lagoons and saltpans. DE: v, GU: lcw, HA: v, MP: v, RA: nr?, UP: v.

Glossy Ibis *Plegadis falcinellus* 55–65 cm

a ADULT BREEDING, **b** ADULT NON-BREEDING and **c** JUVENILE Small, dark ibis with rather fine down-curved bill. Adult breeding is deep chestnut, glossed with purple and green, with metallic green-and-purple wings; has narrow white surround to bare lores. Adult non-breeding is duller, with white streaking on dark brown head and neck. Juvenile similar to adult non-breeding, but is dark brown with white mottling on head, and only faint greenish gloss to upperparts. Inland wetlands. DE: np, GU: nr, HA: cr, JK: v, MP: np, PU: nr, RA: nr, UP: nw, UR: np.

Black-headed Ibis *Threskiornis melanocephalus* 75 cm

a ADULT BREEDING and **b** IMMATURE Stocky, mainly white ibis with stout down-curved black bill. Adult breeding has naked black head, white lower-neck plumes, variable yellow wash to mantle and breast, and grey on scapulars and elongated tertials. Adult non-breeding has all-white body and lacks neck-plumes. Immature has grey feathering on head and neck, and black-tipped wings. Flooded fields, marshes, rivers and pools. DE: cr, GU: cr, HA: cr, MP: nr, PU: nr, RA: lcr, UP: lcr, UR: np.

Black Ibis *Pseudibis papillosa* 68 cm

ADULT Stocky, dark ibis with relatively stout down-curved bill. Has white shoulder-patch and reddish legs. Adult has naked black head with red patch on rear crown and nape, and is dark brown with green-and-purple gloss. Immature dark brown, including feathered head. Marshes, lakes and fields, sometimes in dry cultivation. DE: lcr, GU: cr, HA: cr, HP: v, MP: cr, PU: nr, RA: lcr, UP: cr, UR: nr.

Eurasian Spoonbill *Platalea leucorodia* 80–90 cm

a ADULT BREEDING and **b** JUVENILE White, with spatulate-tipped bill. Adult has black bill with yellow tip; when breeding, has crest and yellow breast-patch. Juvenile has pink bill; in flight, shows black tips to primaries. Marshes, lakes and large rivers. DE: cw, GU: lcr, HA: lcr, MP: nr, PU: nr, RA: lcr, UP: lcr, UR: np.

1 Great White Pelican *Pelecanus onocrotalus* 140–175 cm

a ADULT BREEDING, **b** **c** ADULT NON-BREEDING, **d** IMMATURE and **e** JUVENILE Adult and immature have black underside to primaries and secondaries that contrasts strongly with white (or largely white) underwing-coverts. Feathering of forehead narrower than on Dalmatian, and tapers to a point at bill-base (as orbital skin more extensive). Adult breeding has white body and wing-coverts tinged with pink, bright yellow pouch and pinkish skin around eye. Adult non-breeding has duller bare parts and lacks pink tinge and white crest. Immature has variable amounts of brown on wing-coverts and scapulars. Juvenile has largely brown head, neck and upperparts, including upperwing-coverts, and brown flight feathers; upperwing appears more uniform brown, and underwing shows pale central panel contrasting with dark inner coverts and flight feathers; greyish pouch becomes yellower with age. Large lakes and lagoons. DE: nw, GU: lcw, HA: lcw, RA: nw, UP: nw, UR: nw.

2 Dalmatian Pelican *Pelecanus crispus* 160–180 cm

a ADULT BREEDING, **b** **c** ADULT NON-BREEDING and **d** IMMATURE In all plumages, has greyish underside to secondaries and inner primaries (becoming darker on outer primaries) that lacks strong contrast with pale underwing-coverts and often with whiter central panel. Forehead feathering broader across upper mandible (orbital skin more restricted than on Great White). Legs and feet always dark grey (pinkish on Great White). Larger than Spot-billed, with cleaner and whiter appearance at all ages; lacks 'spotting' on upper mandible, and bill usually darker than pouch. Adult breeding has orange pouch and purple skin around eye, and curly or bushy crest. Adult non-breeding is more dirty white; pouch and skin around eye are paler. Immature is dingier than adult non-breeding, with some pale grey-brown on upperwing-coverts and scapulars. Juvenile has pale grey-brown mottling on hind-neck and upperparts, including upperwing-coverts; pouch greyish-yellow. Large inland waters and coastal lagoons. DE: v, GU: nw, HA: nw, RA: nw, UP: nw.

3 Spot-billed Pelican *Pelecanus philippensis* 140 cm

a **b** ADULT, **c** IMMATURE and **d** JUVENILE Much smaller than Great White and Dalmatian pelicans, with dingier appearance, rather uniform pinkish bill and pouch (except in breeding condition), and black spotting on upper mandible (except juveniles). Tufted crest/hind-neck usually apparent even on young birds. Underwing pattern similar to Dalmatian (and quite different from Great White), showing little contrast between wing-coverts and flight feathers, and with paler greater coverts producing distinct central panel. Adult breeding has cinnamon-pink rump, underwing-coverts and undertail-coverts; head and neck appear greyish; purplish skin in front of eye, and pouch is pink to dull purple and blotched with black. Adult non-breeding is dirtier greyish white, with pinkish pouch. Immature has variable grey-brown markings on upperparts. Juvenile has brownish head and neck, brown mantle and upperwing-coverts (fringed with pale buff), and brown flight feathers; spotting on bill initially lacking (and still indistinct at 12 months). Large rivers. Globally threatened (Vulnerable). DE: v, GU: np, HA: nw, MP: np, RA: nw, UP: nw, UR: np.

1

Painted Stork *Mycteria leucocephala* 93–100 cm

a **b** ADULT and **c** **d** IMMATURE Adult has down-curved yellow bill, bare orange-yellow or red face, and red legs; white barring on mainly black upperwing-coverts, pinkish tertials and black barring across breast. Juvenile is dirty greyish white, with grey-brown (feathered) head and neck, and brown lesser coverts; bill and legs duller than adult's. Marshes and lakes. DE: cr, GU: cr, HA: cr, HP: np, MP: lcr, PU: nr, RA: lcr, UP: lcr, UR: nr.

2

Asian Openbill *Anastomus oscitans* 68 cm

a ADULT BREEDING and **b** **c** ADULT NON-BREEDING Stout, dull-coloured 'open bill'. Largely white (breeding) or greyish-white (non-breeding), with black flight feathers and tail; legs usually dull pink, brighter in breeding condition. Juvenile has brownish-grey head, neck and breast, and brownish mantle and scapulars slightly paler than the blackish flight feathers. At a distance in flight, best told from White Stork by dull-coloured bill and black tail. Marshes and lakes. DE: lcr, GU: nr, HA: cr, MP: lcr, PU: nr, RA: lcr, UP: cr, UR: nr.

3

Woolly-necked Stork *Ciconia episcopus* 75–92 cm

a **b** ADULT Stocky, largely blackish stork with 'woolly' white neck, black 'skullcap', and white vent and undertail-coverts. In flight, upperwing and underwing entirely dark. Juvenile is similar to adult but with duller brown body and wings, and feathered forehead. Flooded fields, marshes and lakes. DE: lcr, GU: cr, HA: cr, HP: nr, JK: nr, MP: lcr, PU: nw, RA: lcr, UP: cr, UR: nr.

4

White Stork *Ciconia ciconia* 100–125 cm

a **b** ADULT Mainly white stork, with black flight feathers, and striking red bill and legs. Generally has cleaner black-and-white appearance than Asian Openbill. Juvenile is similar to adult but with brown greater coverts and duller brownish-red bill and legs. Red bill and white tail help separate it from Asian Openbill at a distance in flight. Wet grassland and fields. DE: v, GU: nw, HA: np, MP: np, PU: nw, RA: nw, UP: nw, UR: nw.

2/27/14 RANTHANBOR

1b

1d

1a

1c

2a

2/27/14
RANTHANBOR

3a

3b

2b

4a

2c

4b

1

Black Stork *Ciconia nigra* 90–100 cm

a **b** ADULT and **c** IMMATURE Adult mainly glossy black, with white lower breast and belly, and red bill and legs; in flight, white underparts and axillaries contrast strongly with black neck and underwing. Juvenile has brown head, neck and upperparts flecked with white; bill and legs greyish green. Marshes and rivers. DE: v, GU: nw, HA: v, HP: nw, JK: np, MP: nw, PU: nw, RA: nw, UP: nw, UR: nw.

2

Black-necked Stork *Ephippiorhynchus asiaticus* 129–150 cm

a **b** ADULT and **c** **d** IMMATURE Large, black-and-white stork with long red legs and huge black bill. In flight, wings white except for broad black band across coverts, and tail black. Male has brown iris; yellow in female. Juvenile has fawn-brown head, neck and mantle, mainly brown wing-coverts and mainly blackish-brown flight feathers; legs dark. Marshes and large rivers. DE: nr, GU: nr, HA: nr, HP: np, JK: v, MP: nr, PU: nr, RA: nr, UP: nr, UR: nr.

3

Lesser Adjutant *Leptoptilos javanicus* 110–120 cm

a ADULT BREEDING and **b** **c** ADULT NON-BREEDING Flies with neck retracted, as Greater Adjutant. Smaller than Greater, with slimmer bill that has straighter ridge to culmen. Compared with Greater, adult shows pale frontal plate on head, and denser feathering on head and hind-neck that forms small crest. Adult has glossy black mantle and wings, largely black underwing (with white axillaries), white undertail-coverts and largely black neck-ruff (appearing as black patch on breast sides in flight); in breeding plumage, has narrow white fringes to scapulars and inner greater coverts, and copper spots on median coverts. Juvenile similar to adult, but upperparts dull black, and head and neck more densely feathered. Marshes, pools and wet fields. Globally threatened (Vulnerable). DE: v, GU: v, HA: v, MP: v, RA: np, UP: nr, UR: np.

4

Greater Adjutant *Leptoptilos dubius* 120–150 cm

a **b** **c** ADULT BREEDING and **d** IMMATURE Larger than Lesser Adjutant, with stouter, conical bill with convex ridge to culmen. Adult breeding has bluish-grey mantle, silvery-grey panel across greater coverts, greyish or brownish underwing-coverts, grey undertail-coverts and more extensive white neck-ruff. Further, has blackish face and forehead (with appearance of dried blood) and has neck pouch (visible only when inflated). Adult non-breeding and immature have darker grey mantle and inner wing-coverts, and brown greater coverts (which barely contrast with rest of wing); immature has brownish (rather than pale) iris. Marshes. Globally threatened (Endangered). DE: xp, GU: v, HA: xp, MP: v, PU: np, RA: np, UP: np.

1

Hooded Pitta *Pitta sordida* 19 cm
a ADULT and **b** JUVENILE   Black head with chestnut crown, green breast and flanks, and black belly-patch. Song is an explosive double whistle, *wienw-wienw*. Calls include a *skyeew*. Broadleaved evergreen and moist deciduous forest with thick undergrowth. HP: ns, UR: ns.

2

Indian Pitta *Pitta brachyura* 19 cm
a ADULT and **b** JUVENILE   Bold black stripe through eye, white throat and supercilium, buff lateral crown-stripes, and buff breast and flanks. Song is a sharp two-noted whistle, second note descending, *pree-treer*. Broadleaved forest with dense undergrowth. Breeds locally up to 1200 m. DE: v, GU: ns, HA: ns?, HP: ns, MP: cs, PU: ns, RA: ns, UP: lcs, UR: ns.

3

Long-tailed Broadbill *Psarisomus dalhousiae* 28 cm
a ADULT and **b** JUVENILE   Long tail, which is often held cocked. Green, with black cap, and yellow 'ear' spot and throat. Juvenile has green cap. Has a loud, piercing *pieu-wienw-wienw-wienw...*, usually five to eight notes on the same pitch. Moist broadleaved forest. Up to 2000 m. UR: nr.

4

Blue-winged Leafbird *Chloropsis cochinchinensis* 20 cm
a MALE and **b** FEMALE   Male has smaller black throat-patch than Golden-fronted, with yellowish forehead. Female and juvenile have yellowish border to turquoise throat. Race occurring in region (*C. c. jerdoni*) lacks the blue wing panel and blue sides to tail that are present in the nominate race. Open forest and well-wooded areas. GU: nr, MP: lcr, RA: nr, UP: nr.

5

Golden-fronted Leafbird *Chloropsis aurifrons* 19 cm
ADULT   Adult has golden-orange forehead, yellowish border to black throat, and green underparts. Juvenile has green head, with hint of turquoise moustachial stripe. Broadleaved forest and secondary growth. Up to 1800 m. GU: nr, HA: nr, HP: nr, MP: nr, UP: lcr, UR: lcr.

6

Orange-bellied Leafbird *Chloropsis hardwickii* 20 cm
a MALE and **b** FEMALE   Male has orange belly, and black of throat extends to breast. Has purplish-blue edges to flight feathers and tail, which appear blackish at distance. Female has orange belly centre and large blue moustachial stripe. Juvenile has green head; some have touch of orange on belly. Broadleaved forest. Resident; mainly 1300–2135 m. HP: nr, UP: nw, UR: nr.

1 Red-backed Shrike *Lanius collurio* 17 cm

a MALE, **b** FEMALE and **c** 1ST-WINTER Male lacks broad black forehead, has rufous mantle, and lacks white wing-patch (*compare with* Bay-backed). Female has grey cast to head and nape, and dark brown tail. First-winter similar to female, but has barred upperparts. Bushes and cultivation in dry country. GU: np, JK: np, RA: np.

2 Rufous-tailed Shrike *Lanius isabellinus* 18–19 cm

a MALE, **b** FEMALE and **c** 1ST-WINTER *L. i. phoenicuroides*; **d** MALE, **e** FEMALE and **f** 1ST-WINTER *L. i. isabellinus* Typically, has paler sandy-brown/grey-brown mantle and warmer rufous rump and tail than Brown. Male has small white patch at base of primaries, which is lacking in Brown. Female is similar to male but lacks white patch in wing, has grey-brown (rather than blackish) ear-coverts, and usually has some scaling on underparts. First-winter birds are similar to female but with pale fringes and dark subterminal lines to scapulars, wing-coverts and tertials. *L. i. phoenicuroides* has rufous cast to crown and nape, contrasting with grey-brown mantle. Open dry scrub country. DE: lcw, GU: cw, HA: nw, HP: np, JK: np, MP: nw, PU: nw, RA: lcw, UP: v, UR: nw.

3 Brown Shrike *Lanius cristatus* 18–19 cm

a MALE and **b** 1ST-WINTER Compared with Rufous-tailed, typically has darker rufous-brown upperparts (lacking clear contrast between mantle and tail); also thicker bill and more graduated tail. Female has a darker mask than female Rufous-tailed, with more prominent white supercilium. Forest edges, scrub, open forest and bushy hillsides. Up to 2100 m in Himalayas. DE: v, GU: v, HA: nw, HP: v, MP: nw, PU: v, RA: v, UP: nw, UR: v.

4 Bay-backed Shrike *Lanius vittatus* 17 cm

a ADULT, **b** IMMATURE and **c** JUVENILE Adult has black forehead and mask contrasting with pale grey crown and nape, deep maroon mantle, whitish rump and white patch at base of primaries. Juvenile told from juvenile Long-tailed by smaller size and shorter tail, more uniform greyish/buffish base colour to upperparts, pale rump, more intricately patterned wing-coverts and tertials (with buff fringes and dark subterminal crescents and central marks), and primary coverts prominently tipped with buff. First-year like washed-out version of adult; lacks black forehead. Open dry scrub, and bushes in cultivation. Locally up to 2000 m. DE: cr, GU: cr, HA: cr, HP: lcs, JK: ns, MP: cr, PU: cr, RA: lcr, UP: nr, UR: lcr.

5 Long-tailed Shrike *Lanius schach* 25 cm

a ADULT and **b** JUVENILE *L. s. erythronotus*; **c** ADULT *L. s. tricolor* Two intergrading races occur: *L. s. tricolor* chiefly in central areas and eastwards; *L. s. erythronotus* in the west. Adult *L. s. erythronotus* has grey mantle, rufous scapulars and upper back, narrow black forehead, rufous sides to black tail and small white patch on primaries. Juvenile has (dark-barred) rufous-brown scapulars, back and rump; dark greater coverts and tertials fringed rufous. Adult *L. s. tricolor* has black head. Bushes in cultivation and in open country, lightly wooded areas and gardens. Breeds up to 3000 m, winters below 2200 m. DE: cr, GU: cr, HA: cr, HP: lcr, JK: lcr, MP: cr, PU: cr, RA: cr, UP: cr, UR: lcr.

6 Grey-backed Shrike *Lanius tephronotus* 25 cm

a ADULT and **b** JUVENILE Adult has dark grey upperparts (no rufous on scapulars or upper back). Also usually lacks, or has only very indistinct, white patch at base of primaries, and lacks, or has very narrow, black forehead-band. Juvenile has cold grey base colour to upperparts. Bushes in cultivation, scrub and secondary growth. Summers 2700–3600 m, winters down to plains. DE: v, HA: v, HP: nr, JK: nr, RA: v, UP: nw, UR: nr.

7 Southern Grey Shrike *Lanius meridionalis* 24 cm

a ADULT and **b** JUVENILE Adult has narrow black forehead and broad black mask, grey mantle with white scapulars, broad white tips to secondaries, white sides and tip to tail, and white underparts. Juvenile has sandy cast to grey upperparts, buff tips to tertials and coverts, and grey mask. *See* Appendix for comparison with Lesser Grey Shrike. Open dry scrub country. DE: lcw, GU: cr, HA: nr, HP: nr, JK: nr, MP: nr, PU: cr, RA: cr, UP: nr, UR: nr.

1b

1c

1a

2c

2f

2b

2e

2d

2a

3b

3a

4c

4a

4b

5b

5c

6a

5a

6b

7b

7a

2/24/14 · NEEMRANA

INDIA

1

Eurasian Jay *Garrulus glandarius* 32–36 cm
ADULT Reddish-brown head and body, black moustachial stripe and blue barring on wings. White rump contrasts with black tail in flight. Broadleaved forest, mainly of oaks. Resident; mainly 1800–2440 m (900–2750 m). HP: nr, JK: nr, UR: nr.

2

Black-headed Jay *Garrulus lanceolatus* 33 cm
ADULT Black face and crest, streaked throat and pinkish-fawn body; blue barring on wings and tail. Oak and mixed broadleaved forest. Resident; 915–2500 m. HP: lcr, JK: nr, UR: lcr.

3

Yellow-billed Blue Magpie *Urocissa flavirostris* 61–66 cm
ADULT Blue upperparts with very long, graduated, black-and-white-tipped tail. Separated from Red-billed by yellow bill, and white on head restricted to crescent on nape. Juvenile has olive-yellow bill. Broadleaved and coniferous forests. Resident; breeds 1800–3300 m, winters down to 1000 m. HA: nw, HP: cr, JK: lcr, UR: nr.

4

Red-billed Blue Magpie *Urocissa erythrorhyncha* 65–68 cm
ADULT Separated from Yellow-billed by red bill, and extensive white hind-crown and nape. Underparts are white. Juvenile has duller red bill and more extensive white crown compared with adult. Broadleaved and mixed forests. Resident; from 300 m (winter) up to 1800 m. HA: nr, HP: lcr, UR: lcr.

5

Common Green Magpie *Cissa chinensis* 37–39 cm
ADULT Green, with red bill and legs, black mask, chestnut wings, and white tips to tertials and tail feathers. Moist broadleaved forest. Resident; from base of hills up to 1200 m. UR: nr.

6

Rufous Treepie *Dendrocitta vagabunda* 46–50 cm
ADULT Slate-grey hood, rufous-brown mantle, pale grey wing panel, buffish underparts and rump, and whitish subterminal tail-band. Juvenile has brown hood. Open wooded country, groves and trees at edges of cultivation. Up to 2000 m. DE: cr, GU: cr, HA: cr, HP: nr, JK: nr, MP: cr, PU: cr, RA: lcr, UP: cr, UR: lcr.

7

Grey Treepie *Dendrocitta formosae* 36–40 cm
ADULT Dark grey face, grey underparts and rump, and black wings with white patch at base of primaries. Juvenile duller version of adult. Broadleaved forest and secondary growth. Resident; summers chiefly 600–1500 m, winters 915–1525 m. HA: nw, HP: nr, UR: lcr.

8

Black-billed Magpie *Pica pica* 43–50 cm
ADULT Black and white, with long metallic-green/purple tail. Open cultivated upland valleys. 2000–4500 m. HP: nr, JK: lcr, UR: nr?.

1

Hume's Groundpecker *Pseudopodoces humilis* 19 cm
ADULT Down-curved black bill. Sandy-brown upperparts, buffish underparts and white tail sides. Ground-dwelling and very active; flicks wings and moves quickly by bounding hops. Tibetan steppe country. Resident in the trans-Himalayan region; 4200–5500 m. JK: nr

2

Spotted Nutcracker *Nucifraga caryocatactes* 32–35 cm
a ADULT *N. c. multipunctata*; **b** ADULT *N. c. hemispila* Mainly brown, with white spotting on head and body (*multipunctata* of Western Himalayas is more heavily spotted and has white tips to wing feathers). In flight, shows white sides and tip to tail. Call is a far-carrying, dry and harsh *kraaaak*. Coniferous forest. Resident; mainly 2000–3000 m. HP: lcr, JK: nr, UR: lcr.

3

Red-billed Chough *Pyrrhocorax pyrrhocorax* 36–40 cm
ADULT Curved red bill (shorter and orange-brown on juvenile). Call is a far-carrying, penetrating and nasal *chaow…chaow*. Gregarious throughout year, often in flocks of several hundred. High mountains, alpine pastures and cultivation. Resident; 3000–4500 m, forages up to 6000 m, winters down to 1800 m. HP: lcr, JK: lcr, UR: lcr.

4

Yellow-billed Chough *Pyrrhocorax graculus* 37–39 cm
ADULT Almost straight yellow bill (olive-yellow on juvenile). Call is a far-carrying, rippling *preeep*, and a descending whistled *sweeeoo*. Habits are similar to Red-billed, and often found in mixed flocks, but generally occurs at higher altitude. High mountains, alpine pastures and cultivation. Resident; chiefly above 3500 m and up to at least 6250 m. HP: lcr, JK: lcr, UR: nr.

5

Eurasian Jackdaw *Corvus monedula* 34–39 cm
ADULT Small size. Grey nape and hind-neck. Adult has pale grey iris. Open cultivated valleys. Breeds 1500–2100 m, with post-breeding dispersal up to 3600 m, occasionally winters down to the plains. HA: v, JK: lcr, PU: v, UP: v.

6

House Crow *Corvus splendens* 40 cm
a ADULT *C. s. splendens*; **b** ADULT *C. s. zugmayeri* Two-toned appearance, with paler nape, neck and breast (most pronounced in *C. s. zugmayeri* of northwest). Around human habitation and cultivation. Up to 2100 m. DE: cr, GU: cr, HA: cr, HP: lcr, JK: lcr, MP: cr, PU: cr, RA: lcr, UP: cr, UR: lcr.

7

Rook *Corvus frugilegus* 47 cm
a b ADULT and **c** JUVENILE Long, pointed bill, steep forehead and baggy 'trousers'. Adult has bare white skin at base of bill and on throat. Cultivation and pastures. JK: v, PU: v.

8

Carrion Crow *Corvus corone* 48–56 cm
a b ADULT *C. c. orientalis*; **c** ADULT *C. c. sharpii* Resident (*C. c. orientalis*) and winter visitor (*C. c. sharpii*). Comparatively straight bill and flat crown. Race *sharpii* two-toned like House Crow, but has black head and breast, and grey mantle. Open country with cultivation. 2700–3600 m. JK: nr.

9

Large-billed Crow *Corvus macrorhynchos* 46–59 cm
a b ADULT *C. m. intermedius*; **c d** ADULT *C. m. culminatus* All black, lacking paler collar of House Crow. Domed head, and large bill with arched culmen. Two races are known from Northern India. The Himalayan *intermedius* is bigger and with heavier bill, wedge-shaped tail and harsher calls compared with *culminatus* from the lowlands. *C. m. intermedius* is best told from Common Raven by absence of throat hackles, shorter and broader wings, less strongly wedge-shaped tail, squarer or domed crown, and dry *kaaa-kaaa* call. Forest, cultivation and open country above the treeline. Usually associated with towns and villages. Up to 4500 m. DE: lcr, GU: cr, HA: lcr, HP: cr, JK: lcr, MP: cr, PU: cr, RA: nr, UP: cr, UR: cr.

10

Common Raven *Corvus corax* 58–69 cm
a b ADULT Very large; long and angular wings, prominent throat hackles and wedge-shaped tail. Call is a loud, deep, resonant, croaking *wock…wock* call, different from other crows. Dry rocky areas above the treeline. DE: v, GU: v, HA: v, HP: nr, JK: nr, MP: v, PU: cw, RA: nr, UR: nr.

1

2a

2b

3

4

5

6b

2/21/14
DELHI

AIRPORT

6a

7a

7b

7c

8b

8a

9b

9a

8c

9c

10a

10b

9d

2/22/14
TAZ PALACE
DELHI

1 Ashy Woodswallow *Artamus fuscus* 19 cm
a b ADULT Slate-grey head, pinkish-grey underparts and narrow whitish horseshoe-shaped band across uppertail-coverts. Spends much time hawking insect prey on the wing, with mostly gliding interspersed with short bouts of rapid wing-flapping. Open wooded country. Up to 1700 m. DE: v, GU: nr, HA: np?, HP: nr, MP: v, RA: nr, UP: nr, UR: nr.

2 Eurasian Golden Oriole *Oriolus oriolus* 25 cm
a MALE, **b** FEMALE and **c** IMMATURE Male golden-yellow, with black mask and mainly black wings. Female and immature variable, usually with streaking on underparts and yellowish-green upperparts. *See* Appendix for comparison with Black-naped Oriole. Song is a loud, fluty *weela-wheo-oh*. Open woodland, and trees in cultivation. Breeds up to 1800 m, recorded up to 4400 m. DE: lcs, GU: lcr, HA: cs, HP: lcr, JK: lcs, MP: cs, PU: cs, RA: lcs, UP: cr, UR: lcs.

3 Black-hooded Oriole *Oriolus xanthornus* 25 cm
a MALE, **b** FEMALE and **c** IMMATURE Adult has black head and breast; female's upperparts duller than male's. Immature has yellow forehead and black-streaked white throat. Song is a mixture of mellow, fluty notes, *uye-you* or *uye-you-you*. Open broadleaved forest and well-wooded areas. Up to 1200 m. DE: v, GU: nr, HA: nr, HP: nr, MP: nr, PU: nr, RA: nr, UP: lcr, UR: nr.

4 Maroon Oriole *Oriolus traillii* 27 cm
a MALE, **b** FEMALE and **c** IMMATURE Maroon rump and tail. Male has maroon underparts. Female has whitish belly and flanks, streaked with maroon-grey. Immature has brown-streaked white underparts. Dense broadleaved forest. Resident; in hills up to 3100 m, winters down to adjacent plains. DE: v, HA: nr?, HP: nr, UP: nw, UR: nr.

5 Large Cuckooshrike *Coracina macei* 30 cm
a MALE and **b** FEMALE Large and mainly pale grey in coloration. Female has grey barring on underparts. Song is a rich, fluty *pi-io-io*. Open woodland, and trees in cultivation. Up to 1200 m. DE: v, GU: lcr, HA: nr?, HP: lcr, JK: nr, MP: lcr, PU: nr, RA: nr, UP: lcr, UR: lcr.

6 Black-winged Cuckooshrike *Coracina melaschistos* 24 cm
a MALE and **b** FEMALE Male slate-grey, with black wings and bold white tips to tail feathers. Female paler grey, with faint barring on underparts. Open forest and groves. Summers from foothills up to 2100 m, winters in plains and foothills. HP: nr, JK: v, MP: np, PU: v, RA: np, UP: np, UR: nr.

7 Black-headed Cuckooshrike *Coracina melanoptera* 18 cm
a MALE and **b** FEMALE Male has slate-grey head and breast, and pale grey mantle. Female has whitish supercilium, barred underparts, pale grey back and rump contrasting with blackish tail, and broad white fringes to coverts and tertials. Open broadleaved forest and secondary growth. Up to 1500 m. GU: nr, HA: np?, HP: ns, MP: nr, PU: nr, RA: nr, UP: ns, UR: ns.

1

Rosy Minivet *Pericrocotus roseus* 20 cm
a MALE and **b** FEMALE Male has grey-brown upperparts, white throat, and pinkish under-parts and rump. Female has greyish forehead, white throat, pale yellow underparts and dull olive-yellow rump. *See* Appendix for description of Ashy Minivet. Broadleaved forest. Breeds up to 1800 m, winters in plains and foothills. DE: v, HP: ns, JK: ns, MP: v, UR: ns.

2

Small Minivet *Pericrocotus cinnamomeus* 16 cm
a MALE and **b** FEMALE Small size. Male has grey upperparts, dark grey throat and orange on underparts. Female has pale throat and orange wash on underparts. Open wooded areas. Up to 1600 m. DE: nr, GU: cr, HA: nr, HP: lcr, JK: nr, MP: cr, PU: cr, RA: lcr, UP: cr, UR: nr.

3

White-bellied Minivet *Pericrocotus erythropygius* 15 cm
a MALE and **b** FEMALE White wing patch and orange rump. Male has black head and upper-parts, and white underparts with orange breast. Female has brown upperparts and white under-parts. Dry open scrub and forest. DE: xnw, GU: nr, HA: nw?, HP: v, MP: nr, PU: nr?, RA: nr, UP: nr.

4

Long-tailed Minivet *Pericrocotus ethologus* 20 cm
a MALE and **b** FEMALE Male has extension of red wing-patch down secondaries. Female has narrow, indistinct yellow wash on forehead and supercilium, grey ear-coverts and paler yellow throat than breast. Distinctive *pi-ru* whistle. Forest; also well-wooded areas in winter. Resident; summers 1200–3400 m, winters in plains and hills up to 1500 m. DE: lcw, GU: nw, HA: nw, HP: lcr, JK: lcr, MP: nw, PU: nw, RA: nw, UP: cw, UR: lcr.

5

Short-billed Minivet *Pericrocotus brevirostris* 20 cm
a MALE and **b** FEMALE Male lacks extension of red wing-patch down secondaries shown by Long-tailed. Further, male is more crimson-red (rather than scarlet-red) on underparts than Long-tailed, black on throat extends further onto breast, and has glossier black upperparts (although these features are variable and often difficult to detect in the field). Female has yellow forehead and cast to ear-coverts, and deep-yellow throat concolorous with rest of underparts. Distinctive monotone whistle. Broadleaved forest and forest edges. Resident; breeds above 1800 m, descends to foothills in winter. UP: nw, UR: nr.

6

Scarlet Minivet *Pericrocotus flammeus* 20–22 cm
a MALE and **b** FEMALE Best told by large size and isolated patch of colour on secondaries, red in male and yellow in female. Male is more orange-red than Long-tailed and Short-billed. Head pattern of female closest to female Short-billed. Broadleaved and coniferous forests. Up to 1800 m. GU: nr, HA: nr, HP: nr, JK: nr, MP: lcr, PU: nw, RA: nw, UP: lcw, UR: lcr.

7

Bar-winged Flycatcher-shrike *Hemipus picatus* 15 cm
a MALE and **b** FEMALE *H. p. picatus*; **c** MALE *H. p. capitalis* Dark cap contrasts with white sides of throat; has white wing-patch and white rump. Female has brown cap. Black-backed *H. p. picatus* occurs in south of region. Broadleaved forest and forest edges. Breeds 600–1800 m, wintering in foothills and adjacent plains. GU: nr, HA: cr, HP: nr, MP: nr, UP: lcr, UR: nr.

8

Yellow-bellied Fantail *Rhipidura hypoxantha* 13 cm
MALE Long fanned tail, yellow supercilium, dark mask and yellow underparts. Forests and high-altitude shrubberies. Resident; breeds from 1800 m up to the treeline, winters down to the edge of the plains. HA: nr, HP: nr, JK: nr, PU: v, UP: lcw, UR: lcr.

9

White-throated Fantail *Rhipidura albicollis* 19 cm
a ADULT *R. a. canescens*; **b** ADULT *R. a. albogularis* Narrow white supercilium and white throat; lacks spotting on wing-coverts. Broadleaved forest and secondary growth. Up to 2000 m. *R. a. albogularis* occurs in south of region. GU: nr, HA: nr, HP: lcr, JK: nr, MP: nr, PU: nr, RA: nr, UP: cw, UR: lcr.

10

White-browed Fantail *Rhipidura aureola* 18 cm
ADULT Broad white supercilia that meet over forehead, blackish throat, white breast and belly, and white spotting on wing-coverts. Forest undergrowth. Up to 1000 m. DE: np, GU: lcr, HA: nr, HP: lcr, JK: nr, MP: cr, PU: cr, RA: lcr, UP: cr, UR: lcr.

2/22/14 GANDI'S MEMORIAL DELHI

1 Black Drongo *Dicrurus macrocercus* 28 cm

a ADULT and **b** IMMATURE Adult has glossy blue-black underparts and white rictal spot. Tail-fork may be lost during moult. Immature has black underparts with bold whitish fringes. Around habitation and cultivation. Up to 1500 m. DE: cr, GU: cr, HA: cr, HP: lcr, JK: nr, MP: cr, PU: cr, RA: lcr, UP: cr, UR: lcr.

2 Ashy Drongo *Dicrurus leucophaeus* 29 cm

a ADULT and **b** IMMATURE Adult has dark grey underparts and slate-grey upperparts with blue-grey gloss; iris bright red. Immature has brownish-grey underparts with indistinct pale fringes. Broadleaved and coniferous forests. Breeds from foothills up to 3000 m, winters in the plains. DE: nw, GU: lcw, HA: np, HP: lcs, JK: lcs, MP: lcw, PU: v, RA: nw, UP: nw, UR: lcr.

3 White-bellied Drongo *Dicrurus caerulescens* 24 cm

a ADULT and **b** IMMATURE Similar to Ashy Drongo, but with white belly and shorter tail with shallower tail-fork. Immature is similar to adult but throat and breast is browner and border with white belly is less clearly defined. Open forest and well-wooded areas. Up to 1800 m. DE: v, GU: nr, HA: nr, MP: lcr, RA: nr, UP: lcr, UR: lcr.

4 Crow-billed Drongo *Dicrurus annectans* 28 cm

a ADULT and **b** IMMATURE Adult has stout bill, and widely splayed tail with shallow fork. Immature has white spotting on breast and belly. Moist broadleaved forest. UP: np, UR: np.

5 Bronzed Drongo *Dicrurus aeneus* 24 cm

ADULT Adult small, with shallow tail-fork. Heavily spangled. Clearings and edges of moist broadleaved forest. Resident; summers up to 2000 m, usually winters below 1220 m. HA: nr, MP: v, UR: nr.

6 Lesser Racket-tailed Drongo *Dicrurus remifer* 25 cm

a ADULT and **b** IMMATURE Tufted forehead without crest, square-ended tail, and smaller size and bill than Greater Racket-tailed. Tail rackets are smaller, flattened and webbed on both sides of shaft, while Greater has longer rackets that are twisted and webbed on only one side. Moist broadleaved forest. Resident; from foothills up to 2000 m. UP: nw, UR: lcr.

7 Spangled Drongo *Dicrurus hottentottus* 32 cm

ADULT Broad tail with upward-twisted corners, and long down-curved bill. Adult has extensive spangling and hair-like crest. Moist broadleaved forest, associated with flowering trees, especially silk cotton. From plains up to 1400 m. GU: nr, HA: nr, HP: v, MP: nr, PU: nr, RA: v, UP: ns, UR: cr.

8 Greater Racket-tailed Drongo *Dicrurus paradiseus* 32 cm

a ADULT and **b** IMMATURE Larger and with larger bill than Lesser Racket-tailed. Has prominent crest and forked tail; crest much reduced in immature. Open broadleaved forest. Up to 1500 m. GU: nr, HA: nr, MP: lcr, RA: v, UP: lcr, UR: nr.

1 Black-naped Monarch *Hypothymis azurea* 16 cm
a MALE and **b** FEMALE Male mainly blue, with black nape and gorget. Female lacks these features and is duller, with grey-brown mantle and wings. Middle storey of broadleaved forest. Plains and hills up to 1050 m. GU: v, MP: lcr, RA: v, UP: nw, UR: nr.

2 Asian Paradise-flycatcher *Terpsiphone paradisi* 20 cm
a WHITE MALE, **b** RUFOUS MALE and **c** FEMALE Male has black head and crest, with white or rufous upperparts and long tail-streamers. Female and immatures have reduced crest and lack streamers. Open forest, groves and gardens. Breeds mainly in the lower hills, locally up to 2400 m. DE: np, GU: lcr, HA: ns, HP: lcs, JK: lcs, MP: lcr, PU: ns, RA: ns, UP: lcs, UR: lcs.

3 Common Iora *Aegithina tiphia* 14 cm
a MALE BREEDING, **b** MALE NON-BREEDING and **c** FEMALE Green upperparts, yellow underparts and prominent white wing-bars. Male has black tail, and black on crown and nape in breeding plumage. Female has green tail. Open broadleaved forest and well-wooded areas. Plains and hills up to 1500 m. GU: lcr, HA: lcr, HP: nr, MP: lcr, PU: cr, RA: lcr, UP: cr, UR: lcr.

4 Marshall's Iora *Aegithina nigrolutea* 14 cm
a MALE BREEDING and **b** FEMALE Extensive white on black tail in all plumages (Common Iora lacks white in tail). Breeding male has black crown and nape, yellow hind-collar and blackish mantle with yellowish-green mottling. Scrub and groves. DE: xnr, GU: nr, HA: x?r, MP: nr, RA: nr, UP: nr.

5 Large Woodshrike *Tephrodornis gularis* 23 cm
a MALE and **b** FEMALE Male has black mask and grey crown and nape; mask, crown and nape browner in female. Larger than Common Woodshrike, and lacks white supercilium and white on tail. Broadleaved forest and well-wooded areas. Plains and hills up to 1000 m. GU: nr, UR: nr.

6 Common Woodshrike *Tephrodornis pondicerianus* 18 cm
ADULT Smaller than Large Woodshrike, with broad white supercilium and white tail sides. Open broadleaved forest, secondary growth and well-wooded areas. Usually below 200 m, but locally up to 1200 m. DE: cr, GU: cr, HA: cr, HP: nr, JK: nr, MP: cr, PU: cr, RA: lcr, UP: cr, UR: lcr.

7 White-throated Dipper *Cinclus cinclus* 20 cm
a ADULT and **b** JUVENILE Adult has white throat and breast. Juvenile has dark scaling on grey upperparts, and grey scaling on whitish underparts. Rocky fast-flowing mountain streams. Resident in the trans-Himalayan region; 3000–4800 m, may descend in winter but rare below 2400 m. HP: nr, JK: nr, UR: nr.

8 Brown Dipper *Cinclus pallasii* 20 cm
a ADULT and **b** JUVENILE Adult entirely brown. Juvenile has pale spotting on brown upperparts and underparts. Rocky fast-flowing mountain streams and small lakes. Resident; breeds 450–3900 m. HP: cr, JK: cr, UR: lcr.

2c 2a 2b 1a 1b 3a 5b 3b 3c 5a 4a 4b 6 7a 7b 8a 8b

1   **Blue-capped Rock Thrush** *Monticola cinclorhynchus*   17 cm

a MALE BREEDING, **b** FEMALE and **c** 1ST-WINTER MALE Male has white wing-patch, blue crown and throat, and orange rump and underparts; bright coloration obscured by pale fringes in non-breeding and first-winter plumages. Female has uniform olive-brown upperparts including tail; lacks buff neck-patch of Chestnut-bellied. *See* Appendix for comparison with Rufous-tailed Rock Thrush. Open dry forest and rocky slopes with scattered trees. Breeds 1000–3000 m, winters in the plains. DE: v, GU: nw, HA: ns, HP: cs, JK: lcs, MP: nw, PU: np, RA: nw, UP: nw, UR: lcr.

2   **Chestnut-bellied Rock Thrush** *Monticola rufiventris*   23 cm

a MALE and **b** FEMALE Male has chestnut-red underparts, and blue rump and uppertail-coverts; lacks white on wing. Female has orange-buff neck-patch, dark barring on slaty olive-brown upperparts and heavy scaling on underparts. Juvenile has pale spotting on upperparts; male has blue on wing. Open broadleaved and coniferous forests on rocky slopes. Resident; summers mainly 1200–3300 m, winters from 2800 m down to the foothills. HA: nw, HP: nr, JK: nr, PU: nw, UR: lcr.

3   **Blue Rock Thrush** *Monticola solitarius*   20 cm

a MALE BREEDING, **b** FEMALE and **c** 1ST-WINTER MALE Male indigo-blue, with bright coloration obscured by pale fringes in non-breeding and first-winter plumages. Female has bluish cast to slaty-brown upperparts, and buff scaling on underparts. Breeds on open rocky slopes and cliffs, 1200–4500 m, winters along streams, rivers and amongst old buildings. DE: nw, GU: lcw, HA: nw, HP: nr, JK: cs, MP: lcw, PU: nr, RA: lcw, UP: np, UR: np.

4   **Malabar Whistling Thrush** *Myophonus horsfieldii*   25 cm

ADULT Adult blackish, with blue forehead and shoulders. Juvenile more sooty-brown and lacks blue forehead. Rocky hill streams in forest and well-wooded areas. GU: nr, MP: nr, RA: nr.

5   **Blue Whistling Thrush** *Myophonus caeruleus*   33 cm

ADULT Adult blackish, spangled with glistening blue; yellow bill. Juvenile browner and lacks blue spangling. Forest and wooded areas, usually close to streams or rivers. Resident; summers from 1000 m up to the treeline, winters below 2745 m. HA: nw, HP: cr, JK: lcr, PU: nw, UP: np, UR: lcr.

6   **Pied Thrush** *Zoothera wardii*   22 cm

a MALE and **b** FEMALE Male black and white, with white supercilium and wing-bars, and yellow bill. Female has buff supercilium, buff wing-bars and tips to tertials, and scaled underparts. Open broadleaved forest and secondary growth. Summer visitor; mainly 1200–2400 m. HP: ns, UR: ns.

7   **Orange-headed Thrush** *Zoothera citrina*   21 cm

a MALE and **b** FEMALE *Z. c. citrina*; **c** MALE and **d** FEMALE *Z. c. cyanotus* Adult has orange head and underparts, male with blue-grey mantle, female with olive-brown wash to mantle. *Z. c. cyanotus* occurs in the south of the region. Damp, shady places in forest, often in wet ravines. Breeds up to 1600 m, winters in plains and foothills. DE: np, GU: nr, HA: np?, HP: nr, MP: nr, PU: nw, RA: nw, UP: lcr, UR: lcr.

1

Plain-backed Thrush *Zoothera mollissima* 27 cm

ADULT Best told from Long-tailed by absent or indistinct wing-bars. Further subtle differences are more rufescent coloration to upperparts, less pronounced pale wing-panel, more extensive black scaling on belly and flanks, and shorter-looking tail. Summers on rocky and grassy slopes with bushes; winters in forest and open country with bushes. Resident; summers 2700–4300 m, winters 600–2400 m. HP: nr, JK: nr, UR: nr.

2

Long-tailed Thrush *Zoothera dixoni* 27 cm

ADULT Adult has prominent wing-bars; belly and flanks more sparsely marked than on Plain-backed, flanks more barred than scaled, and appears longer-tailed. Undergrowth in forests of birch, fir or juniper; thick forest, often streams in winter. Resident; summers 2100–4200 m, winters 450–2700 m. HP: nr, UR: nr.

3

Scaly Thrush *Zoothera dauma* 26–27 cm

ADULT Boldly scaled upperparts and underparts. Juvenile has spotted breast. Thick forest with dense undergrowth, often near streams. Breeds 2100–3600 m, winters from foothills up to 1800 m and sparsely in plains. HA: v, HP: nr, JK: nr, MP: nw, PU: nw, RA: nw, UP: nw, UR: nr.

4

Long-billed Thrush *Zoothera monticola* 28 cm

ADULT Huge bill and short tail. Differs from Dark-sided in larger bill with prominent hook, dark lores, dark slate-olive upperparts, darker and more uniform sides of head and underparts, and dark spotting on belly. Moist, dense forest, usually near streams. Resident; breeds 2000–3000 m, winters down to the foothills. HP: nr, UR: nr.

5

Dark-sided Thrush *Zoothera marginata* 25 cm

ADULT Long bill and short tail. Differs from Long-billed in rufescent-brown upperparts, pale lores, more strongly marked sides of head (dark ear-covert patch with pale crescent behind), paler underparts with more prominent scaling on breast and flanks, and rufous panel on wing. Moist, dense forest near streams. Resident; Himalayas. UR: nr.

6

Tickell's Thrush *Turdus unicolor* 21 cm

a MALE, **b** FEMALE and **c** 1ST-WINTER MALE Small thrush. Male is pale bluish grey, with whitish belly and vent. Female and first-winter male have pale throat and submoustachial stripe, dark malar stripe, and often have spotting on breast. Open broadleaved forest. Breeds 1200–2200 m, winters in foothills and plains. DE: v, HP: nr, JK: lcr, MP: lcw, PU: nw, RA: nw, UR: ns.

7

White-collared Blackbird *Turdus albocinctus* 27 cm

a MALE and **b** FEMALE Male black, with white collar. Female brown, with variable pale collar. Broadleaved and coniferous forests and forest edges. Resident; breeds 2100–4000 m, winters below 3000 m. HP: nr, JK: nr, UR: lcr.

8

Grey-winged Blackbird *Turdus boulboul* 28 cm

a MALE and **b** FEMALE Male black, with greyish wing-panel. Female olive-brown, with pale rufous-brown wing-panel. Moist broadleaved forest and forest edges. Resident; breeds 1800–2700 m, winters down to the foothills, rarely to the plains. HA: nw, HP: nr, JK: nr, PU: nw, RA: v, UP: nw, UR: lcr.

9

Eurasian Blackbird *Turdus merula* 25–28 cm

a MALE and **b** FEMALE Male is entirely black and female mainly brown, both lacking pale collar or pale wing-panel shown by similar species. Juniper scrub. Breeds mainly 3300–4500 m and winters below 3000 m. GU: nw, HA: nw, HP: v, JK: nr, MP: lcr, PU: v, RA: nr, UR: nr.

1 Chestnut Thrush *Turdus rubrocanus* 27 cm

a MALE and **b** FEMALE Greyish head with chestnut upperparts and underparts. Male has pale collar; female has more uniform brownish-grey head/neck. Open wooded areas with fruiting trees. Resident; breeds 2100–3200 m, winters 1200–3050 m. HP: nr, JK: nr, UR: nr.

2 Dark-throated Thrush *Turdus ruficollis* 25 cm

a MALE, **b** FEMALE and **c** 1ST-WINTER FEMALE *T. r. ruficollis*; **d** MALE, **e** FEMALE and **f** 1ST-WINTER FEMALE *T. r. atrogularis* Uniform grey upperparts and wings. *T. r. ruficollis* has red throat and/or breast, and red on tail; first-winter has rufous wash to supercilium and breast. *T. r. atrogularis* has black throat and/or breast; first-winter has grey streaking on breast and flanks. *See* Appendix for comparison with Dusky Thrush. Forest, forest edges, cultivation and pastures with scattered trees. Winter visitor; below 4200 m. DE: nw, GU: nw, HA: nw, HP: cw, JK: nw, MP: nw, PU: nw, RA: nw, UP: lcw, UR: lcw.

3 Mistle Thrush *Turdus viscivorus* 27 cm

ADULT Large size, pale grey-brown upperparts, whitish edges to wing feathers, and spotted breast. *See* Appendix for description of Song Thrush. Summers in open coniferous forest and shrubberies; winters on grassy slopes and at forest edges. Resident; breeds from 1800 m to the treeline, winters 1200–3000 m. HA: v, HP: nr, JK: nr, MP: v, UR: lcr.

4 Gould's Shortwing *Brachypteryx stellata* 13 cm

ADULT Adult with chestnut upperparts, slate-grey underparts, and white star-shaped spotting on belly and flanks. Breeds in rhododendron and juniper shrubberies near the treeline; winters in forest. Resident; Himalayas. UR: nr.

5 Lesser Shortwing *Brachypteryx leucophrys* 13 cm

a 'BLUE' MALE and **b** FEMALE Smaller and shorter-tailed than White-browed, with pinkish legs. Male is pale slaty-blue with white throat and belly. Female is brown with white throat and belly. Both sexes have fine white supercilium that may be obscured. Immature male shows intermediate plumage. Undergrowth in moist broadleaved forest and secondary growth. Himalayas. UR: nr?

6 White-browed Shortwing *Brachypteryx montana* 15 cm

a MALE, **b** FEMALE and **c** IMMATURE MALE Larger than Lesser with longer tail and dark legs. Male dark slaty-blue, with fine white supercilium. Rufous-orange lores and more uniform brownish underparts of female are features separating it from female Lesser. Immature male has fine white supercilium. Dense undergrowth in moist forest, often near streams. Himalayas. HP: nr, UR: nr?

1

Spotted Flycatcher *Muscicapa striata* 15 cm
ADULT Large size, large and mainly dark bill, streaking on forehead and crown, indistinct eye-ring, and streaked throat and breast. Open forests. DE: v, GU: nw, HA: v, HP: np, JK: np, PU: v, RA: np.

2

Dark-sided Flycatcher *Muscicapa sibirica* 14 cm
ADULT Small dark bill, and long primary projection. Breast and flanks heavily marked, with narrow pale line down centre of belly. Canopy of open forest. Resident; breeds 2100 m to the treeline, locally to 1500 m. HP: cr, JK: lcr, PU: v, UR: lcr.

3

Asian Brown Flycatcher *Muscicapa dauurica* 13 cm
ADULT Large bill with prominent pale base to lower mandible. Shorter primary projection than Dark-sided, and lores are more extensively pale than in that species. Pale underparts, with light brownish wash to breast and flanks. *See* Appendix for comparison with Brown-breasted Flycatcher. Open broadleaved forest. Breeds 900–1900 m, locally to 2230 m. DE: v, GU: nr, HA: np, HP: lcs, JK: ns, MP: nr, PU: nw, RA: nr?, UP: nr, UR: ns.

4

Rusty-tailed Flycatcher *Muscicapa ruficauda* 14 cm
ADULT Rufous uppertail-coverts and tail, rather plain face, and pale orange lower mandible. Fir, birch and oak forests. Summer visitor and passage migrant; breeds 2100–3600 m. DE: v, HA: v, HP: ns, JK: cs, RA: v, UR: ns.

5

Ferruginous Flycatcher *Muscicapa ferruginea* 13 cm
ADULT Rufous-orange uppertail-coverts and tail, rufous-orange flanks and undertail-coverts, and grey cast to head. Moist broadleaved forest. UR: nr?

6

Rufous-gorgeted Flycatcher *Ficedula strophiata* 14 cm
a MALE and **b** FEMALE Rufous gorget, and white sides to black tail. Female duller than male. Broadleaved and coniferous forests. Resident; breeds 2400–3700 m, winters down to foothills. HA: nw, HP: nr, JK: nr, MP: v, UP: nw, UR: lcr.

7

Red-throated Flycatcher *Ficedula parva* 11.5–12.5 cm
a MALE and **b** FEMALE *F. p. parva*; **c** MALE *F. p. albicilla* White sides to tail. Male has reddish-orange throat. Female and many males have creamy-white to greyish-white underparts. Male *F. p. albicilla* has grey breast-band. Open forest, bushes and wooded areas. DE: cw, GU: cw, HA: cw, HP: np, JK: np, MP: cw, PU: nw, RA: np, UP: cw, UR: lcw.

8

Kashmir Flycatcher *Ficedula subrubra* 13 cm
a MALE and **b** FEMALE Male has more extensive and deeper red on underparts than Red-throated, with diffuse black border to throat and breast. Female and first-winter male can rather resemble some male Red-throated, but coloration of throat is more rufous, and this coloration is often more pronounced on breast than throat and often continues as wash onto belly and/or flanks. Open broadleaved forest. Summer visitor, 1800–2700 m. Globally threatened (Vulnerable). HP: v, JK: ns, UR: v?.

9

Snowy-browed Flycatcher *Ficedula hyperythra* 11 cm
a MALE and **b** FEMALE Small size and short tail. Both sexes have rufous-brown wings. Male has short white supercilium, slaty-blue upperparts and orange throat/breast. Female has orange-buff supercilium and eye-ring. Dense undergrowth in moist broadleaved forest. Resident; breeds above 1900 m, winters down to foothills. HA: nr?, JK: v, MP: v, UR: nr.

10

Little Pied Flycatcher *Ficedula westermanni* 10 cm
a MALE and **b** FEMALE Male black and white, with broad white supercilium. Female has grey-brown upperparts, brownish-grey wash to breast and rufous cast to rump/uppertail-coverts. Breeds in broadleaved forest; also winters in open wooded country. Resident; breeds above 1200 m, winters down to the foothills and plains. HP: nr, UP: lcw, UR: nr.

1   **Ultramarine Flycatcher** *Ficedula superciliaris*   12 cm
a MALE, **b** FEMALE and **c** 1ST-SUMMER MALE   Male has deep blue upperparts and sides of neck/breast, and white underparts. Female has greyish-brown breast side-patches and lacks rufous on rump/uppertail-coverts. Breeds in forest, 1800–3000 m, winters in open woodland and wooded areas down to the plains. DE: v, GU: v, HA: cw, HP: nr, JK: lcr, MP: nw, PU: v, RA: v, UP: lcw, UR: lcr.

2   **Slaty-blue Flycatcher** *Ficedula tricolor*   13 cm
a MALE and **b** FEMALE   Male has white throat and white on tail; belly and flanks greyish. Female has white throat and rufous tail. Breeds in subalpine shrubberies, dense bushes and forest edges; winters in forest undergrowth and ravines. Resident; breeds 1800–3300 m, winters in foothills below 1200 m. HA: cw, HP: nr, JK: cr, PU: nw, RA: v, UP: v, UR: lcr.

3   **Verditer Flycatcher** *Eumyias thalassina*   15 cm
a MALE and **b** FEMALE   Male greenish blue, with black lores. Female duller and greyer, with dusky lores. Open forest and wooded areas, especially of broadleaves. Breeds 1200–3000 m, winters in foothills and plains. DE: np, GU: nw, HA: v, HP: nr, JK: nr, MP: nw, PU: nw, RA: nw, UP: nw, UR: lcr.

4   **Small Niltava** *Niltava macgrigoriae*   11 cm
a MALE and **b** FEMALE   Small size. Male dark blue, with brilliant blue forehead and neck-patch. Female has indistinct blue neck-patch and rufescent wings and tail; lacks oval throat-patch of female Rufous-bellied. Bushes in broadleaved forest, along streams, edges of tracks and forest clearings. Resident; breeds 1000–2100 m, winters in foothills. UR: nr.

5   **Rufous-bellied Niltava** *Niltava sundara*   18 cm
a MALE and **b** FEMALE   Male has brilliant blue crown and neck-patch, and orange on underparts extending to vent. Female has oval-shaped throat-patch. Undergrowth in broadleaved forest and secondary growth. Resident; breeds 1800–3200 m, winters down to foothills. HA: nw, HP: nr, JK: nr, PU: v, UR: nr.

6   **Pale-chinned Flycatcher** *Cyornis poliogenys*   18 cm
ADULT   Greyish head and well-defined cream throat; creamy-orange breast and flanks that merge with belly. Bushes and undergrowth in broadleaved forest. Resident; in low hills. UR: nr.

7   **Pale Blue Flycatcher** *Cyornis unicolor*   18 cm
a MALE and **b** FEMALE   Male confusable with Verditer Flycatcher, but has longer bill, and is pale blue rather than turquoise in coloration and with distinctly greyer belly. Has shining blue fore-crown and dusky lores. Female very different from Verditer and more like other *Cyornis*; best told by large size and uniform greyish underparts. Moist broadleaved forest. Resident; breeds around 1500 m, winters in foothills. UR: lcr.

8   **Blue-throated Flycatcher** *Cyornis rubeculoides*   14 cm
a MALE and **b** FEMALE   Male has blue throat (some with orange wedge), and well-defined white belly and flanks. Female has poorly defined creamy-orange throat, orange breast well demarcated from white belly, and creamy lores (compare with Pale-chinned). Olive-brown head and upperparts and rufescent tail are best features separating it from female Tickell's. Open forest and wooded areas. Partial migrant; breeds from the foothills up to 1500 m; winters in foothills and plains. DE: v, HP: ns, JK: ns?, PU: nw, UP: nw, UR: lcr.

9   **Tickell's Blue Flycatcher** *Cyornis tickelliae*   14 cm
a MALE and **b** FEMALE   Male has orange throat and breast, with clear horizontal division from white flanks and belly. Female has greyish-blue upperparts (especially rump and tail). Open dry broadleaved forest. GU: lcr, HA: cw, MP: lcr, PU: nr, RA: nr, UP: nr, UR: nr.

10   **Grey-headed Canary Flycatcher** *Culicicapa ceylonensis*   13 cm
ADULT   Grey head and breast, rest of underparts yellow, and upperparts greenish. Forest and wooded areas. Partial migrant; breeds 1500–2400 m, winters in foothills and plains. DE: nw, GU: nw, HA: lcw, HP: cs, JK: ns, MP: lcw, PU: nw, RA: nw, UP: cw, UR: lcr.

Siberian Rubythroat *Luscinia calliope* 14 cm

a MALE and **b** FEMALE Olive-brown upperparts and tail, and white supercilium and moustachial stripe. Male has ruby-red throat and grey breast. Female has olive-buff wash to breast. Legs pale brown. Bushes and thick undergrowth, often near water. DE: v, HP: v, MP: nw, RA: nw, UP: lcw, UR: lcw.

White-tailed Rubythroat *Luscinia pectoralis* 14 cm

a MALE and **b** FEMALE Male has ruby-red throat, black breast-band and white on tail. Female has grey upperparts, grey breast-band and white tip to tail. Legs black. Breeds in subalpine shrubberies and on alpine slopes; winters in scrub and tall grass in marshes. Resident; breeds 2700–4800 m, winters in the foothills. HP: nr, JK: lcr, PU: nw, RA: v, UP: nw, UR: lcr.

Bluethroat *Luscinia svecica* 15 cm

a MALE NON-BREEDING, **b** 1ST-WINTER FEMALE *L. s. svecica*; **c** MALE BREEDING *L. s. abbotti* White supercilium and rufous tail sides. Male has variable blue, black and rufous patterning to throat and breast (patterning obscured by whitish fringes in fresh plumage). Female is less brightly coloured but usually with blue and rufous breast-bands. First-winter female may have just black submoustachial stripe and band of black spotting across breast. Summers in scrub along streams and lakes, 2600–3800 m, winters in scrub and tall grass in foothills and plains. DE: cw, GU: cw, HA: cw, HP: nr, JK: nr, MP: nw, PU: nw, RA: cp, UR: cw, UR: lcw.

Indian Blue Robin *Luscinia brunnea* 15 cm

a MALE and **b** FEMALE Male has blue upperparts and orange underparts, with white supercilium and black ear-coverts. Female has olive-brown upperparts, and buffish underparts with white throat and belly. Breeds in forest undergrowth, winters in forest, secondary scrub and plantations. Summer visitor 1600–3300 m. GU: v, HP: lcs, JK: lcs, UR: lcs.

Orange-flanked Bush Robin *Tarsiger cyanurus* 14 cm

a MALE and **b** FEMALE White throat, orange flanks, blue tail and redstart-like stance. Male has blue upperparts and breast sides. Female has olive-brown upperparts and breast sides. Forest understorey and bushes at clearings and edges of forest. Resident; summers mainly 2700–4400 m, winters 150–3000 m. HA: nw, HP: lcr, JK: lcr, PU: v, UR: lcr.

Golden Bush Robin *Tarsiger chrysaeus* 15 cm

a MALE and **b** FEMALE Orange to orange-buff underparts, with orange tail sides. Pale legs. Male has broad orange supercilium, dark mask and orange scapulars. Female duller, with less distinct supercilium. Summers in subalpine shrubberies and forest undergrowth; winters in forest undergrowth and dense scrub. Resident; summers 3000–3600 m, winters 1400–2000 m. HP: nr, UR: nr.

White-browed Bush Robin *Tarsiger indicus* 15 cm

a MALE and **b** FEMALE Upright stance, long tail, fine and down-curved supercilium, and dark legs (compared with Indian Blue Robin). Male has slaty-blue upperparts and rufous-orange underparts. Female has olive-brown upperparts and dirty orange-buff underparts. Subalpine shrubberies and bushes at forest edges. Resident; summers 3000–4200 m, winters 2000–3000 m. UR: nr.

Rufous-tailed Scrub Robin *Cercotrichas galactotes* 15 cm

ADULT Long rufous tail, tipped white and with black subterminal markings. Sandy-grey upperparts and creamy-white underparts, with whitish supercilium and dark eye-stripe and moustachial stripe. Dry scrub jungle. DE: v, GU: np, PU: v, RA: np.

1 Oriental Magpie Robin *Copsychus saularis* 23 cm

[a] MALE and [b] FEMALE Black/slate-grey and white, with white on wing and at sides of tail. Gardens, groves, open broadleaved forest and secondary growth. Resident; up to 2000 m. DE: cr, GU: cr, HA: cr, HP: lcr, JK: nr, MP: cr, PU: cr, RA: lcr, UP: cr, UR: lcr.

2 White-rumped Shama *Copsychus malabaricus* 22 cm

[a] MALE and [b] FEMALE Long, graduated tail and white rump. Male has glossy blue-black upperparts and breast, and rufous-orange underparts. Female duller, with brownish-grey upperparts. Undergrowth in broadleaved forest. Resident; below 365 m. GU: nr, HA: nr, HP: nr, UP: lcr, UR: lcr.

3 Indian Robin *Saxicoloides fulicata* 19 cm

[a] MALE and [b] FEMALE Reddish vent and black tail in all plumages. Male has white shoulders and black underparts. Female has greyish underparts. Dry stony areas with scrub, and cultivation edges. Up to 1500 m. DE: cr, GU: cr, HA: cr, HP: lcr, JK: nr, MP: cr, PU: cr, RA: lcr, UP: lcr, UR: lcr.

4 Rufous-backed Redstart *Phoenicurus erythronota* 16 cm

[a] MALE BREEDING, [b] 1ST-WINTER MALE and [c] FEMALE Large size. Often holds tail slightly cocked. Male has rufous mantle and throat, white on wing, and black mask; plumage heavily obscured by pale fringes in non-breeding and first-winter plumages. Female has double buffish wing-bar. Scrub and stone walls bordering fields in dry habitats. Winter visitor, from base of hills up to 2100 m. HP: nw, JK: nw.

5 Blue-capped Redstart *Phoenicurus coeruleocephalus* 15 cm

[a] MALE BREEDING, [b] FEMALE and [c] 1ST-WINTER MALE Male has blue-grey cap, black tail and white on wing; the dark areas have pale fringes in non-breeding and first-winter plumages. Female has grey underparts, prominent double wing-bar, blackish tail and chestnut rump. Summers on rocky slopes with open forest, 2400–3900 m; winters in open forest and secondary growth, from foothills up to 3500 m. HA: lcw, HP: nr, JK: nr, PU: v, UR: nr.

6 Black Redstart *Phoenicurus ochruros* 15 cm

[a] MALE and [b] FEMALE *P. o. phoenicuroides*; [c] MALE *P. o. rufiventris* Male has black upperparts and breast (*phoenicuroides* has greyer crown), and rufous underparts. Female is mainly dusky brown with rufous tail. *See* Appendix for comparison with Common and Hodgson's redstarts. Breeds in Tibetan steppe habitat, 2400–5100 m; winters in cultivation, stony areas and thin scrub, below 1700 m. DE: cw, GU: cw, HA: cw, HP: nr, JK: lcr, MP: cw, PU: cw, RA: cw, UP: lcw, UR: lcr.

7 White-winged Redstart *Phoenicurus erythrogaster* 18 cm

[a] MALE and [b] FEMALE Large size and stocky appearance. Male has white cap and large white patch on wing. Female has buff-brown upperparts and buffish underparts. Breeds in rocky alpine meadows, 3600–5200 m; winters in stony pastures and scrub patches, 1525–4800 m. HP: nr, JK: nr, UR: nr.

1 Blue-fronted Redstart *Phoenicurus frontalis* 15 cm

a MALE and **b** FEMALE Orange rump and tail sides, with black centre and tip to tail. Male has blue head and upperparts, and chestnut-orange underparts; plumage heavily obscured by rufous-brown fringes in non-breeding and first-winter plumage. Female has dark brown upperparts and underparts, with orange wash to belly; tail pattern best feature separating it from other female redstarts. Breeds in subalpine shrubberies; winters in bushes and open forest. Resident; breeds 2700–4500 m, winters 1000–2700 m. HA: nw, HP: lcr, JK: lcr, RA: v, UR: lcr.

2 White-capped Water Redstart *Chaimarrornis leucocephalus* 19 cm

ADULT White cap, and rufous tail with broad black terminal band. Mainly mountain streams and rivers. Resident; breeds 1830–4880 m, winters mainly from foothills up to 1500 m. HA: nw, HP: cr, JK: cr, PU: nw, UR: cr.

3 Plumbeous Water Redstart *Rhyacornis fuliginosus* 12 cm

a MALE and **b** FEMALE Male slaty-blue, with rufous-chestnut tail. Female and first-year male have black-and-white tail and white spotting on grey underparts. Mountain streams and rivers, also summers in alpine meadows and rocky areas far from water. Resident; breeds 1200–4300 m, winters from 2400 m down to foothills, rarely to plains. DE: v, HA: nw, HP: cr, JK: cr, PU: nw, UR: cr.

4 White-bellied Redstart *Hodgsonius phaenicuroides* 18 cm

a MALE and **b** FEMALE Long, graduated tail that is often held cocked and fanned. Male has white belly, rufous tail sides and white spots on alula. Female has white throat and belly, and chestnut on tail. Breeds in subalpine shrubberies; winters in thick undergrowth and forest edges at lower levels. Resident; breeds 2440–3900 m, winters from 1500 m down to foothills. HP: nr, JK: lcr, UR: nr.

5 White-tailed Robin *Myiomela leucura* 18 cm

a MALE and **b** FEMALE White patches on tail. Male blue-black, with glistening blue forehead and shoulders. Female olive-brown, with whitish lower throat. Undergrowth in moist broadleaved forest, often near streams. Resident; breeds 1200–2700 m, winters from 1500 m down to foothills. HP: nr, MP: v, UR: nr.

6 Grandala *Grandala coelicolor* 23 cm

a MALE and **b** FEMALE Slim and long-winged; a strong flier and often in flocks. Male purple-blue, with darker wings and tail. Female and immature male have white patches on wing, and streaked head and underparts. Rocky slopes and stony meadows; alpine zone in summer, lower altitudes in winter. Resident; breeds 3900–5500 m, winters 3000–4300 m. HP: nr, JK: nr, UR: nr.

7 Little Forktail *Enicurus scouleri* 12 cm

ADULT Small and plump, with short tail. White forehead. Mountain streams; also slower-moving streams in winter. Resident; breeds 1800–3700 m, winters from 1000 m up to at least 2000 m. HP: nr, JK: nr, UR: nr.

8 Black-backed Forktail *Enicurus immaculatus* 25 cm

ADULT Black crown and mantle, and more white on forehead than Slaty-backed. Fast-flowing streams in moist broadleaved forest. Resident; from 1450 m down to plains. UR: nr.

9 Slaty-backed Forktail *Enicurus schistaceus* 25 cm

ADULT Slaty-grey crown and mantle; less white on forehead and larger bill than Black-backed. Fast-flowing streams in forest and wooded lake margins. Resident; breeds 300–1600 m, winters down to base of hills. UR: nr.

10 Spotted Forktail *Enicurus maculatus* 25 cm

ADULT Large size; white forehead, white spotting on mantle, and black breast. Rocky streams in forest. Resident; breeds 1000–3000 m, winters 600–2300 m. HA: v, HP: lcr, JK: nr, UR: lcr.

1 Purple Cochoa *Cochoa purpurea* 30 cm
a MALE and **b** FEMALE Lilac crown, wing-panelling and tail (latter with dark tip). Male is purplish brown. Female has rufous-brown upperparts and brownish-orange underparts. Song is a broad flute-like *peeeeee*; also *peee-you-peee*. Mainly dense, moist, broadleaved forest. Possibly resident; 1000–3000 m. HP: nr?, UR: nr.

2 Green Cochoa *Cochoa viridis* 28 cm
a MALE and **b** FEMALE Mainly green, with bluish head, and blue tail with black band. Male has blue wing-panelling. Female has green in blue wing-panels. Song is a pure, drawn-out monotone whistle that is thinner and weaker than Purple Cochoa's. Dense broadleaved evergreen forest. Resident; 700–1830 m. UR: nr?

3 Stoliczka's Bushchat *Saxicola macrorhyncha* 17 cm
a MALE BREEDING, **b** MALE NON-BREEDING and **c** FEMALE Male has white supercilium, white primary coverts and much white on tail; upperparts and ear-coverts appear blackish when worn (breeding) and streaked when fresh (non-breeding). Female differs from female Common Stonechat in longer bill and tail, more prominent supercilium, and broad buffish edges and tips to tail feathers. Sandy desert plains with scattered bushes. Globally threatened (Vulnerable). Resident. GU: nw, HA: v, RA: nr?, UP: v.

4 Hodgson's Bushchat *Saxicola insignis* 17 cm
a MALE NON-BREEDING and **b** FEMALE Large size. Male has white throat extending to form almost complete white collar, and more white on wing than Common Stonechat. Female has broad buffish-white wing-bars and tips to primary coverts. Grassland, and tall grasses and reeds along rivers. Globally threatened (Vulnerable). Local winter visitor. HA: v, UP: nw, UR: nw.

5 Common Stonechat *Saxicola torquata* 17 cm
a MALE BREEDING, **b** MALE NON-BREEDING and **c** FEMALE Male has black head, white patch on neck, orange breast and whitish rump (features obscured in fresh plumage); lacks white in tail. Female has streaked upperparts and orange on breast and rump. Tail darker than in female White-tailed. Summers in open country with bushes, including high-altitude semi-desert; winters in scrub, reedbeds and cultivation. Resident, winter visitor and passage migrant; breeds 1500–3300 m, winters in plains and up to 2200 m. DE: lcw, GU: cw, HA: cw, HP: nr, JK: lcr, MP: cw, PU: cw, RA: cw, UP: cw, UR: lcr.

6 White-tailed Stonechat *Saxicola leucura* 12.5–13 cm
a MALE BREEDING and **b** FEMALE Male has largely white inner webs to tail feathers. Female has greyer upperparts than Common, with diffuse streaking and paler grey-brown tail. Reeds and tall grassland. Resident; mainly in terai below 700 m. DE: lcr, HA: nr, PU: lcr, UP: nr, UR: nr.

7 Pied Bushchat *Saxicola caprata* 13.5 cm
a MALE BREEDING, **b** FEMALE and **c** 1ST-WINTER MALE Male black, with white rump and wing-patch; rufous fringes to body in non-breeding and first-winter plumages. Female has dark brown upperparts and rufous-brown underparts, with rufous-orange rump. Mainly cultivation and open country with scattered bushes or tall grass. Resident up to 1500 m. DE: cr, GU: nr, HA: cr, HP: cr, JK: lcr, MP: nr, PU: cr, RA: cr, UP: lcr, UR: lcr.

8 Grey Bushchat *Saxicola ferrea* 15 cm
a MALE and **b** FEMALE Male has white supercilium and dark mask; upperparts grey to almost black, depending on extent of feather wear. Female has buff supercilium, and rufous rump and tail sides. Secondary growth, forest edges and scrub-covered hillsides. Resident; breeds 1500–3300 m, winters from 2400 m down to foothills and plains. DE: v, HA: nw, HP: cr, JK: lcr, MP: nw, PU: nw, RA: nw, UP: lcw, UR: lcr.

9 Brown Rock-chat *Cercomela fusca* 17 cm
ADULT Both sexes brown, with more rufescent underparts. Buildings in open country. Up to 1800 m. DE: cr, GU: lcr, HA: cr, HP: nr, JK: nr, MP: cr, PU: cw, RA: lcr, UP: lcr, UR: nr.

1 Hume's Wheatear *Oenanthe alboniger* 17 cm

ADULT All-black head and largely white underparts. Told from *picata* race of Variable by stockier appearance and domed head, larger bill and glossy sheen to black of plumage (except when worn); also, black of throat does not extend so far down on breast and white of rump extends further up lower back. Barren stony slopes with boulders. Resident. JK: v.

2 Northern Wheatear *Oenanthe oenanthe* 15 cm

a MALE BREEDING, **b** FEMALE BREEDING and **c** 1ST-WINTER Breeding male has blue-grey upperparts, black mask and pale orange breast. Breeding female greyish to olive-brown above; lacks rufous patch on ear-coverts of Finsch's and never shows dark grey/black on throat. Compared with Isabelline, adult winter and first-winter have blackish centres to wing-coverts and tertials, and show more white at sides of tail. Open stony ground and cultivation. HP: v, MP: v, RA: v.

3 Variable Wheatear *Oenanthe picata* 14.5 cm

a MALE and **b** FEMALE *O. p. picata*; **c** MALE and **d** FEMALE *O. p. capistrata*; and **e** MALE and **f** FEMALE *O. p. opistholeuca* Very variable. Males can be mainly black, have black head with white underparts, or white crown and white underparts. Females can be mainly sooty-brown or have greyish upperparts with variable greyish-white underparts. Both sexes show extensive white at sides of tail. Cultivation and rocky areas. Winter visitor. DE: nw, GU: cw, HA: nw, HP: nw, JK: nw, MP: nw, PU: cw, RA: cw, UP: nw, UR: v.

4 Pied Wheatear *Oenanthe pleschanka* 14.5 cm

a MALE, **b** FEMALE, **c** 1ST-WINTER MALE and **d** 1ST-WINTER FEMALE Different tail pattern from Variable: always shows black edge to outer feathers (lacking in Variable) and often has only a narrow and broken terminal black band (broad and even on Variable). On breeding male, white of nape extends to mantle, black of throat does not extend to upper breast, and breast is washed with buff (features separating it from *capistrata* race of Variable). Non-breeding and first-winter male and female have pale fringes to upperparts and wings (not apparent on fresh-plumaged Variable). Open stony country with lowlands; breeds around 4000 m. HP: ns, JK: ns.

5 Rufous-tailed Wheatear *Oenanthe xanthoprymna* 14.5 cm

a MALE BREEDING and **b** MALE NON-BREEDING Rufous-orange lower back and rump, and rufous tail sides. Male has black lores. Summers on dry rocky slopes; winters in semi-desert. Winter visitor. DE: v, GU: nw, HA: nw, HP: np, RA: nw.

6 Desert Wheatear *Oenanthe deserti* 14–15 cm

a MALE BREEDING, **b** MALE NON-BREEDING, **c** FEMALE BREEDING and **d** FEMALE NON-BREEDING Sandy-brown upperparts, with largely black tail and contrasting white rump. Male has black throat (partly obscured by pale fringes in fresh plumage). Female has blackish centres to wing-coverts and tertials in fresh plumage, and largely black wings when worn (useful distinction from Isabelline). Dry semi-desert in Tibetan plateaux country. Breeds 3000–5100 m, winters in plains. DE: nw, GU: cw, HA: nw, HP: ns, JK: ns, MP: nw, PU: nw, RA: cw, UP: nw, UR: v.

7 Isabelline Wheatear *Oenanthe isabellina* 16.5 cm

ADULT Rather plain sandy-brown and buff. Tail shorter than in Desert and with more white at base and sides. Has paler, sandy-brown wings with contrasting dark alula (lacking black centres to coverts and tertials/secondaries). Dry cultivation. DE: nw, GU: cw, HA: nw, HP: v, JK: np, MP: nw, PU: v, RA: cw, UP: nw, UR: v.

1

2128114
RANTHAHTOR

3f

3a

3b

3e

2c

2a

2b

3d

3c

4a

4b

4c

4d

5a

5b

6a

6d

6c

6b

7

1

Spot-winged Starling *Saroglossa spiloptera* 19 cm
a MALE and **b** FEMALE White wing-patch and whitish iris. Male has blackish mask, red-dish-chestnut throat, and dark-scalloped greyish upperparts. Female has browner upperparts, and greyish-brown markings on throat and breast. Juvenile similar to female, with buff wing-bars. Open broadleaved forest and well-wooded areas, favours flowering trees. Foothills up to 2000 m. HP: ns, UR: ns.

2

Chestnut-tailed Starling *Sturnus malabaricus* 20 cm
a ADULT and **b** JUVENILE Adult has grey upperparts, rufous underparts and chestnut tail. Juvenile is rather uniform, with rufous sides and tips to outer tail feathers. Open wooded areas and groves. Up to 2000 m. DE: v, GU: nr, HA: v, HP: ns, MP: nr, PU: v, RA: v, UP: nr, UR: ns.

3

Brahminy Starling *Sturnus pagodarum* 21 cm
a ADULT and **b** JUVENILE Adult has black crest, and rufous-orange sides to head and under-parts. Juvenile lacks crest; has grey-brown cap and paler orange-buff underparts. Dry, well-wooded areas and thorn scrub. Up to 1800 m. DE: cr, GU: cr, HA: cr, HP: lcs, JK: ns, MP: cr, PU: cr, RA: lcr, UP: lcr, UR: lcr.

4

Rosy Starling *Sturnus roseus* 21 cm
a ADULT and **b** JUVENILE Adult has blackish head with shaggy crest, pinkish mantle and underparts, and blue-green gloss to wings. Plumage much duller in non-breeding and first-winter; pink of plumage partly obscured by buff fringes, black by greyish fringes. Juvenile main-ly sandy-brown, with stout yellowish bill and broad pale fringes to wing feathers. Cultivation and damp grassland. DE: lcp, GU: cw, HA: cp, HP: np, JK: np, MP: nwp, PU: cw, RA: lcw, UP: cw.

5

Common Starling *Sturnus vulgaris* 21 cm
a ADULT BREEDING, **b** ADULT NON-BREEDING and **c** JUVENILE Adult metallic-green and purple; heavily marked with buff and white in winter. Juvenile dusky-brown with whiter throat. Cultivation and damp grassland. Breeds 1500–2500 m, winters in plains. DE: cw, GU: nw, HA: lcw, HP: nw, JK: lcs, MP: nw, PU: cw, RA: nw, UP: cw, UR: nw.

6

Asian Pied Starling *Sturnus contra* 23 cm
a ADULT and **b** JUVENILE Adult is black and white, with orange orbital skin and large, pointed, yellowish bill. Juvenile has brown plumage in place of black. Cultivation, damp grass-land and habitation. Up to 800 m. DE: cr, GU: nr, HA: cr, HP: nr, JK: nr, MP: lcr, PU: cr, RA: nr, UP: cr, UR: lcr.

7

Common Myna *Acridotheres tristis* 25 cm
a **b** ADULT Brownish myna with yellow orbital skin, white wing-patch and white tail-tip. Juvenile duller. Habitation and cultivation. Up to 3000 m. DE: cr, GU: cr, HA: cr, HP: lcr, JK: lcr, MP: cr, PU: cr, RA: lcr, UP: cr, UR: lcr.

8

Bank Myna *Acridotheres ginginianus* 23 cm
a **b** ADULT and **c** JUVENILE Orange-red orbital patch, orange-yellow bill, and tufted fore-head. Wing-patch, underwing-coverts and tail-tip orange-buff. Adult is bluish grey with black-ish cap. Juvenile duller and browner than adult. Cultivation, damp grassland near villages, often associated with grazing animals. Up to 800 m. DE: cr, GU: cr, HA: cr, HP: nr, JK: nr, MP: nr, PU: cr, RA: lcr, UP: cr, UR: lcr.

9

Jungle Myna *Acridotheres fuscus* 23 cm
a ADULT and **b** JUVENILE Tufted forehead, and white wing-patch and tail-tip; lacks bare orbital skin. Juvenile browner, with reduced forehead tuft. Cultivation near well-wooded areas, and edges of habitation. Up to 2100 m. DE: v, GU: cr, HA: nr, HP: lcr, JK: nr, MP: nr, PU: cr, RA: ?nr, UP: lcr, UR: lcr.

10

Hill Myna *Gracula religiosa* 25–29 cm
ADULT Large myna with yellow wattles, large orange-yellow bill and white wing-patches. Juvenile has duller bill, paler yellow wattles and less gloss to plumage. Moist broadleaved forest. Resident; Himalayan foothills. UR: nr.

1   **Kashmir Nuthatch** *Sitta cashmirensis*   12 cm
a MALE and **b** FEMALE Compared with female Chestnut-bellied, has uniform undertail-coverts and lacks clearly defined white cheeks. Appears larger and longer-billed than White-tailed, with more pronounced white cheeks, no white at base of tail, and distinctive, rasping jay-like call. Deciduous and broadleaved/coniferous forest. Resident; breeds 1800–3000 m. HP: nr, JK: nr.

2   **Chestnut-bellied Nuthatch** *Sitta castanea*   12 cm
a MALE and **b** FEMALE Male has deep chestnut underparts and white cheeks. Female paler cinnamon-brown on underparts, although white cheeks more pronounced than on similar species; has pale fringes to undertail-coverts. Calls include an explosive *siditit*. Broadleaved forest and groves. Up to 1800 m in Himalayas. DE: xnr, HA: nw, MP: nr, PU: nr, RA: nr, UP: lcr, UR: lcr.

3   **White-tailed Nuthatch** *Sitta himalayensis*   12 cm
ADULT White at base of tail (difficult to see); less distinct white cheek-patch than Kashmir; uniform undertail-coverts. Calls include a hard *chak, kak*, which may be repeated as a rattle. Mainly broadleaved forest. Resident; breeds 1500–3500 m, winters down to 950 m. HA: nw, HP: nr, UR: lcr.

4   **White-cheeked Nuthatch** *Sitta leucopsis*   12 cm
ADULT Black crown and nape, white face, and whitish underparts with rufous flanks and under-tail-coverts. Call likened to bleating of a young goat. Coniferous and mixed forest. Resident; breeds from 2100 m up to the treeline, winters locally down to 1800 m. HP: nr, JK: lcr, UR: nr.

5   **Velvet-fronted Nuthatch** *Sitta frontalis*   10 cm
a MALE and **b** FEMALE Violet-blue upperparts, black forehead, black-tipped red bill, and lilac underparts. Female lacks black eye-stripe. Open broadleaved forest and well-wooded areas. Up to 2200 m in Himalayas. GU: nr, HA: lcr, MP: nr, UR: lcr.

6   **Wallcreeper** *Tichodroma muraria*   16 cm
a MALE BREEDING and **b** ADULT NON-BREEDING Long, down-curved bill. Largely crimson wing-coverts; shows white primary spots in flight. Breeding male has black throat. Rock cliffs and gorges; also stony river beds in winter. Breeds chiefly from 3300 m up to the snowline, winters down to foothills and adjacent plains. DE: v, HA: nw, HP: lcw, JK: nr, PU: nw, UR: nr.

7   **Eurasian Treecreeper** *Certhia familiaris*   12 cm
ADULT Unbarred tail, and whitish throat and breast. Mainly conifer/birch forest. Resident; breeds mainly from 2700 m up to the timberline. HA: nw, HP: nr, JK: nr, UR: nr.

8   **Bar-tailed Treecreeper** *Certhia himalayana*   12 cm
ADULT Dark barring on tail, white throat, and dull whitish or dirty greyish-buff underparts. Mainly coniferous forest. Resident; breeds from 1500 m up to the timberline, winters from 2400 m down to the foothills. DE: v, HA: nw, HP: lcr, JK: cr, PU: nw, UP: nw, UR: lcr.

9   **Rusty-flanked Treecreeper** *Certhia nipalensis*   12 cm
ADULT Buffish supercilium continues around dark ear-coverts, unbarred tail, white throat and rufous flanks. Mainly oak, also coniferous/broadleaved forest. Resident; around 3000 m. UR: nr.

10   **Brown-throated Treecreeper** *Certhia discolor*   12 cm
ADULT Brownish-buff throat and breast; unbarred tail. Mainly broadleaved forest, especially mossy oak; also coniferous/broadleaved forest. Resident; around 2500 m. UR: nr.

11   **Spotted Creeper** *Salpornis spilonotus*   13 cm
ADULT Long, down-curved bill, and shortish tail. Plumage spotted with white. Open deciduous forest and groves. Resident. DE: xnr, GU: nr, HA: v, MP: nr, RA: nr, UP: nr.

1

White-crowned Penduline Tit *Remiz coronatus* 10 cm

a FRESH MALE, **b** FEMALE and **c** JUVENILE Male has blackish mask and nape, whitish crown and whitish collar. Female has pale grey crown and collar, and lacks black nape-band. Juvenile lacks dark mask. Reedbeds and riverine forest. DE: v, PU: nw.

2

Fire-capped Tit *Cephalopyrus flammiceps* 10 cm

a MALE BREEDING, **b** MALE NON-BREEDING and **c** FEMALE Flowerpecker-like, with greenish upperparts and yellowish to whitish underparts. Lacks crest. Breeding male has bright orange-scarlet fore-crown. Deciduous forest and deciduous/coniferous forest. Breeds 2000–3500 m, winters down to plains. DE: v, HA: v, HP: ns, JK: ns, MP: v, RA: v, UP: nw, UR: ns.

3

Rufous-naped Tit *Parus rufonuchalis* 13 cm

ADULT Large size. Extensive black bib (to upper belly) and grey belly. Lacks wing-bars. Mainly coniferous forest. Resident; breeds 2400–3600 m, winters down to 1500 m. HP: lcr, JK: lcr, UR: nr.

4

Rufous-vented Tit *Parus rubidiventris* 12 cm

ADULT Smaller than Rufous-naped, with smaller black bib and rufous belly. Lacks wing-bars. Coniferous forest and conifer/birch forest; also rhododendron shrubberies. Resident; breeds 2550–4250 m, winters down to 2135 m. HP: nr, JK: nr, UR: nr.

5

Spot-winged Tit *Parus melanolophus* 11 cm

ADULT Small size. Broad white tips to median and greater coverts, blue-grey mantle, rufous breast sides and dark grey belly. Mainly coniferous forest, also coniferous/broadleaved forest. Resident; breeds 2000–3300 m, winters down to 600 m. HP: cr, JK: lcr, UR: lcr.

6

Coal Tit *Parus ater* 11 cm

ADULT Small size. Whitish tips to median and greater coverts, olive-grey mantle and creamy-buff underparts. Mainly coniferous forest, also fir/birch forest. Around 2500 m. UR: ?nr.

7

Grey-crested Tit *Parus dichrous* 12 cm

ADULT Greyish crest and upperparts, whitish collar and orange-buff underparts. Mainly broad-leaved, also coniferous/rhododendron and coniferous forests. Resident; breeds 2400–3300 m, winters down to 2200 m. HP: nr, JK: nr, UR: nr.

8

Great Tit *Parus major* 14 cm

ADULT Black breast-centre and line down belly, greyish mantle, greyish-white breast sides and flanks, and white wing-bar. Juvenile has yellowish-white cheeks and underparts, and yellowish-olive wash to mantle. Open forest and well-wooded country, favours broadleaves. Breeds up to 3600 m in Ladakh. DE: v, GU: lcr, HA: nr?, HP: lcr, JK: lcr, MP: cr, PU: cw, RA: lcr, UP: lcr, UR: lcr.

9

Green-backed Tit *Parus monticolus* 12.5 cm

ADULT Green mantle and back, and yellow on underparts. Forest; prefers moister habitat than Great Tit. Resident; breeds 1600–2800 m, winters down to the foothills. HP: cr, JK: nr, PU: v, UR: lcr.

Winter Wren *Troglodytes troglodytes* 9.5 cm
ADULT Small and squat, with stubby tail. Brown, with dark-barred wings, tail and underparts. High-altitude rocky and bushy slopes, also in forest undergrowth in winter. Resident; breeds 2400–3900 m, winters 1200–3000 m. HP: lcr, JK: cr, UR: nr.

White-naped Tit *Parus nuchalis* 12 cm
ADULT Black mantle and wing-coverts (grey on Great Tit); much white on tertials and at bases of secondaries and primaries. Thorn-scrub forest. Globally threatened (Vulnerable). Resident. GU: nr, RA: nr.

Black-lored Tit *Parus xanthogenys* 13 cm
a ADULT *P. x xanthogenys*; **b** MALE and **c** FEMALE *P. x. aplonotus* Prominent black crest, and black or grey centre to yellow throat and breast. Yellowish or whitish wing-bars. *P. x. aplonotus* occurs in south of region. Open forest, forest edges and groves. Breeds 1500–2100 m in Himalayas. GU: nr, HP: nr, JK: nr, MP: lcr, RA: nr, UR: nr.

Yellow-browed Tit *Sylviparus modestus* 10 cm
ADULT Very small, with slight crest and rather stubby bill. Olive-green upperparts, yellowish eye-ring, fine yellow supercilium and yellowish-buff underparts. Broadleaved forest; favours oaks. Resident; breeds 2100–3600 m, winters 1200–2900 m. HP: nr, JK: nr, UR: nr.

White-cheeked Tit *Aegithalos leucogenys* 11 cm
ADULT Black throat, cinnamon crown, yellowish iris and grey-brown mantle. Juvenile has buffish-white throat and streaking on breast. Scrub forest. Resident; around 1800 m. HP: nr, JK: nr, UR: nr.

Black-throated Tit *Aegithalos concinnus* 10.5 cm
ADULT Chestnut crown, white chin and black throat, white cheeks and grey mantle. Juvenile has white throat and indistinct black-spotted breast-band. Broadleaved and broadleaved/coniferous forest and secondary growth. Resident; breeds 1400–2400 m, winters down to 900 m. HP: nr, JK: nr, UR: lcr.

White-throated Tit *Aegithalos niveogularis* 11 cm
ADULT White forehead and fore-crown, and whitish throat; iris brownish. Diffuse blackish mask and cinnamon underparts, with darker breast-band. Juvenile has dusky throat, more prominent breast-band, and paler lower breast and belly. Bushes in birch/coniferous forest and high-altitude shrubberies. Resident; breeds 2400–3600 m, winters down to 1800 m. HP: nr, JK: nr, UR: nr.

1   **Sand Martin** *Riparia riparia*   13 cm

a **b** **c** ADULT White throat and half-collar, and brown breast-band. Very similar to Pale Martin; upperparts darker brown, breast-band clearly defined and tail-fork deeper. Rivers and lakes. DE: nw, GU: np, HA: np, MP: nw, UP: nw, UR: np.

2   **Pale Martin** *Riparia diluta*   13 cm

a **b** **c** ADULT Upperparts paler and greyer than on Sand and Plain martins; throat greyish white, breast-band not clearly defined and tail-fork very shallow. Rivers and lakes. DE: np, GU: nw, HA: np?, HP, ns, JK: np, PU: ?ns, RA: np, UP: np.

3   **Plain Martin** *Riparia paludicola*   12 cm

a **b** **c** ADULT Pale brownish-grey throat and breast, merging into dingy-white rest of underparts; some have suggestion of breast-band. Underwing darker than on Sand and Pale, flight weaker and more fluttering, and has shallower indent to tail. Upperparts darker than on Pale. Rivers and lakes. Up to 1500 m. DE: cr, GU: lcr, HA: cr, HP: nr, JK: nr, MP: cr, PU: nr?, RA: nr, UP: cr, UR: lcr.

4   **Eurasian Crag Martin** *Hirundo rupestris*   15 cm

a **b** **c** ADULT Larger and stockier than the *Riparia* martins. Dark underwing-coverts, dusky throat, and brown flanks and undertail-coverts (latter with pale fringes). Lacks breast-band. Shows white spots in tail when spread. *See* Appendix for comparison with Pale Crag Martin. Rocky cliffs and gorges. Resident; breeds 1200–4500 m, winters from 2000 m down to the plains. GU: nw, HA: nw, HP: nr, JK: lcr, MP: nw, RA: v, UP: nw, UR: lcr.

5   **Dusky Crag Martin** *Hirundo concolor*   13 cm

a **b** **c** ADULT Upperparts and underparts dark brown and rather uniform. Cliffs, gorges and old buildings. Resident. DE: cr, GU: cr, HA: lcr, HP: nr, MP: lcr, PU: nr, RA: nr, UP: nr, UR: lcr.

6   **Barn Swallow** *Hirundo rustica*   18 cm

a **b** **c** ADULT and **d** JUVENILE Reddish throat, long tail-streamers and blue-black breast-band. Juvenile duller; lacks tail-streamers. Cultivation, habitation, lakes and rivers. Breeds from foothills up to 3000 m, winters mainly in plains. DE: cw, GU: cw, HA: cw, HP: ns, JK: lcs, MP: nw, PU: cw, RA: nw, UP: cw, UR: nr.

1 **Wire-tailed Swallow** *Hirundo smithii* 14 cm

    a **b** **c** ADULT and **d** JUVENILE Chestnut crown, white underparts and fine tail projections. Juvenile has brownish cast to blue upperparts, and dull brownish crown. Open country and cultivation near fresh waters. Plains and foothills up to 1500 m. DE: cr, GU: lcr, HA: lcr, HP: lcs, JK: ns, MP: cr, PU: cs, RA: nr, UP: cr, UR: lcr.

2 **Red-rumped Swallow** *Hirundo daurica* 16–17 cm

    a **b** **c** ADULT and **d** JUVENILE Rufous-orange neck sides and rump, finely streaked buffish-white underparts and black undertail-coverts. Cultivation and upland pastures. Breeds 1000–3300 m in Himalayas, in plains and up to 1600 m south of the Himalayas. DE: lcr, GU: cr, HA: lcr, HP: lcs, JK: lcs, MP: cr, PU: nr, RA: nr, UP: cw, UR: lcr.

3 **Streak-throated Swallow** *Hirundo fluvicola* 11 cm

    a **b** **c** ADULT and **d** JUVENILE Small, with slight fork to long, broad tail. Chestnut crown, streaked throat and breast, white mantle streaks and brownish rump. Juvenile is duller, with browner crown. Rivers and lakes. Up to 700 m. DE: cs, GU: nr, HA: lcr, HP: ns, JK: ns, MP: nr, PU: nr, RA: nr, UP: nr, UR: lcr.

4 **Northern House Martin** *Delichon urbica* 12 cm

    a **b** **c** ADULT Distinguished from Asian by whiter underparts and underwing-coverts, longer deeply forked tail, and whiter and more extensive rump-patch. Mountain valleys. Breeds 3000–4500 m in Himalayas, small numbers on passage south of Himalayas. DE: v, GU: v, HA: v, HP: np, JK: ns, MP: v, PU: v, UR: v.

5 **Asian House Martin** *Delichon dasypus* 12 cm

    a **b** **c** ADULT Dusky-white underparts and rump, shallow tail-fork, dusky underwing and (not always) dusky centres to undertail-coverts. Grassy slopes with cliffs, forest, mountain villages. Resident; breeds 1800–4800 m, winters at lower altitudes, rarely down to plains. HP: nr, JK: lcr, MP: v, PU: v, UR: nr.

6 **Nepal House Martin** *Delichon nipalensis* 13 cm

    a **b** **c** ADULT Square-cut tail, narrow white rump, blackish underwing-coverts and undertail-coverts, and blackish throat (just chin in some). Mountain ridges with cliffs, forest, villages. Resident; breeds 1000–4000 m, winters 300–2000 m. UR: nr.

1 Black-crested Bulbul *Pycnonotus melanicterus* 19 cm
ADULT Crested black head, yellow underparts, and greenish wings and tail. Moist broadleaved forest and thick secondary growth. Resident; terai up to 1500 m. HP: ?nr, MP: nr, PU: nr?, UP: nr, UR: nr.

2 Red-whiskered Bulbul *Pycnonotus jocosus* 20 cm
ADULT Black crest, red 'whiskers', white underparts with complete or broken breast-band, and red vent. Juvenile duller and lacks 'whiskers'. Open forest and secondary growth. Up to 1500 m in Himalayas. DE: cr, GU: lcr, HA: nr, HP: nr, MP: nr, PU: cr, RA: nr, UP: lcr, UR: nr.

3 White-eared Bulbul *Pycnonotus leucotis* 20 cm
a ADULT *P. l. leucotis*; **b** ADULT *P. l. humii* White-cheeked bulbul with black crown and nape, and short (in northwest part of range) or non-existent crest. Thorn scrub and dry, open cultivation. DE: lcr, GU: lcr, HA: cr, MP: nr, PU: nr, RA: lcr, UP: nr.

4 Himalayan Bulbul *Pycnonotus leucogenys* 20 cm
ADULT Brown crest and nape, white cheeks with black throat, and yellow vent. Dry scrub, secondary growth and bushes around habitation. Resident; 30–2400 m. HA: nr, HP: lcr, JK: lcr, PU: np?, UR: lcr.

5 Red-vented Bulbul *Pycnonotus cafer* 20 cm
ADULT Blackish head with slight crest, scaled appearance to upperparts and breast, red vent and white rump. Open deciduous forest, secondary growth and trees around habitation. Up to 1830 m in the Himalayas. DE: cr, GU: cr, HA: cr, HP: lcr, JK: nr, MP: cr, PU: cr, RA: lcr, UP: cr, UR: lcr.

6 White-browed Bulbul *Pycnonotus luteolus* 20 cm
ADULT White supercilium and crescent below eye, and dark eye-stripe and moustachial stripe. Otherwise nondescript. Dry scrub and forest edges. Resident. DE: v, GU: nr, RA: nr.

7 White-throated Bulbul *Alophoixus flaveolus* 22 cm
ADULT Brownish crest, white throat, yellow breast and belly, and rufous cast to wings and tail. Undergrowth in broadleaved evergreen forest and secondary growth; lower hills. UR: nr?

8 Ashy Bulbul *Hemixos flavala* 20 cm
ADULT Grey crest and upperparts, black mask and tawny ear-coverts, and olive-yellow wing-patch. Broadleaved forest; also forest edges in winter. Resident; 700–1600 m. UR: nr.

9 Mountain Bulbul *Hypsipetes mcclellandii* 24 cm
ADULT Brown crest, greyish throat with white streaking, cinnamon-brown breast with buff streaking, and greenish upperparts. Forest and secondary growth. Resident; breeds 900–2700 m, winters down to the foothills. UR: nr.

10 Black Bulbul *Hypsipetes leucocephalus* 25 cm
ADULT Slate-grey bulbul with black crest. Has shallow fork to tail, and red bill, legs and feet. Juvenile lacks crest; has whitish underparts with diffuse grey breast-band, and brownish cast to upperparts. Mainly broadleaved forest. Resident; breeds 1000–3200 m, winters down to the foothills and adjacent plains. DE: v, HA: nw?, HP: lcr, JK: lcr, MP: v, PU: nw, UR: lcr.

11 Grey Hypocolius *Hypocolius ampelinus* 25 cm
a MALE and **b** FEMALE Crested, with long tail and white on primaries. Male has black mask and tail-band. Female rather uniform sandy-brown. Thorn scrub and date-palm groves in semi-desert. Winter visitor. GU: nw.

TAZ PALACE
2/22/14
DE4461
↕
2/22/14

Rufous-vented Prinia *Prinia burnesii* 17 cm

ADULT Large size. Streaked upperparts, whitish lores/eye-ring, broad tail, and rufous vent. Tall grassland and reedbeds. Resident. PU: nr, RA: nr?, UP: nr?

Striated Prinia *Prinia criniger* 16 cm

a ADULT BREEDING and b ADULT NON-BREEDING Large size. Streaked upperparts and stout bill. In breeding plumage has dark bill and lores, and indistinct streaking to grey-brown upperparts. In non-breeding has prominently streaked, rufous-brown upperparts and buff lores. Scrub and grass hillsides and terraced cultivation. Resident; breeds 600–2100 m, winters 300–2100 m. HA: nr, HP: lcr, JK: nr, PU: nw, UR: lcr.

Grey-crowned Prinia *Prinia cinereocapilla* 11 cm

ADULT Orange-buff supercilium, dark blue-grey crown and nape, and rufous-brown mantle and back. Grassland in forest clearings and at forest edges, and secondary growth. From edge of plains up to 1350 m. Globally threatened (Vulnerable). UR: nr.

Rufous-fronted Prinia *Prinia buchanani* 12 cm

ADULT Rufous-brown crown and broad white tips to tail (very prominent in flight). Call is a distinctive rippling trill. Rufous to crown may be difficult to see when worn. Upperparts uniform pale rufous-brown on juvenile. Scrub in semi-desert. Resident. DE: lcr, GU: cr, HA: nr, HP: nr, JK: nr, MP: nr, PU: cr, RA: lcr, UP: lcr.

Grey-breasted Prinia *Prinia hodgsonii* 11 cm

a ADULT BREEDING and b ADULT NON-BREEDING Small size. Diffuse grey breast-band in summer. In non-breeding plumage has fine dark bill, fine whitish supercilium, brown upperparts with rufescent cast, and greyish wash to sides of neck and breast. Bushes at forest edges, scrub and secondary growth. From base of hills up to 1600 m. DE: cr, GU: lcr, HA: lcr, HP: lcr, JK: nr, MP: lcr, PU: nr, RA: nr, UP: cr, UR: lcr.

Jungle Prinia *Prinia sylvatica* 13 cm

a ADULT BREEDING and b ADULT NON-BREEDING Larger than Plain, with stouter bill and uniform wings. Song is a loud, pulsing *zong zee chu*, repeated monotonously; calls include a dry rattle and a loud *tiu*. In breeding plumage has greyer upperparts, dark lores and bill, and shorter tail with prominent white outertail feathers. More rufescent in non-breeding plumage, with prominent supercilium and longer tail. Scrub and tall grass in open dry areas. Plains and hills up to 1500 m. DE: xnr, GU: lcr, HA: nr, HP: lcr, JK: nr, MP: nr, PU: nr, RA: nr, UP: nr, UR: lcr.

Yellow-bellied Prinia *Prinia flaviventris* 13 cm

ADULT White throat and breast, and yellow belly. Slate-grey cast to crown and olive-green cast to upperparts. Juvenile has uniform yellowish olive-brown upperparts and yellow underparts. Tall grassland by wetlands. Plains and foothills up to 800 m. DE: lcr, HA: lcr, PU: nr, UP: lcr, UR: nr.

Ashy Prinia *Prinia socialis* 13 cm

a ADULT BREEDING and b ADULT NON-BREEDING Slate-grey crown and ear-coverts, red eyes, slate-grey or rufous-brown upperparts, and orange-buff wash to underparts. Tall grass and scrub, open secondary growth, reedbeds and forest edges. Plains and hills up to 1200 m. DE: cr, GU: lcr, HA: cr, HP: nr, JK: nr, MP: cr, PU: cr, RA: lcr, UP: cr, UR: lcr.

Plain Prinia *Prinia inornata* 13 cm

a ADULT BREEDING and b ADULT NON-BREEDING Smaller than Jungle, with finer bill, and pale or rufous fringes to tertials. Song is a rapid wheezy trill, *tlick-tlick-tlick* etc.; calls include a plaintive *tee-tee-tee* and nasal *beep*. In breeding plumage has greyer upperparts, dark bill, and shorter tail with prominent white outertail feathers. More rufescent in non-breeding plumage, with longer tail. Reeds, grassland, edges of cultivation, scrub and forest edges. Plains and hills up to 1200 m. DE: cr, GU: cr, HA: cr, HP: lcr, JK: nr, MP: cr, PU: nr, RA: lcr, UP: cr, UR: lcr.

1 **Graceful Prinia** *Prinia gracilis* 11 cm
ADULT Small, with fine bill and streaked upperparts. Tall grass and scrub along river banks in the terai. DE: lcr, GU: lcr, HA: lcr, JK: nr, PU: nr, RA: lcr, UP: nr.

2 **Zitting Cisticola** *Cisticola juncidis* 10 cm
a ADULT BREEDING and **b** ADULT NON-BREEDING Small, with short tail that has prominent white tips. Bold streaking on buff upperparts, including nape, and thin whitish supercilium. Song, uttered in display flight, is a repetitive *pip pip pip…*; call is a single *plit*. Fields and grassland. Plains and hills up to 1800 m. DE: cr, GU: cr, HA: cr, HP: nr, MP: cr, PU: nr, RA: lcr, UP: cr, UR: nr.

3 **Bright-headed Cisticola** *Cisticola exilis* 10 cm
a MALE BREEDING and **b** NON-BREEDING Breeding males have unstreaked rufous crown. In other plumages very similar to Zitting; typically shows unstreaked rufous nape, rufous supercilium and neck sides, blacker crown and mantle with less distinct pale streaking, and longer and more uniformly dark tail with narrow buff tips. Song is a *cheeezz…joo-ee, di-do*, given in display flight or from perch; the *cheeezz* often given alone. Tall grassland. Plains and foothills up to 1200 m. MP: nr, UP: lcr, UR: lcr.

4 **Oriental White-eye** *Zosterops palpebrosus* 10 cm
ADULT Black lores and white eye-ring, bright yellow throat and breast, and whitish belly. Open broadleaved forest and wooded areas. Up to 2100 m in breeding season in Himalayas. DE: cr, GU: cr, HA: cr, HP: nr, JK: lcr, MP: cr, PU: nr, RA: lcr, UP: cr, UR: lcr.

5 **Chestnut-headed Tesia** *Tesia castaneocoronata* 8 cm
ADULT Adult has chestnut head and yellow underparts. Juvenile lacks chestnut head and has dark rufous underparts. Thick undergrowth in moist forest. Resident; breeds 1800–3355 m, winters from 1800 m down to the foothills. HP: nr, UR: lcr.

6 **Grey-bellied Tesia** *Tesia cyaniventer* 9 cm
ADULT Pale grey underparts, green upperparts with bright yellowish-green supercilium, and dark eye-stripe. Thick undergrowth in moist forest; favours streamsides. Resident; breeds 1500–2550 m, winters from 1800 m down to the foothills. UP: nw, UR: nr.

7 **Common Tailorbird** *Orthotomus sutorius* 13 cm
a MALE and **b** FEMALE Rufous forehead, greenish upperparts, and whitish underparts including undertail-coverts. Bushes in gardens, cultivation edges and forest edges. Up to 1800 m. DE: cr, GU: cr, HA: cr, HP: lcr, JK: lcr, MP: cr, PU: cr, RA: lcr, UP: cr, UR: lcr.

8 **White-browed Tit Warbler** *Leptopoecile sophiae* 10 cm
a MALE and **b** FEMALE Whitish supercilium, rufous crown, and lilac and purple in plumage. Dwarf scrub in semi-desert. Breeds 3000–3900 m, winters down to 1800 m. JK: nr.

1   Pale-footed Bush Warbler *Cettia pallidipes*   11 cm

ADULT Upperparts more rufescent, underparts whiter, and supercilium more prominent compared with Brownish-flanked. Pale pinkish legs and feet. (*See also* Table 7 on p.295.) Song is a loud, explosive *zip...zip-tschuck-o-tschuck*. Tall grass and bushes at forest edges. Resident; chiefly below 250 m. UR: nr.

2   Brownish-flanked Bush Warbler *Cettia fortipes*   12 cm

ADULT Underparts duskier and upperparts more olive-tinged than Pale-footed. Brownish legs and feet. (*See also* Table 7 on p.295.) Song is a *weeee chiwiyou*. Open forest and thickets. Resident; breeds 1800–3200 m, winters from 1800 m down to the foothills. HA: v, HP: lcr, JK: lcr, PU: v, UR: lcr.

3   Chestnut-crowned Bush Warbler *Cettia major*   13 cm

ADULT Chestnut crown. Told from Grey-sided by larger size, rufous-buff on fore supercilium, and whiter underparts. (*See also* Table 7 on p.295.) Song has an introductory note, then an explosive warble. Summers in rhododendron shrubberies and bushes in forest; winters in reedbeds. Resident; breeds 3300–4000 m, winters below 250 m. UR: nr.

4   Aberrant Bush Warbler *Cettia flavolivacea*   12 cm

ADULT Greenish upperparts, and yellowish supercilium and underparts. (*See also* Table 7 on p.295.) Song is short warble, followed by inflected whistle *dir dir-tee teee-weee*. Bushes at forest edges and shrubberies. Resident; breeds 2400–3600 m, winters 700–2700 m. HP: nr, UR: nr.

5   Yellowish-bellied Bush Warbler *Cettia acanthizoides*   9.5 cm

ADULT Small size, pale rufous-brown upperparts, whitish throat and breast, and yellowish belly and flanks. (*See also* Table 7 on p.295.) Song is a thin, high-pitched *see-saw see-saw see-saw* etc. Mainly bamboo stands. Resident; summers 2400–3300 m. UR: nr.

6   Grey-sided Bush Warbler *Cettia brunnifrons*   10 cm

ADULT Chestnut crown. Told from Chestnut-crowned by small size, shorter whitish supercilium and greyer underparts. (*See also* Table 7 on p.295.) Song is a loud, wheezy, repeated *sip ti ti sip*. Summers in high-altitude shrubberies and bushes at forest edges; winters in scrub and forest undergrowth. Resident; breeds 2745–4000 m, winters 915–2135 m. HA: nw?, HP: nr, JK: nr, PU: nw, UP: nw, UR: nr.

7   Cetti's Bush Warbler *Cettia cetti*   14 cm

ADULT Large size with big tail; white breast and indistinct supercilium, greyish breast sides and flanks, and whitish tips to undertail-coverts. (*See also* Table 7 on p.295.) Song is an explosive *chit...chit...chitity chit...chitity chit*; call is an explosive *chit*. Reedbeds and tamarisks. HA: v, PU: nw, RA: nw.

8   Spotted Bush Warbler *Bradypterus thoracicus*   13 cm

ADULT Spotting on throat and breast (can be indistinct). Shortish bill, grey ear-coverts and breast, and olive-brown flanks; boldly patterned undertail-coverts. Song is a repeated *trick-i-di*. Summers in high-altitude shrubberies, winters in reedbeds and tall grass. Resident; breeds 3000–4000 m. JK: nr, UP: nw, UR: nr.

9   Long-billed Bush Warbler *Bradypterus major*   13 cm

ADULT Spotting on throat and breast (can be indistinct). Long bill, white underparts and unmarked undertail-coverts. Song is monotonous *pikha-pikha-pikha* etc. Bushy hillsides, and thickets at forest edges. Resident; breeds 2400–3600 m. JK: nr.

1

Lanceolated Warbler *Locustella lanceolata* 12 cm

a **b** ADULT Streaking on throat, breast and flanks (weak on some). Some can be very similar to Grasshopper; streaking on undertail-coverts is less extensive but blacker and more clear cut, and tertials are darker with clear-cut pale edges. Tall grassland, and bush/grassland. Winter visitor. DE: v, GU: v?, HA: v, RA: v, UP: nw.

2

Grasshopper Warbler *Locustella naevia* 13 cm

a **b** ADULT Olive-brown upperparts, indistinct supercilium, and (usually) unmarked or only lightly streaked throat and breast. *See* Appendix for comparison with Rusty-rumped Warbler. Tall grassland, reedbeds and paddy-fields. Winter visitor. DE: v, GU: np, HA: nw?, HP: np, MP: nw, RA: v, UP: nw.

3

Moustached Warbler *Acrocephalus melanopogon* 12.5 cm

ADULT Broad white supercilium, blackish eye-stripe and boldly streaked rufous-brown mantle. *See* Appendix for comparison with Sedge Warbler. Tall reedbeds and tamarisks. Winter visitor in the plains. DE: np, GU: nw, HA: lcw, JK: np, MP: nw, PU: nw, RA: nw, UP: nw, UR: nw.

4

Greater Whitethroat *Sylvia communis* 14 cm

a MALE and **b** FEMALE Larger and longer-tailed than Lesser, with broad, well-defined, sandy-brown to pale rufous-brown fringes to greater coverts and tertials, pale base to lower mandible, and orange-brown to pale brown (not grey) legs and feet. Standing crops and bushes. DE: np, GU: lcp, HA: np, HP: np, JK: v, PU: v, RA: np, UP: v.

5

Lesser Whitethroat *Sylvia curruca* 13 cm

a ADULT *S. c. blythi*; **b** ADULT *S. c. minula*; **c** ADULT *S. c. althaea* Brownish-grey upperparts, grey crown with darker ear-coverts, blackish bill, and dark grey legs and feet. *S. c. althaea* ('Hume's Whitethroat') is the largest and darkest race; *minula* ('Small Whitethroat') is the most finely built, with pale, sandy grey-brown upperparts. Scrub. Breeds 1500–3700 m, winters in plains and hills up to 900 m. DE: cw, GU: cw, HA: cw, HP: np, JK: lcs, MP: lcw, PU: nw, RA: cw, UP: cw, UR: lcw.

6

Desert Warbler *Sylvia nana* 11.5 cm

ADULT Small size, sandy-brown upperparts, rufous rump and tail, yellow iris, and yellowish legs and feet. Scrub in desert and rocky hills. DE: v, GU: nw, HA; v, MP: v, PU: nw, RA: lcw, UR: v.

7

Orphean Warbler *Sylvia hortensis* 15 cm

a ADULT MALE, **b** ADULT FEMALE and **c** 1ST-WINTER Larger and bigger-billed than Lesser Whitethroat; more ponderous movements, and heavier appearance in flight. Adult has blackish crown, pale grey mantle, blackish tail and pale iris. First-year has crown concolorous with mantle, darker grey ear-coverts and dark iris; very similar to many Lesser Whitethroats. Orphean often shows darker-looking uppertail, lacks or has indistinct eye-ring, and has greyish centres and pale fringes to undertail-coverts; these features are variable and difficult to observe in the field. Winters in scrub and groves. DE: lcp, GU: lcw, HA: nw, HP: v, MP: nw, PU: nw, RA: nw, UP: nw, UR: np.

Paddyfield Warbler *Acrocephalus agricola* 13 cm

a ADULT FRESH and **b** ADULT WORN Prominent white supercilium behind eye, and stout bill with dark tip. Often shows dark edge to supercilium. Rufous cast to upperparts in fresh plumage. Typically shows dark centres and pale edges to tertials (wings usually uniform in Blyth's Reed). (*See also* Table 8 on p.296.) *See* Appendix for comparison with Black-browed Reed. Reedbeds and damp grassland. DE: lcp, GU: cw, HA: cp, HP: np, JK: np, MP: nw, PU: np, RA: np, UP: np.

Blunt-winged Warbler *Acrocephalus concinens* 13 cm

a ADULT FRESH and **b** ADULT WORN Longer and stouter bill than Paddyfield, with pale lower mandible. Supercilium indistinct behind eye. Lacks dark edge to supercilium and eye-stripe is less striking than in Paddyfield. (*See also* Table 8 on p.296.) Reedbeds, and tall grass near water. Breeds 1525–3000 m, no winter records. JK: lcs, RA: v.

Blyth's Reed Warbler *Acrocephalus dumetorum* 14 cm

a ADULT FRESH and **b** ADULT WORN Long bill, olive-brown to olive-grey upperparts, and uniform wings. Supercilium indistinct compared with Paddyfield, barely apparent behind eye. (*See also* Table 8 on p.296.) Bushes and trees at edges of forest and cultivation. Plains and hills up to 2100 m. DE: cp, GU: cw, HA: cp, HP: cp, JK: np, MP: cw, PU: cp, RA: lcp, UP: np, UR: np.

Large-billed Reed Warbler *Acrocephalus orinus* 14 cm

NOT ILLUSTRATED Very similar in appearance to Blyth's Reed Warbler. Compared with this species in fresh plumage, is less olive and more rufous-tinged. Structurally has a longer and slightly broader bill, more-rounded wings, and longer and more-graduated tail with more-pointed tail feathers. Smaller with weaker bill and feet than Clamorous Reed. (*See also* Table 8 on p.296.) Known only from the type specimen collected in the Sutlej Valley, Himachal Pradesh, in 1867. Subject to some taxonomic debate, recent DNA studies have made the case for it to be regarded as a distinct species. HP: nr?

Clamorous Reed Warbler *Acrocephalus stentoreus* 19 cm

ADULT Large size, long bill, short primary projection, and whitish supercilium. *See* Appendix for comparison with Great Reed. Reedbeds and bushes around wetlands. Breeds up to 1500 m in Kashmir, winters in plains and peninsular hills up to 1800 m. DE: lcr, GU: cw, HA: lcr, HP: ns, JK: lcs, MP: np, PU: nw, RA: nr, UP: nr?, UR: lcr.

Thick-billed Warbler *Acrocephalus aedon* 19 cm

ADULT Large size. Short, stout bill and rounded head. 'Plain-faced' appearance, lacking prominent supercilium or eye-stripe. Tall grass, scrub, reeds and bushes at edges of forest and cultivation. GU: v, RA: v, UR: v.

Striated Grassbird *Megalurus palustris* 25 cm

a ADULT WORN and **b** ADULT FRESH Streaked upperparts, finely streaked breast and long, graduated tail. Has longer and finer bill and more prominent supercilium than Bristled. Tall damp grassland and reedbeds. DE: lcr, HA: nr?, HP: v, MP: nr, PU: nr, UP: nr.

Bristled Grassbird *Chaetornis striatus* 20 cm

ADULT Streaked upperparts and fine streaking on lower throat. Has shorter, stouter bill and less prominent supercilium than Striated, also shorter and broader tail with buffish-white tips. Short grassland with scattered bushes and some tall vegetation. Globally threatened (Vulnerable). DE: xnr, GU: nr, HA: nr, MP: nr?, PU: nr?, UP: nr.

Rufous-rumped Grassbird *Graminicola bengalensis* 18 cm

ADULT Rufous and whitish streaking on black upperparts, white-tipped blackish tail, and white underparts with rufous-buff breast sides and flanks. Tall grass and reeds. UP: lcr.

1 Booted Warbler *Hippolais caligata* 12 cm

a ADULT *H. c. caligata*; **b** ADULT *H. c. rama* Small size and *Phylloscopus*-like behaviour. Tail looks long and square-ended, and undertail-coverts look short. Often shows faint whitish edges and tip to tail, and fringes to tertials. (*See also* Table 8 on p.296.) Scrub and bushes at cultivation edges in dry habitats. DE: cp, GU: nw, HA: np?, MP: nw, PU: ns, RA: np, UP: np, UR: np.

2 Common Chiffchaff *Phylloscopus collybita* 11 cm

ADULT Brownish to greyish upperparts; olive-green edges to wing-coverts, remiges and rectrices. Black bill and legs. No wing-bar. (*See also* Table 2 on p.292.) Forest, bushes and secondary growth. Up to 2100 m. DE: cw, GU: cw, HA: cw, HP: nw, JK: np, MP: lcw, PU: cw, RA: lcw, UP: cw, UR: nw.

3 Mountain Chiffchaff *Phylloscopus sindianus* 11 cm

ADULT Much as Common Chiffchaff, but generally lacks olive-green tone to back and to edges of wing-coverts, remiges and rectrices. (*See also* Table 2 on p.292.) Different call. Breeds in bushes; winters in riverine trees and bushes. Breeds in Himalayas 2500–4400 m, winters in plains and foothills. DE: v, HA: v, HP: ns, JK: ns, PU: v, RA: v.

4 Plain Leaf Warbler *Phylloscopus neglectus* 10 cm

ADULT Much as Common Chiffchaff, but smaller, with shorter tail, no olive-green or yellow in plumage, and different call. (*See also* Table 2 on p.292.) Breeds in juniper and pine forest; winters in open wooded areas. Has bred in hills of Kashmir but current status unknown; winters in lowlands. DE: v, HP: np?, JK: ns, RA: nw.

5 Dusky Warbler *Phylloscopus fuscatus* 11 cm

ADULT Brown upperparts and whitish underparts, with buff flanks. Prominent supercilium, and hard *chack* call. *See* Appendix for comparison with Radde's Warbler. (*See also* Table 2 on p.292.) Bushes and long grass, especially near water. DE: v, HP: v, JK: v, MP: nw, PU: v, RA: nw, UP: nw, UR: nw.

6 Smoky Warbler *Phylloscopus fuligiventer* 10 cm

ADULT Very dark, with short yellowish supercilium, and yellowish centre to throat and belly. (*See also* Table 2 on p.292.) Call is a throaty *thrup thrup*. Breeds in dwarf juniper and other shrubberies at 3960–4270 m; winters in dense undergrowth near water in plains and foothills. PU: v, RA: nw, UP: nw, UR: nw.

7 Tickell's Leaf Warbler *Phylloscopus affinis* 11 cm

ADULT FRESH Dark greenish to greenish-brown upperparts, and bright yellow supercilium and underparts. (*See also* Table 2 on p.292.) *Chit* call. Breeds in open country with bushes at 3300–4800 m; widespread in winter in bushes at edges of forest and cultivation, chiefly in the hills, from the base up to 2100 m. DE: v, GU: np, HA: np, HP: ns, JK: lcs, MP: nw, PU: v, RA: np, UR: ns.

8 Sulphur-bellied Warbler *Phylloscopus griseolus* 11 cm

ADULT FRESH Dark greyish upperparts, bright yellow supercilium, and dusky yellow underparts strongly washed with buff. (*See also* Table 2 on p.292.) Soft *quip* call. Has distinctive habit of climbing about rocks and nuthatch-like on tree trunks and branches. Summers in open dry, stony mountain slopes with scattered trees and bushes, winters in rocky areas and around old buildings. DE: np, GU: nw, HA: np, HP: ns, JK: ns, MP: nw, PU: np, RA: np, UP: np, UR: np.

1

Buff-barred Warbler *Phylloscopus pulcher*   10 cm
ADULT FRESH   Buffish-orange wing-bars, yellowish supercilium and wash to underparts, white on tail, and small yellowish rump-patch. (*See also* Table 5 on p.294.) Breeds in subalpine shrubberies and forest 2800–4300 m; winters in broadleaved forest 500–2800 m. DE: v, HP: lcr, JK: nr, PU: v, UR: nr.

2

Ashy-throated Warbler *Phylloscopus maculipennis*   9 cm
ADULT FRESH   Small size. Greyish throat and breast, yellow belly and flanks, white supercilium and crown-stripe, yellow rump and white on tail. (*See also* Table 5 on p.294.) Broadleaved and broadleaved/coniferous forest; also secondary growth in winter. Resident; breeds 2500–3400 m, winters from 2900 m down to the foothills. HP: nr, JK: nr, UR: nr.

3

Lemon-rumped Warbler *Phylloscopus chloronotus*   9 cm
ADULT FRESH   Yellowish crown-stripe and rump-band, dark crown-sides, dark panel across greater coverts, and whitish underparts. (*See also* Table 5 on p.294.) Forest; also secondary growth in winter. Resident; breeds 2200–4200 m, winters from 2100 m down to the foothills. HA: nw, HP: cr, JK: cr, PU: v, UR: cr.

4

Brooks's Leaf Warbler *Phylloscopus subviridis*   9 cm
a ADULT FRESH and **b** ADULT WORN   Yellow supercilium and ear-coverts; variable yellow wash to throat and breast. Lacks dark lateral crown-stripes and has indistinct pale rump-band. (*See also* Table 5 on p.294.) Winters in bushes and well-wooded areas in plains and hills. DE: nw, HA: np, HP: np, JK: v, MP: nw, PU: nw, RA: nw, UP: v.

5

Hume's Warbler *Phylloscopus humei*   10–11 cm
ADULT FRESH   Lacks rump-band and well-defined crown-stripe. Has buffish or whitish wing-bars and supercilium. Bill appears all dark, and legs are normally blackish brown. (*See also* Table 5 on p.294.) Call is a rolling *whit-hoo*. See Appendix for comparison with Yellow-browed Warbler. Breeds in coniferous forest and subalpine shrubberies; winters in forest and secondary growth. Resident; breeds 2100–3600 m, winters in plains and hills up to 1800 m. DE: cw, GU: nw, HA: cw, HP: lcr, JK: lcs, MP: nw, PU: nw, RA: nw, UP: cw, UR: lcs.

6

Greenish Warbler *Phylloscopus trochiloides*   10–11 cm
a ADULT FRESH *P. t. viridanus*; **b** ADULT FRESH *P. t. trochiloides*; **c** ADULT FRESH *P. t. nitidus*   *P. t. trochiloides* is a summer visitor, chiefly 3000–4270 m, *P. t. viridanus* is a winter visitor below 1830 m, and a passage migrant. *P. t. nitidus* is a spring passage migrant below 2135 m. Slurred, loud *chli-wee* call. No crown-stripe; fine wing-bar (sometimes two). (*See also* Table 4 on p.293.) Breeds in forest and subalpine shrubberies 2700–4300 m; winters in well-wooded areas in plains and hills up to 2200 m. DE: cp, GU: cw, HA: cp, HP: cp, JK: lcs, MP: cw, PU: cp, RA: nw, UP: cw, UR: lcs.

7

Large-billed Leaf Warbler *Phylloscopus magnirostris*   13 cm
ADULT FRESH   Clear, loud *der-tee* call is best feature separating it from Greenish. Large, with large dark bill. Very bold yellow-white supercilium and broad dark eye-stripe. (*See also* Table 4 on p.293.) Forest along mountain rivers and streams. Summer visitor, 1800–3600 m. DE: v, HP: ns, JK: lcs, MP: v, PU: v, RA: v, UR: lcs.

8

Tytler's Leaf Warbler *Phylloscopus tytleri*   11 cm
ADULT FRESH   Slender, mainly dark bill, long fine supercilium, no wing-bars and shortish tail. (*See also* Table 2 on p.292.) Oak/rhododendron forest and shrubberies at forest edges. Summer visitor, 2400–3600 m. HP: np, JK: ns, UP: np?

1

Western Crowned Warbler *Phylloscopus occipitalis*   11 cm

ADULT FRESH Large size. Crown-stripe, greyish-green upperparts and greyish-white underparts. Head and wing pattern tends to be less striking than on Blyth's Leaf. (*See also* Table 6 on p.295.) Breeds in broadleaved and coniferous forests 1800–3200 m, winters mainly in hills below 2100 m. DE: np, GU: np, HA: np, HP: lcs, JK: lcs, MP: lcw, PU: np, RA: np, UP: lcw, UR: lcs.

2

Blyth's Leaf Warbler *Phylloscopus reguloides*   11 cm

ADULT FRESH Crown-stripe, yellowish on underparts, and broad wing-bars with dark panel across greater coverts. (*See also* Table 6 on p.295.) Summers in broadleaved and coniferous forests, winters in bushes and open forest. Resident; breeds 2000–3700 m, winters from 1500 m down to the plains. HA: v, HP: nr, JK: nr, PU: v, UR: nr.

3

Golden-spectacled Warbler *Seicercus burkii*   10 cm

ADULT Yellow eye-ring, and yellowish-green face. Forest understorey and secondary growth. Resident; altitudinal range uncertain, probably summers 1550–2050 m, winters down to 250 m, occasionally to 150 m. HA: nw, MP: v, RA: v, UP: v, UR: cr.

4

Whistler's Warbler *Seicercus whistleri*   10 cm

ADULT Very similar in plumage to Golden-spectacled; dark sides of crown are not as black and are diffuse on forehead, and yellow eye-ring is broader at rear. Generally, upperparts are duller greyish-green, underparts are duller yellow and wing-bar is usually more distinct. Shows more white in outer tail feathers; in particular, there is much white on basal half of outerweb of outermost tail feathers (generally lacking white in this area in Golden-spectacled). Song lacks tremelos and trills that are present in Golden-spectacled's and this is best means of identification. Forest understorey, secondary growth and high-altitude shrubberies. Resident; altitudinal range uncertain, probably summers 2130–3800 m, winters below 2135 m. HA: v, HP: nr, JK: np, PU: v, UR: nr.

5

Grey-hooded Warbler *Seicercus xanthoschistos*   10 cm

ADULT *Phylloscopus*-like appearance. Whitish supercilium, and grey crown with pale central stripe; yellow underparts and no wing-bars. Lower canopy and bushes in forest and secondary growth. Resident; breeds 900–2700 m, winters from 2000 m down to the foothills. GU: v, HA: cr/w, HP: lcr, JK: nr, PU: nw, UR: lcr.

6

Grey-cheeked Warbler *Seicercus poliogenys*   10 cm

ADULT White eye-ring, and dark grey head with poorly defined lateral crown-stripes; grey ear-coverts, grey lores and white chin. Evergreen broadleaved forest. Resident; breeds from 1700–3050 m, winters from 1890 m down to the foothills. UR: nr.

7

Chestnut-crowned Warbler *Seicercus castaniceps*   9.5 cm

ADULT Chestnut crown, white eye-ring and grey ear-coverts; white belly, yellow rump and wing-bars, and white on tail. Mainly oak forest. Resident; breeds 1200–2500 m, winters 150–2300 m. UR: nr.

8

Black-faced Warbler *Abroscopus schisticeps*   9 cm

ADULT Black mask, yellow supercilium and throat, and grey crown. Moist broadleaved forest. Resident; around 1500 m. UR: nr.

9

Goldcrest *Regulus regulus*   9 cm

ADULT Small size. Plain face, lacking supercilium, but with dark eye and pale eye-ring. Yellow centre to crown. Coniferous forest. Resident; breeds 2200 m to treeline, winters 1500–3000 m. HP: nr, JK: nr, PU: v, UR: nr.

1

White-throated Laughingthrush *Garrulax albogularis* 28 cm
ADULT White throat and upper breast, rufous-orange belly and broad white tip to tail. Broadleaved and mixed forest and secondary growth. Resident; summers chiefly 1800–2440 m, occasionally to 3500 m, winters from 1220 m up to at least 2255 m. HP: nr, JK: nr, UR: lcr.

2

White-crested Laughingthrush *Garrulax leucolophus* 28 cm
ADULT White crest and black mask, white throat and upper breast, and chestnut mantle. Broadleaved forest and secondary growth. Resident; 305–2135 m, mainly 800–1980 m. HA: nw, HP: nr, UR: lcr.

3

Striated Laughingthrush *Garrulax striatus* 28 cm
ADULT Crested appearance, white streaking on head and body, and stout black bill. Broadleaved forest. Resident; 1200–2700 m, summers mainly above 2000 m. HP: nr, UR: lcr.

4

Rufous-chinned Laughingthrush *Garrulax rufogularis* 22 cm
ADULT Blackish cap, rufous chin and throat, black barring on upperparts, bold patterning on wing, and rufous-orange tip and black subterminal band to tail. Undergrowth in broadleaved forest. Resident; 600–1800 m. HP: nr, JK: nr, UR: lcr.

5

Spotted Laughingthrush *Garrulax ocellatus* 32 cm
ADULT White spotting on chestnut upperparts, black throat and barring on breast, and white tips to chestnut, grey and black tail. Undergrowth in forest and rhododendron shrubberies. Resident; chiefly 2135–3660 m. UR: nr.

6

Streaked Laughingthrush *Garrulax lineatus* 20 cm
ADULT Small, and mainly grey-brown with fine pale streaking. Grey-tipped olive tail, and grey panel in wings. Scrub-covered hills, secondary growth and bushes in cultivation. Resident; summers chiefly 2100–3000 m, winters 1000–2700 m. HA: nw, HP: cr, JK: lcr, PU: nr, UR: cr.

7

Variegated Laughingthrush *Garrulax variegatus* 24 cm
ADULT Black eye-patch and throat, rufous-buff forehead, black patches on greyish wings, and grey tip to tail. Forest undergrowth and rhododendron shrubberies. Resident; breeds 1700–3355 m, winters 1200–2100 m. HP: cr, JK: lcr, PU: v, UR: lcr.

8

Chestnut-crowned Laughingthrush *Garrulax erythrocephalus* 28 cm
ADULT Chestnut crown, dark scaling/spotting on mantle and breast, and olive-yellow wings and tail sides. Undergrowth in broadleaved forest. Resident; summers chiefly 1800–3400 m, winters mainly 1200 m to at least 2000 m. HP: lcr, UR: lcr.

1
Puff-throated Babbler *Pellorneum ruficeps* 15 cm
ADULT Rufous crown, prominent buff supercilium, white throat (often puffed out), and bold brown spotting/streaking on breast and sides of neck. Song is a halting, impulsive *swee ti-ti-hwee hwee hwee ti swee-u*, rambling up and down the scale. Undergrowth in broadleaved forest and secondary growth. Resident; 300–1200 m. GU: nr, HA: lcr, HP: nr, JK: nr, MP: nr, PU: nr, RA: nr, UR: lcr.

2
Rusty-cheeked Scimitar Babbler *Pomatorhinus erythrogenys* 25 cm
ADULT Rufous sides to head and neck, and rufous sides to breast and flanks contrasting with white of rest of underparts. Forest undergrowth and thick scrub. Resident; 450–2200 m. HP: lcr, JK: nr, PU: nr, UR: lcr.

3
Indian Scimitar Babbler *Pomatorhinus horsfieldii* 22 cm
a ADULT *P.h. horsfieldii*; **b** *P.h. obscurus* Upperparts, breast sides and flanks greyish. Forest and secondary growth in lower hills. Resident. *P.h. horsfieldii* occurs in S. Gujarat. GU: nr, MP: nr, RA: nr.

4
White-browed Scimitar Babbler *Pomatorhinus schisticeps* 22 cm
ADULT White centre to breast and belly, and chestnut sides to neck and breast; usually has slate-grey crown. Forest undergrowth and thick scrub. Resident; from plains edge up to 1500 m. HA: nr, HP: nr, PU: nr?, UR: lcr.

5
Streak-breasted Scimitar Babbler *Pomatorhinus ruficollis* 19 cm
ADULT Smaller and smaller-billed than White-browed, with olive-brown crown. Also has olive-brown streaking on breast and belly, and distinct rufous neck-patch extending diffusely across nape. Forest undergrowth and dense scrub. Resident; breeds 1400–3330 m, winters down to 800 m. UR: nr.

6
Scaly-breasted Wren Babbler *Pnoepyga albiventer* 10 cm
a ADULT WHITE and **b** ADULT FULVOUS MORPH Bold scaly white on white or fulvous underparts, and olive-brown upperparts. Usually has buff spotting on crown and sides of neck, occasionally extending on to mantle. Song is a strong warbling *tze-tze-zit tzu-stu-tzit*, rising and ending abruptly. Tall herbage in moist forest. Resident; summers chiefly 2400–3600 m, winters down to 1000 m. HP: nr, PU: v, UR: lcr.

7
Nepal Wren Babbler *Pnoepyga immaculata* 10 cm
a ADULT WHITE and **b** ADULT FULVOUS MORPH Very similar to Scaly-breasted, but has narrower black centres to underpart feathers, and lacks buff spotting on crown, neck-sides and wings. Different song from Scaly-breasted: eight high-pitched piercing notes, fairly quickly delivered *si-su-si-si-swi-si-si-si*. Tall herbage at forest edges or in open forest near running water. HP: nr?, UR: nr?

1

Black-chinned Babbler *Stachyris pyrrhops* 10 cm
ADULT Black chin and lores, and orange-buff underparts. Undergrowth in open forest and secondary growth. Resident; 245–2440 m, breeds mainly 1500–2000 m. HA: lcr, HP: nr, JK: nr, PU: nr, UR: lcr.

2

Tawny-bellied Babbler *Dumetia hyperythra* 13 cm
a ADULT *D. h. hyperythra*; **b** ADULT *D. h. abuensis* Rufous-brown forehead and fore-crown, and orange-buff underparts. *D. h. abuensis*, occurring in the southern part of the region, has a white throat. Thorny scrub and tall grass. Up to 900 m. DE: v, GU: nr, HA: lcr, HP: nr, MP: lcr, PU: lcr, RA: nr, UP: lcr, UR: lcr.

3

Striped Tit Babbler *Macronous gularis* 11 cm
ADULT Rufous-brown cap, pale yellow supercilium, and finely streaked pale yellow throat and breast. Undergrowth in broadleaved forest. Resident; *c.* 300 m. UP: lcr.

4

Chestnut-capped Babbler *Timalia pileata* 17 cm
ADULT Chestnut cap and black mask contrasting with white forehead and supercilium. Tall grass, reedbeds and scrub. Resident; below 305 m. UP: lcr, UR: nr.

5

Yellow-eyed Babbler *Chrysomma sinense* 18 cm
ADULT Yellow iris and orange eye-ring, white lores and supercilium, and white throat and breast. Tall grass, bushes and reeds. Up to 1200 m. DE: lcr, GU: lcr, HA: nr, HP: nr, JK: nr, MP: cr, PU: cr, RA: lcr, UP: cr, UR: lcr.

6

Common Babbler *Turdoides caudatus* 23 cm
ADULT Streaked upperparts. Unstreaked whitish throat and breast centre. Legs and feet are yellowish. Dry cultivation and scrub. Occasionally up to 2100 m in Himalayas. DE: cr, GU: cr, HA: cr, HP: nr, JK: nr, MP: cr, PU: cr, RA: lcr, UP: cr, UR: lcr.

7

Striated Babbler *Turdoides earlei* 21 cm
ADULT Streaked upperparts. Brown mottling on fulvous throat and breast. Legs and feet are greyish to olive-brown. Reedbeds and tall grass in wet habitats. Below 305 m. DE: lcr, HA: lcr, HP: nr, PU: nr, RA: nr, UP: lcr, UR: nr.

8

Large Grey Babbler *Turdoides malcolmi* 28 cm
ADULT Dull white sides to long, graduated tail; unmottled pinkish-grey throat and breast, pale grey forehead and dark grey lores. Open dry scrub and cultivation. Up to 1200 m. DE: cr, GU: cr, HA: cr, MP: cr, PU: cr, RA: lcr, UP: lcr, UR: nr.

9

Jungle Babbler *Turdoides striatus* 25 cm
ADULT Uniform tail; variable dark mottling and streaking on throat and breast. Cultivation and secondary scrub. Up to 1200 m, locally to 1800 m in Himalayas. DE: cr, GU: lcr, HA: cr, HP: lcr, JK: nr, MP: cr, PU: cr, RA: nr, UP: cr, UR: lcr.

1 **Silver-eared Mesia** *Leiothrix argentauris* 15 cm
MALE Black crown, grey ear-coverts, orange-yellow throat and breast, and crimson wing-panel. Male has crimson uppertail-coverts and undertail-coverts. Female has olive-yellow uppertail-coverts and orange-buff undertail-coverts. Bushes in broadleaved evergreen forest. Local resident; 365–1220 m. HP: nr, UR: nr.

2 **Red-billed Leiothrix** *Leiothrix lutea* 13 cm
MALE Red bill, yellowish-olive crown, yellow throat and orange breast, and forked black tail. Male has some crimson edgings to flight feathers; in female the crimson is replaced by yellow. Undergrowth in moist broadleaved forest. Resident; 1000–2400 m. HP: nr, JK: nr, UR: lcr.

3 **Cutia** *Cutia nipalensis* 20 cm
a MALE and **b** FEMALE Grey crown and dark mask, blue-grey panel in wings, and black barring on flanks. Female has spotted mantle. Mossy broadleaved forest. Very local resident; favours 2100–2300 m. UR: nr.

4 **White-browed Shrike Babbler** *Pteruthius flaviscapis* 16 cm
a MALE and **b** FEMALE Male has rufous tertials, black cap with white supercilium, and grey mantle. Female has grey cap and olive mantle; larger size and rufous tertials best distinguish it from Green. Broadleaved forest, favouring oaks. Resident; breeds 1500–2700 m, winters 1350–2000 m. HP: lcr, JK: nr, UR: nr.

5 **Green Shrike Babbler** *Pteruthius xanthochlorus* 13 cm
MALE Grey crown and nape, narrow white or yellowish-white wing-bar, greyish-white throat and breast, and yellowish flanks. Broadleaved and coniferous forests. Resident; breeds 1800–3000 m, winters 1200–2400 m. HP: nr, UR: nr.

6 **Blue-winged Minla** *Minla cyanouroptera* 15 cm
ADULT Blue on crown and on wings and tail; vinaceous-grey underparts. Bushes in forest. Resident; breeds 1500–2500 m, winters 1000–2200 m. UR: nr.

7 **Chestnut-tailed Minla** *Minla strigula* 14 cm
ADULT Orange crown, black-and-white barring on throat, and yellow sides to tail. Mainly broadleaved forest. Resident; breeds 2100–3600 m, winters 1300–2250 m. HP: nr, UR: lcr.

8 **White-browed Fulvetta** *Alcippe vinipectus* 11 cm
ADULT Broad white supercilium, dark ear-coverts and black panel in flight feathers. Subalpine shrubberies and bushes in temperate and subalpine forest. Resident; breeds 2700 m to over 3000 m, winters 1500–2700 m. HP: nr, UR: lcr.

9 **Brown-cheeked Fulvetta** *Alcippe poioicephala* 15 cm
ADULT Nondescript, lacking any patterning to head or wings. Undergrowth in moist forest and secondary growth. Resident. GU: nr, MP: nr.

1   Rufous Sibia *Heterophasia capistrata*   21 cm
ADULT Black cap, and rufous collar and underparts; black and grey bands on rufous tail. Mainly broadleaved forest, especially oak. Resident; breeds 1800–2700 m, winters 1200–2100 m. HP: nr, JK: nr, PU: v, UR: lcr.

2   Whiskered Yuhina *Yuhina flavicollis*   13 cm
ADULT Pale hind-collar and black moustachial stripe. Broadleaved forest and secondary growth. Resident; breeds 1700–3000 m, winters 1200–2300 m. HA: nw, HP: nr, PU: nr, UR: nr.

3   Stripe-throated Yuhina *Yuhina gularis*   14 cm
ADULT Large size, streaked throat, and black and orange wing-panels. Broadleaved and broadleaved/coniferous forests. Resident; breeds 2400–3700 m, winters 1700–3000 m. UR: nr.

4   Black-chinned Yuhina *Yuhina nigrimenta*   11 cm
ADULT Black lores and chin, black crest with grey streaking, and red lower mandible. Moist broadleaved forest. Resident; 610–2200 m. UR: nr.

5   White-bellied Yuhina *Yuhina zantholeuca*   11 cm
ADULT Olive-yellow upperparts and white underparts. Broadleaved forest. Resident; 180–2600 m, mainly below 1600 m. UR: nr.

6   Great Parrotbill *Conostoma oemodium*   28 cm
ADULT Huge conical yellow bill, greyish-white forehead and dark brown lores. Bamboo stands in forest. Resident; 2600–3660 m. UR: nr.

7   Black-throated Parrotbill *Paradoxornis nipalensis*   10 cm
ADULT Greyish crown and ear-coverts, blackish lateral crown-stripes and throat, and white malar patch. Bamboo and dense forest undergrowth. Resident; 2100–2700 m. UR: nr.

1 **Thick-billed Flowerpecker** *Dicaeum agile* 10 cm
ADULT Thick bill; diffuse malar stripe, streaking on breast, and indistinct white tip to tail. Broadleaved forest and well-wooded country. Resident; below 800 m all year, summers up to 1500 m. DE: v, GU: nr, HA: nr?, HP: lcr, MP: nr, PU: nr, RA: nr, UP: lcr, UR: nr.

2 **Yellow-bellied Flowerpecker** *Dicaeum melanoxanthum* 13 cm
a MALE and **b** FEMALE Large size and stout bill; white centre to throat and breast, dark breast sides, and yellow belly and vent. Broadleaved forest. Resident; *c.* 2500 m. UR: nr.

3 **Pale-billed Flowerpecker** *Dicaeum erythrorynchos* 8 cm
ADULT Pale bill. Greyish-olive upperparts and pale grey underparts. Open broadleaved forest and well-wooded areas. Below 300 m. DE: xnr, GU: nr, HP: nr, MP: lcr, PU: nr, RA: nr, UP: nr, UR: lcr.

4 **Plain Flowerpecker** *Dicaeum concolor* 9 cm
ADULT Dark bill. Olive-green upperparts and dusky greyish-olive underparts. Edges of broadleaved forest and well-wooded areas. UP: nr.

5 **Fire-breasted Flowerpecker** *Dicaeum ignipectus* 9 cm
a MALE and **b** FEMALE Male has metallic-blue/green upperparts, and buff underparts with red breast. Female has olive-green upperparts, and orange-buff throat and breast. Broadleaved forest and secondary growth. Resident; summers mainly 1400–2500 m, winters from foothills up to 2500 m. HP: nr, JK: nr, PU: nw, UR: nr.

6 **Ruby-cheeked Sunbird** *Anthreptes singalensis* 11 cm
a MALE, **b** FEMALE and **c** JUVENILE Rufous-orange throat and yellow underparts. Male has metallic-green upperparts and 'ruby' cheeks. Juvenile is uniform yellow below. Open broadleaved forest and forest edges in foothills; favours evergreens. HA: nr?.

7 **Purple-rumped Sunbird** *Nectarinia zeylonica* 10 cm
a MALE, **b** FEMALE and **c** JUVENILE Male has narrow maroon breast-band, maroon head-sides and mantle, and greyish-white flanks. Female has greyish-white throat, yellow breast, whitish flanks and rufous-brown on wing. Juvenile uniform yellow below, with rufous-brown on wing. Calls include a high-pitched *ptsee-ptsee* and a metallic *chit*. Cultivation and secondary growth. Resident. GU: nr, RA: nr.

8 **Crimson-backed Sunbird** *Nectarinia minima* 8 cm
a MALE, **b** FEMALE and **c** ECLIPSE MALE Smaller and finer-billed than Purple-rumped. Male has broad crimson breast-band and mantle. Female has crimson rump. Eclipse male has crimson back and purple rump. Calls include a flowerpecker-like *thlick-thlick*. Evergreen forest and plantations. Resident. GU: nr.

9 **Purple Sunbird** *Nectarinia asiatica* 10 cm
a MALE, **b** **c** FEMALE and **d** ECLIPSE MALE Male metallic purple. Female has uniform yellowish underparts, with faint supercilium and darker mask; can have greyer upperparts and whiter underparts. Eclipse plumage male is similar to female but with dark stripe down centre of throat. Open forest and gardens. Up to 1700 m in Himalayas. DE: cr, GU: cr, HA: cr, HP: lcs, JK: ns, MP: cr, PU: cr, RA: lcr, UP: cr, UR: lcr.

1

2b

2a

3

4

5b

5a

6c

6b

6a

7c

7b

7a

8c

8b

8a

9b

9d

9a

9c

31/1/14
KALANNO

1

Mrs Gould's Sunbird *Aethopyga gouldiae* 10 cm
a MALE and **b** FEMALE Male has metallic purplish-blue crown, ear-coverts and throat, crimson mantle and back (reaching yellow rump), yellow belly and blue tail. Female has pale yellow rump, yellow belly, short bill and prominent white on tail. Rhododendron and other flowering trees and shrubs in forest. Resident; breeds 1830–3300 m, winters from 2700 m down to the base of the hills. HP: nr, RA: v, UR: nr.

2

Green-tailed Sunbird *Aethopyga nipalensis* 11 cm
a MALE and **b** FEMALE Male has metallic blue-green crown, throat and tail. Upper edge of mantle is maroon; rest of upperparts are olive-green. Lack of well-defined yellow rump-band (although rump can be a slightly paler yellowish green), and longer, graduated tail help separate it from female Mrs Gould's. Oak/rhododendron and mixed forests and secondary growth. Resident; breeds 1800–2900 m, winters down to 150 m. UR: nr.

3

Black-throated Sunbird *Aethopyga saturata* 11 cm
a MALE and **b** FEMALE Male has black throat and breast, greyish-olive underparts, and crimson mantle. Combination of dusky olive-green underparts, yellow rump, and long, dark and noticeably down-curved bill are useful features distinguishing female from other female sunbirds. Bushes in forest and secondary growth. Resident; from the base of the hills in winter up to 2000 m in summer. UR: nr.

4

Crimson Sunbird *Aethopyga siparaja* 11 cm
a MALE and **b** FEMALE *A. s. seheriae;* **c** MALE, **d** FEMALE and **e** ECLIPSE MALE *A. s. vigorsii* Male has crimson mantle, scarlet throat and breast, and grey belly. Female lacks yellow rump; most similar to female Green-tailed but has shorter and squarer tail, with only indistinct pale tips to outer tail feathers, and shorter and broader-based bill with paler lower mandible. Male *vigorsii* (which occurs in the south of the region) is larger, and central tail feathers extend only slightly beyond rest of tail; also has yellow streaking to throat and breast. Female *vigorsii* has greyer underparts than *seheriae*. Light forest, groves and gardens. Resident; breeds from the foothills up to 1800 m, winters down to adjacent plains. GU: nr, HA: lcr, HP: ns, JK: ns, MP: nr, PU: nr, UP: lcr, UR: lcr.

5

Fire-tailed Sunbird *Aethopyga ignicauda* 12 cm
a MALE, **b** ECLIPSE MALE and **c** FEMALE Male has red uppertail-coverts and red on tail. Female has yellowish belly, yellowish wash to rump, and brownish-orange tail sides (which lack white at tip). Breeds in rhododendron shrubberies; winters in broadleaved and mixed forest. Resident; breeds 3000–4000 m, winters 1200–2900 m. HA: nw, HP: nr, UR: lcr.

6

Streaked Spiderhunter *Arachnothera magna* 19 cm
ADULT Very long down-curved bill, and boldly streaked upperparts and underparts. Moist broadleaved forest; favours bananas. Resident; below 450 m. HP: nr?

House Sparrow *Passer domesticus* 15 cm

a MALE and **b** FEMALE Male has grey crown, black throat and upper breast, chestnut nape, and brownish mantle. Female has buffish supercilium and unstreaked greyish-white underparts. Habitation, also nearby cultivation. Breeds up to 4500 m in Ladakh, withdraws from higher altitudes in winter. DE: cr, GU: cr, HA: cr, HP: lcr, JK: lcr, MP: cr, PU: cr, RA: lcr, UP: cr, UR: lcr.

Spanish Sparrow *Passer hispaniolensis* 15.5 cm

a MALE BREEDING, **b** MALE NON-BREEDING and **c** FEMALE Male has chestnut crown, black breast and streaking on flanks, and blackish mantle with pale 'braces'; pattern obscured by pale fringes in non-breeding season. Female told from female House Sparrow by longer whitish supercilium, fine streaking on underparts, and pale 'braces'. Cultivation, semi-desert and reedbeds. Winter visitor. DE: np, HA: lcw, JK: np, MP: nw, PU: cw, RA: lcw, UP: nw.

Sind Sparrow *Passer pyrrhonotus* 13 cm

a MALE and **b** FEMALE Smaller and slimmer than House, with finer bill. Male told from male House by chestnut on head restricted to crescent around ear-coverts; also grey ear-coverts and small black throat-patch. Female separated from female House by more prominent buffish-white supercilium, greyish ear-coverts, and warmer buffish-brown lower back and rump. Trees close to water. DE: nr, GU: nw, HA: nr, PU: lcr.

Russet Sparrow *Passer rutilans* 14.5 cm

a MALE and **b** FEMALE Male lacks black cheek-patch; has bright chestnut mantle and yellowish wash to underparts. Female has prominent supercilium and dark eye-stripe, rufous-brown scapulars and rump, and yellowish wash to underparts. Open forest, forest edges and cultivation. Resident; summers 1200–2900 m, 500–1500 m. HA: nw, HP: lcr, JK: cr, PU: nw, UR: lcr.

Eurasian Tree Sparrow *Passer montanus* 14 cm

ADULT Chestnut crown, and black spot on ear-coverts. Sexes similar. Habitation and nearby cultivation. Resident; breeds up to 2700 m. HP: nr, JK: nr, RA: v, UR: nr.

Chestnut-shouldered Petronia *Petronia xanthocollis* 13.5 cm

a MALE and **b** FEMALE Unstreaked brownish-grey head and upperparts, and prominent wing-bars. Male has some females have yellow on throat. Male has chestnut lesser coverts and white wing-bars; lesser coverts brown and wing-bars buff in female. Open dry forest and scrub. Up to 1200 m. DE: lcr, GU: cr, HA: lcr, HP: lcs, MP: cr, PU: cr, RA: lcr, UP: cr, UR: lcr.

Rock Sparrow *Petronia petronia* 17 cm

ADULT Striking head pattern, including pale crown-stripe. Has whitish patch at base of primaries and tip to tail. Dry stony ground in mountains. JK: v.

Tibetan Snowfinch *Pyrgilauda adamsi* 17 cm

a ADULT and **b** JUVENILE Largely white or buffish-white wing-coverts. Adult has black throat, but head otherwise rather plain grey-brown. *See* Appendix for comparison with White-rumped Snowfinch. Open stony hillsides, plateaux and near upland villages. Resident; recorded from 3800 m up to almost 5000 m. HP: lcr, JK: lcr, UR: v.

Plain-backed Snowfinch *Pyrgilauda blanfordi* 15 cm

ADULT Cinnamon nape and neck sides, black 'spur' dividing white supercilium and black throat; lacks wing-bars. Tibetan steppe country. Breeds at 4500 m. HP: nr, JK: nr.

JAIMER
2/25/14 IHPIR

1a

1b

2a

3a

2b

3b

2c

5

4a

4b

6b

7

6a

8a

9

8b

1 Forest Wagtail *Dendronanthus indicus* 18 cm
ADULT Broad yellowish-white wing-bars, double black breast-band, olive upperparts, white supercilium and whitish underparts. Paths and clearings in forest. DE: v, GU: v, HP: v, MP: np, RA: v, UR: v.

2 White Wagtail *Motacilla alba* 19 cm
a MALE BREEDING, **b** MALE NON-BREEDING and **c** JUVENILE *M. a. alboides*; **d** MALE BREEDING and **e** 1ST-WINTER *M. a. personata*; **f** FEMALE *M. a. dukhunensis* Extremely variable. Head pattern, and grey or black mantle, indicate racial identification of breeding males. Non-breeding and first-winter birds often not racially distinguishable. Never has head pattern of White-browed. Breeds by running waters in open country; winters near water in open country. Resident; breeds 1500–5000 m, winters in plains and hills. DE: cw, GU: cw, HA: cw, HP: lcr, JK: lcr, MP: cw, PU: cw, RA: nw, UP: cw, UR: cw.

3 White-browed Wagtail *Motacilla maderaspatensis* 21 cm
a ADULT and **b** JUVENILE Large black-and-white wagtail. Head black with white supercilium, and black mantle. Juvenile has brownish-grey head, mantle and breast, with white supercilium. Banks of rivers, pools and lakes. Resident; in plains and hills, locally to 1500 m in Himalayas, to 2200 m in the peninsula. DE: lcr, GU: cr, HA: lcr, HP: nr, JK: nr, MP: cr, PU: cw, RA: nr, UP: cr, UR: lcr.

4 Citrine Wagtail *Motacilla citreola* 19 cm
a MALE BREEDING, **b** ADULT FEMALE, **c** JUVENILE and **d** **e** 1ST-WINTER *M. c. calcarata*; **f** MALE BREEDING *M. c. citreola* Broad white wing-bars in all plumages. Male breeding has yellow head and underparts, and black or grey mantle. Female breeding and adult non-breeding have broad yellow supercilium continuing around ear-coverts, grey upperparts and mainly yellow underparts. Juvenile lacks yellow, and has brownish upperparts, buffish supercilium (with dark upper edge) and ear-covert surround, and spotted black gorget. First-winter has grey upperparts; distinguished from Yellow by white surround to ear-coverts, dark border to supercilium, pale brown forehead, pale lores, all-dark bill and white undertail-coverts; by early November, has yellowish supercilium, ear-covert surround and throat. Marshes and wet fields. Breeds 3000–5000 m, widespread in winter, chiefly in the plains. DE: cw, GU: cw, HA: cw, HP: lcw, JK: lcr, MP: nw, PU: cw, RA: nw, UP: lcw, UR: nw.

5 Yellow Wagtail *Motacilla flava* 18 cm
a MALE BREEDING, **b** ADULT FEMALE, **c** JUVENILE and **d** 1ST-WINTER *M. f. beema*; **e** MALE *M. f. leucocephala*; **f** MALE and **g** 1ST-WINTER *M. f. lutea*; **h** MALE *M. f. melanogrisea*; **i** MALE *M. f. superciliaris*; **j** MALE *M. f. zaissanensis*; **k** MALE *M. f. plexa*; **l** MALE *M. f. taivana*; **m** MALE and **n** 1ST-WINTER *M. f. thunbergi* Male breeding has olive-green upperparts and yellow underparts, with considerable variation in coloration of head depending on race. Female extremely variable, but often has some features of breeding male. First-winter birds typically have brownish-olive upperparts, and whitish underparts with variable yellowish wash; in some races can closely resemble Citrine, but these have narrower white supercilium that does not continue around ear-coverts. (*See also* Table 3 on p.293.) Damp grasslands and marshes. Breeds 3600–4500 m, winters in plains and up to 1200 m. DE: cw, GU: cw, HA: cw, HP: cp, JK: nr, MP: lcw, PU: cw, RA: nw, UP: lcw, UR: nw.

6 Grey Wagtail *Motacilla cinerea* 19 cm
a MALE BREEDING, **b** ADULT FEMALE and **c** JUVENILE Longer-tailed than other wagtails. In all plumages, shows white supercilium, grey upperparts, and yellow vent and undertail-coverts. Male has black throat when breeding. Fast-flowing rocky streams in summer, slower streams in winter. Resident; breeds 1800–3900 m, winters in plains and foothills up to 1500 m. DE: lcw, GU: nw, HA: nw, HP: lcr, JK: lcr, MP: cw, PU: nw, RA: nw, UP: lcw, UR: lcr.

1

2b

2d

INDIA
2/24/14

2a

2e

3b

3a

2f

2c

4f

5d

4a

4e

4c

5c

5b

4d

5e

4b

5a

2/22/14
GANDI'S
TOMB

DELHI

5g

6a

6b

6c

5l

5f

5h

5i

5j

5k

5m

5n

1 Richard's Pipit *Anthus richardi* 17 cm

ADULT Large size and loud *schreep* call. Well-streaked upperparts and breast, pale lores, long and stout bill, and long hind-claw. When flushed, typically gains height with deep undulations (compared with Paddyfield). Moist grassland and cultivation. DE: v, HA: np?, HP: np, MP: np, PU: np, RA: np, UR: np.

2 Paddyfield Pipit *Anthus rufulus* 15 cm

ADULT Smaller than Richard's, with *chip-chip-chip* call. Well-streaked breast; lores usually look pale. When flushed, has comparatively weak, rather fluttering flight. Short grassland and cultivation. In plains and hills up to 1800 m. DE: cr, GU: cr, HA: cr, HP: lcr, JK: nr, MP: cr, PU: cr, RA: lcr, UP: cr, UR: lcr.

3 Tawny Pipit *Anthus campestris* 16 cm

a ADULT, **b** 1ST-WINTER and **c** JUVENILE Loud *tchilip* or *chep* call. Adult and first-winter have plain or faintly streaked upperparts and breast. Juvenile more heavily streaked. Useful distinguishing features are dark lores, comparatively fine bill, rather horizontal stance and wagtail-like behaviour. DE: cw, GU: cw, HA: cw, HP: nw, MP: nw, PU: nw, RA: nw, UP: nw, UR: nw.

4 Blyth's Pipit *Anthus godlewskii* 16.5 cm

ADULT Call a wheezy *spzeeu*. Smaller than Richard's, with shorter tail, and shorter and more pointed bill. Shape of centres to adult median coverts distinctive if seen well, but this feature is of no use in first-winter and juvenile plumage; these feathers have square-shaped, well-defined black centres with broad, pale tips (in adult Richard's, centres to median coverts are more triangular in shape, and more diffuse). Pale lores and well-streaked breast useful distinctions from Tawny. Grassland and cultivation. Plains and hills up to 750 m. DE: nw, GU: nw, HA: cw?, HP: v, MP: nw, RA: nw, UP: v.

5 Long-billed Pipit *Anthus similis* 20 cm

ADULT Considerably larger than Tawny, with very large bill and shorter-looking legs. Dark lores. Greyish upperparts and warm buff colour to unstreaked or only lightly streaked underparts. Call is a sparrow-like *chirp*. Breeds on rocky or scrubby slopes 600–1800 m, winters in dry cultivation and scrub below 900 m. DE: nw, GU: nw, HA: nw, HP: lcs, JK: lcs, MP: nw, PU: nw, RA: nw, UP: nw, UR: ns.

6 Upland Pipit *Anthus sylvanus* 17 cm

a **b** ADULT Large, heavily streaked pipit with short and broad bill, and rather narrow, pointed tail feathers. Fine black streaking on underparts, whitish supercilium; ground colour of underparts varies from warm buff to rather cold and grey. Call is a sparrow-like *chirp*. Rocky and grassy slopes. Resident; breeds 1200–3000 m. HA: lcw, HP: nr, JK: nr, PU: nw, UR: lcr.

1 Tree Pipit *Anthus trivialis* 15 cm

a ADULT *A. t. trivialis*; **b** ADULT *A. t. haringtoni* Buffish-brown to greyish ground colour to upperparts (lacking greenish-olive cast), and buffish fringes to greater coverts, tertials and secondaries. Call is an adrupt *teez*. Fallow cultivation and open country with scattered trees. Breeds 2700–4200 m, winters in plains. DE: nw, GU: nw, HA: cw, HP: cp, JK: nr, MP: nw, PU: nw, RA: nw, UP: cw, UR: nw.

2 Olive-backed Pipit *Anthus hodgsoni* 15 cm

a ADULT FRESH and **b** ADULT WORN *A. h. hodgsoni*; **c** ADULT *A. h. yunnanensis* Greenish-olive cast to upperparts, and greenish-olive fringes to greater coverts, tertials and secondaries. Typically, has more striking head pattern than Tree Pipit. *A .h. yunnanensis*, which is a winter visitor, is much less heavily streaked on upperparts than nominate race. Call is a quiet *tees*, softer than call of Tree. Open forest and shrubberies. Resident; summers mainly 2700–4000 m, winters in plains and hills up to 2000 m. DE: lcw, GU: nw, HA: np?, HP: lcr, JK: nr, MP: cw, PU: cw, RA: nw, UP: cw, UR: lcr.

3 Red-throated Pipit *Anthus cervinus* 15 cm

a MALE BREEDING and **b** 1ST-YEAR Adult has reddish throat and upper breast, which tend to be paler on female and on autumn/winter birds. First-year has heavily streaked upperparts, pale 'braces', well-defined white wing-bars, strongly contrasting blackish centres and whitish fringes to tertials, pronounced dark malar patch, and more boldly streaked breast and (especially) flanks. Call a drawn-out *seeeeee*. Marshes, grassland and stubble. DE: v, GU: np, HA: nw, HP: np, JK: np, PU: v, RA: v, UR: np.

4 Rosy Pipit *Anthus roseatus* 15 cm

a **b** ADULT BREEDING and **c** ADULT NON-BREEDING Always has boldly streaked upperparts, olive cast to mantle, and olive to olive-green edges to greater coverts, secondaries and tertials. Adult breeding has mauve-pink wash to underparts. Non-breeding plumage has heavily streaked underparts and dark lores. Call a weak *seep-seep*. Breeds above treeline to 4200 m, winters in marshes, damp grassland, cultivation in plains and foothills up to 1500 m. DE: lcw, GU: v, HA: nw, HP: cr, JK: cr, MP: nw, PU: nw, RA: nw, UR: lcr.

5 Water Pipit *Anthus spinoletta* 15 cm

a ADULT BREEDING and **b** ADULT NON-BREEDING In all plumages, has lightly streaked upperparts, lacks olive-green on wing, has dark legs and usually has pale lores; underparts less heavily marked than on Rosy and Buff-bellied Pipits. Orange-buff wash to supercilium and underparts in breeding plumage. Call is similar to that of Rosy Pipit, perhaps thinner and sharper. Marshes and cultivation in plains and foothills. DE: nw, HA: v, HP: nw, JK: v, PU: nw, RA: nw, UP: v.

6 Buff-bellied Pipit *Anthus rubescens* 15 cm

a ADULT BREEDING and **b** ADULT NON-BREEDING In all plumages, has lightly streaked upperparts, lacks olive-green on wing and has pale lores; underparts more heavily streaked, upperparts darker and legs paler compared with Water Pipit. Call much as Rosy and Water Pipits. Marshes, damp cultivation. HA: v, PU: v, RA: v.

1

Alpine Accentor *Prunella collaris*   15.5–17 cm
ADULT Black barring on throat, grey breast and belly, and black band across greater coverts. Open stony slopes, rocky pastures. Resident; breeds 3600–5500 m, winters 2400–4800 m. HP: nr, JK: nr, UR: nr.

2

Altai Accentor *Prunella himalayana*   15–15.5 cm
ADULT White throat, with black gorget and spotting in malar region; white underparts, with rufous mottling on breast and flanks. Grassy and stony slopes. Winter visitor; 2000–4000 m. HP: lcw, JK: nw, UR: nw.

3

Robin Accentor *Prunella rubeculoides*   16–17 cm
ADULT Uniform grey head, rusty-orange band across breast and whitish belly. Breeds in dwarf scrub near streams and pools, winters in dry stony areas. Resident; summers 3600–5300 m, winters down to 2000 m. HP: nr, JK: nr.

4

Rufous-breasted Accentor *Prunella strophiata*   15 cm
a ADULT and **b** 1ST-WINTER? Rufous band across breast, white-and-rufous supercilium, blackish ear-coverts, and streaking on neck sides and underparts. Breeds on high-altitude slopes, winters in bushes in cultivation and scrub. Resident; summers 2700–4000 m, winters down to 600 m. HA: nw?, HP: lcr, JK: cr, PU: v, UR: lcr.

5

Brown Accentor *Prunella fulvescens*   14.5–15 cm
ADULT White supercilium, faintly streaked upperparts and pale orange-buff underparts. Dry scrubby and rocky slopes. Resident; summers 3300–5100 m, winters down to 1500 m. HP: nr, JK: nr.

6

Black-throated Accentor *Prunella atrogularis*   14.5–15 cm
a ADULT and **b** 1ST-WINTER FEMALE Orange-buff supercilium and submoustachial stripe, and black throat. Some have indistinct (or lack) black on throat, which instead is whitish; note heavily streaked mantle. Bushes near cultivation and dry scrub. In hills up to 2500 m. HA: nw, HP: nw, JK: nw, PU: v, UR: nw.

7

Maroon-backed Accentor *Prunella immaculata*   16 cm
ADULT Grey head and breast, maroon-brown mantle, yellow iris, and grey panel across wing. Moist forest. UR: nw.

8

Plain Mountain Finch *Leucosticte nemoricola*   15 cm
a ADULT BREEDING and **b** JUVENILE Told from Brandt's by boldly streaked mantle with pale 'braces', and distinct patterning on wing-coverts (dark-centred, with well-defined wing-bars). Juvenile warmer rufous-buff than adult. Breeds on alpine slopes; winters in open forest and upland cultivation. Resident; summers 3300–5000 m, winters down to 1000 m. HP: lcr, JK: lcr, UR: lcr.

9

Brandt's Mountain Finch *Leucosticte brandti*   16.5–19 cm
a MALE BREEDING and **b** 1ST-SUMMER Unstreaked to lightly streaked mantle, and rather uniform wing-coverts. More striking white panel on wing and more prominent white edges to tail compared with Plain. Adult breeding has sooty-black head and nape, and brownish-grey mantle with poorly defined streaking. Male has pink on rump. Stony slopes and alpine meadows. Resident; breeds 4200–5250 m, usually winters above 3500 m. HP: nr, JK: nr.

1 Black-breasted Weaver *Ploceus benghalensis* 14 cm
a b MALE BREEDING and **c** NON-BREEDING Breeding male has yellow crown and black breast-band. In female and non-breeding plumages, breast-band can be broken by whitish fringes or restricted to small patches at sides, and may show indistinct, diffuse streaking on lower breast and flanks; head pattern as on female/non-breeding Streaked, except crown, nape and ear-coverts more uniform; rump also indistinctly streaked and, like nape, contrasts with heavily streaked mantle/back. Tall moist grassland, reedy marshes. DE: lcr, GU: lcr, HA: cr, MP: nr, PU: cr, RA: nr, UP: nr, UR: lcr.

2 Streaked Weaver *Ploceus manyar* 14 cm
a MALE BREEDING and **b** NON-BREEDING Breeding male has yellow crown, dark brown head-sides and throat, and heavily streaked breast and flanks. Other plumages typically show boldly streaked underparts; can be only lightly streaked on underparts, when best told from Baya by combination of yellow supercilium and neck-patch, heavily streaked crown, dark or heavily streaked ear-coverts, and pronounced dark malar and moustachial stripes. Reedbeds. DE: lcr, GU: lcr, HA: cr, JK: nr, PU: cr, RA: nr, UP: lcr.

3 Baya Weaver *Ploceus philippinus* 15 cm
a MALE BREEDING, **b** MALE NON-BREEDING and **c** NON-BREEDING Breeding male has yellow crown, dark brown ear-coverts and throat, unstreaked yellow breast, and yellow on mantle and scapulars. Female/non-breeding birds usually have unstreaked buff to pale yellowish underparts; can show streaking as prominent as on some poorly marked Streaked, but generally has less distinct and buffish supercilium, lacks yellow neck-patch, and lacks pronounced dark moustachial and malar stripes. Head pattern of some (non-breeding males?) can, however, be rather similar to Streaked. Cultivation and grassland. Plains and hills up to 1200 m. DE: cr, GU: cr, HA: cr, HP: lcr, JK: nr, MP: cr, PU: cr, RA: lcr, UP: cr, UR: lcr.

4 Finn's Weaver *Ploceus megarhynchos* 17 cm
a MALE BREEDING, **b** FEMALE BREEDING and **c** ADULT NON-BREEDING Large size and bill. Breeding male has yellow underparts and rump, and dark patches on breast (can show as complete breast-band). Breeding female has pale yellow to yellowish-brown head, and pale yellow to buffish-white underparts. Adult non-breeding and immature very similar to non-breeding Baya. Grassland in plains and terai. Globally threatened (Vulnerable). DE: v?, HA: v?, UP: nr, UR: nr.

5 Red Avadavat *Amandava amandava* 10 cm
a MALE BREEDING, **b** FEMALE and **c** JUVENILE Breeding male mainly red with white spotting. Non-breeding male and female have red bill, red rump and uppertail-coverts, and white tips to wing-coverts and tertials. Juvenile lacks red in plumage; has buff wing-bars, pink bill-base, and pink legs and feet. Tall wet grassland, reedbeds. DE: lcr, GU: lcr, HA: lcr, HP: nr, JK: nr, MP: nr, PU: nr, RA: nr, UP: cr, UR: lcr.

6 Green Avadavat *Amandava formosa* 10 cm
a MALE and **b** FEMALE Breeding male green and yellow, with red bill and barred flanks. Female much duller, with weak flank barring. Grass and low bushes, also tall grassland. Globally threatened (Vulnerable). GU: nr, MP: nr, RA: nr.

7 Indian Silverbill *Lonchura malabarica* 11–11.5 cm
a ADULT and **b** JUVENILE Adult has white rump and uppertail-coverts, black tail and rufous-buff barring on flanks. Dry cultivation, grassland and thorn scrub. In plains and hills up to 600 m. DE: cr, GU: cr, HA: cr, HP: lcr, JK: nr, MP: cr, PU: cr, RA: lcr, UP: cr, UR: lcr.

8 White-rumped Munia *Lonchura striata* 10–11 cm
ADULT Dark breast and white rump. Pale streaking on ear-coverts, rufous-brown to whitish fringes to brown breast, and dingy underparts with faint streaking. Open wooded areas and scrub. Plains and hills up to 1675 m. DE: v, GU: nr, MP: nr, RA: nr, UR: nr.

9 Scaly-breasted Munia *Lonchura punctulata* 10.7–12 cm
a ADULT and **b** JUVENILE Adult has chestnut throat and breast, and whitish underparts with dark scaling. Juvenile is plain with black bill. Open forest, bushes, cultivation, plains and hills up to 2400 m. DE: lcr, GU: nr, HA: nr, HP: nr, JK: nr, MP: nr, PU: cr, RA: nr, UP: cr, UR: lcr.

10 Black-headed Munia *Lonchura malacca* 11.5 cm
a ADULT and **b** JUVENILE Black head and breast, rufous-brown upperparts, chestnut lower breast and flanks, and black belly centre and undertail-coverts. Juvenile is plain with bill blue-grey. Cultivation, grassland. DE: nr?, GU: nr, HA: nr, MP: nr, PU: nr?, RA: nr, UP: nr.

1 Chaffinch *Fringilla coelebs* 16 cm
a MALE NON-BREEDING and **b** FEMALE White wing-bars; lacks white rump. Male has blue-grey crown and nape, orange-pink face and underparts, and maroon-brown mantle. Female dull, with greyish-brown mantle and greyish-buff underparts. Upland fields with nearby bushes and coniferous forest. HP: v, UR: v.

2 Brambling *Fringilla montifringilla* 16 cm
a MALE BREEDING, **b** MALE NON-BREEDING and **c** FEMALE White rump and belly, and orange scapulars, breast and flanks. Patterning of head and mantle vary with sex and feather wear. Upland fields and nearby bushes and coniferous forest. Erratic winter visitor. HP: v, JK: v, UR: v.

3 Fire-fronted Serin *Serinus pusillus* 12.5 cm
a MALE, **b** FEMALE and **c** JUVENILE Adult has blackish head with scarlet forehead. Juvenile has cinnamon-brown head. Breeds in Tibetan steppe; winters on stony and bushy slopes. Resident; breeds 2400–4300 m, winters mainly 750–3300 m. HA: v, HP: nr, JK: nr, UR: nr.

4 Yellow-breasted Greenfinch *Carduelis spinoides* 14 cm
a MALE, **b** FEMALE and **c** JUVENILE Yellow supercilium and underparts, dark ear-coverts and malar stripe, and yellow patches on wing. Juvenile heavily streaked. Open forest, shrubberies and cultivation with nearby trees. Resident; breeds 1800–3300 m, winters mainly below 1500 m. HA: v, HP: lcr, JK: cr, PU: nw, UR: lcr.

5 Eurasian Siskin *Carduelis spinus* 11–12 cm
a MALE and **b** FEMALE Yellow wing-bars and yellowish rump. Male has black crown and chin. Forest. HP: v.

6 European Goldfinch *Carduelis carduelis* 13–15.5 cm
a MALE and **b** JUVENILE Red face (lacking on juvenile), and black-and-yellow wings with white tertial markings. Upland cultivation, shrubberies and open coniferous forest. Resident; breeds 2400–3900 m, descends in winter, occasionally to the plains. HA: v, HP: nr, JK: cr, PU: nw, UR: lcr.

7 Twite *Carduelis flavirostris* 13–13.5 cm
a MALE and **b** FEMALE Rather plain and heavily streaked, with small yellowish bill, buff wing-bars, and white edges to remiges and rectrices. Male has pinkish rump. Boulder-strewn alpine meadows and stony hills. Resident; breeds 3600–5000 m, winters down to 3000 m. HP: nr, JK: nr.

8 Eurasian Linnet *Carduelis cannabina* 13–14 cm
a MALE BREEDING, **b** MALE NON-BREEDING and **c** FEMALE Told from Twite by greyish crown and nape contrasting with browner mantle, whitish lower rump and uppertail-coverts, and larger greyish bill. Forehead and breast crimson on breeding male. Open stony slopes and upland meadows. HP: v, JK: v, PU: v.

1   Spectacled Finch *Callacanthis burtoni*   17–18 cm
a MALE and **b** FEMALE Black wings with white tips to feathers. Blackish head with red (male) or orange-yellow (female) 'spectacles'. Juvenile has browner head with buff eye-patch, and buffish wing-bars. Open mixed forest. Resident; breeds 2400 m to the treeline, winters 1800–3000 m. HP: nr, JK: nr, UR: nr.

2   Red Crossbill *Loxia curvirostra*   16–17 cm
a MALE, **b** FEMALE and **c** JUVENILE Dark bill with crossed mandibles. Male rusty-red. Female olive-green, with brighter rump. Juvenile heavily streaked; mandibles are not initially crossed. Coniferous forest; favours hemlocks. Resident; 2700–4000 m. HP: nr, JK: v, UR: nr.

3   Trumpeter Finch *Bucanetes githagineus*   14–15 cm
a MALE and **b** JUVENILE Stocky, with very stout pinkish or yellow bill. Comparatively uniform wings and tail show traces of pink (except on juvenile). Dry rocky hills and stony semi-desert. DE: v, GU: v, HA: v, RA: nw.

4   Mongolian Finch *Bucanetes mongolicus*   14–15 cm
a MALE and **b** FEMALE Whitish panels at bases of greater coverts and secondaries (which can be rather indistinct), whitish outer edges to tail, and a less stout bill than Trumpeter's. Dry stony slopes and gravelly ground in the hills. JK: nr, RA: v.

5   Dark-breasted Rosefinch *Carpodacus nipalensis*   15–16 cm
a MALE and **b** FEMALE Slim, with slender bill. Male has maroon-brown breast-band, dark eye-stripe, and maroon-brown upperparts with indistinct dark streaking. Female has unstreaked underparts, lacks supercilium, and has streaked mantle, buffish wing-bars and tips to tertials, and olive-brown rump and uppertail-coverts. (*See also* Table 9 on p.297–8.) Breeds in high-altitude shrubberies, winters in forest clearings. Resident; summers 3000 m up to the treeline, winters 1800–2700 m. HP: lcr, JK: nr, UR: nr.

6   Common Rosefinch *Carpodacus erythrinus*   14.5–15 cm
a MALE and **b** FEMALE *C. e. roseatus*; **c** MALE and **d** FEMALE *C. e. erythrinus* Compact, with short, stout bill. Male has red head, breast and rump. Female has streaked upperparts and underparts, and double wing-bar. Migrant nominate race has less red in male, and female is less heavily streaked, compared with *roseatus*, which is a resident race. (*See also* Table 9 on p.297–8.) Breeds in high-altitude shrubberies and open forest, winters in cultivation with bushes. Resident and winter visitor; summers 3900–4200 m, winters from 1500 m down to the foothills and plains. DE: lcw, GU: nw, HA: cw, HP: lcp, JK: lcs, MP: np, PU: nw, RA: np, UP: lcw, UR: nr.

7   Beautiful Rosefinch *Carpodacus pulcherrimus*   15 cm
a MALE and **b** FEMALE Male has pale lilac-pink supercilium, rump and underparts; upperparts grey-brown and heavily streaked. Female has poorly defined supercilium and heavily streaked underparts. (*See also* Table 9 on p.297–8.) Breeds in high-altitude shrubberies, winters on bush-covered slopes and cultivation with bushes. Resident; summers mainly 3600–4650 m, winters 2100–3300 m. HP: nr, UR: nr.

8   Pink-browed Rosefinch *Carpodacus rodochrous*   14–15 cm
a MALE and **b** FEMALE Male has deep pink supercilium and underparts, and crimson crown. Female has buff supercilium and fulvous ground colour to rump, belly and flanks. (*See also* Table 9 on p.297–8.) Breeds in high-altitude shrubberies and open forest, winters in oak forest and on bushy slopes. Resident; summers 2745–3660 m, winters 1220–3000 m. HP: lcr, JK: nr, UR: lcr.

1   **Vinaceous Rosefinch** *Carpodacus vinaceus*   13–16 cm

> **a** MALE and **b** FEMALE   Male dark crimson, with pink supercilium and pinkish-white tips to tertials. Female lacks supercilium; has whitish tips to tertials, and streaked underparts. (*See also* Table 9 on p.297–8.) Understorey in moist forest. Resident; 3500 m in August, 2500 m in winter. UR: nr.

2   **Spot-winged Rosefinch** *Carpodacus rodopeplus*   15 cm

> **a** MALE and **b** FEMALE   Male has pink supercilium and underparts, maroon upperparts, and pinkish tips to wing-coverts and tertials. Female has prominent buff supercilium, dark ear-coverts, pale and heavily streaked throat, prominent wing-bars, buff tips to tertials, and fulvous underparts with bold streaking on breast. (*See also* Table 9 on p.297–8.) Breeds in rhododendron shrubberies, winters in forest understorey. Resident; summers 3050–4000 m, winters 2000–3050 m. HP: nr, UR: nr.

3   **White-browed Rosefinch** *Carpodacus thura*   17 cm

> **a** MALE and **b** FEMALE   Large size. Male has pink-and-white supercilium, pink rump and underparts, and heavily streaked brown upperparts. Female has prominent supercilium with dark eye-stripe, ginger-brown throat and breast, and olive-yellow rump. (*See also* Table 9 on p.297–8.) Breeds in high-altitude shrubberies and open forest, winters on bushy hills. Resident; summers mainly 3000–4200 m, winters above 1800 m. HP: nr, JK: nr, UR: nr.

4   **Red-mantled Rosefinch** *Carpodacus rhodochlamys*   18 cm

> **a** MALE and **b** FEMALE   Large size and large bill. Male has pink supercilium and underparts, and pale grey-brown upperparts with pinkish wash. Female pale grey and heavily streaked, with indistinct supercilium. (*See also* Table 9 on p.297–8.) Breeds in dry high-altitude shrubberies and forest, winters in well-wooded areas. Resident, breeds 3400–4000 m, winters 2200–2600 m. HP: nr, JK: nr, UR: nr.

5   **Streaked Rosefinch** *Carpodacus rubicilloides*   19 cm

> **a** MALE and **b** FEMALE   Large size and long tail. Male has crimson-pink head and underparts, and heavily streaked upperparts. Female lacks supercilium and has streaked upperparts. (*See also* Table 9 on p.297–8.) Open stony ground with sparse dry scrub. Resident; 3700–5000 m, winters down to 3000 m. HP: nr, JK: nr.

6   **Great Rosefinch** *Carpodacus rubicilla*   19–20 cm

> **a** MALE and **b** FEMALE   Large size and long tail. Male has pale pink head and underparts, and pale sandy-grey and lightly streaked upperparts. Female lacks supercilium, and has lightly streaked pale sandy-brown upperparts; centres to wing-coverts and tertials are pale grey-brown (much darker brownish-black on female Streaked). (*See also* Table 9 on p.297–8.) Open stony ground with sparse dry scrub. Resident; summers 3300–4800 m. HP: nr, JK: nr.

7   **Red-fronted Rosefinch** *Carpodacus puniceus*   20 cm

> **a** MALE and **b** FEMALE   Large size, conical bill and short tail. On male, red of plumage contrasts with brown crown, eye-stripe and upperparts. Female lacks supercilium, is heavily streaked and may show yellow/olive rump. (*See also* Table 9 on p.297–8.) High-altitude rocky slopes. Resident; breeds 3900–5200 m, winters down to 2700 m. HP: nr, JK: nr, UR: nr.

8   **Scarlet Finch** *Haematospiza sipahi*   18 cm

> **a** MALE, **b** FEMALE and **c** IMMATURE MALE   Male scarlet. Female olive-green, with yellow rump. First-summer male has orange rump. Broadleaved forest. Resident. UR: nr.

1a

1b

2a

2b

3a

3b

4a

4b

5b

5a

6a

6b

7a

7b

8a

8b

8c

1 Brown Bullfinch *Pyrrhula nipalensis* 16–17 cm

a ADULT and **b** JUVENILE Adult has grey-brown mantle, grey underparts, narrow white rump, and long tail. Juvenile has brownish-buff upperparts and warm buff underparts, and lacks adult head pattern. Dense moist broadleaved forest. Resident; summers 2100–3000 m, winters down to 1500 m. HP: nr, UR: nr.

2 Orange Bullfinch *Pyrrhula aurantiaca* 14 cm

a MALE, **b** FEMALE and **c** JUVENILE Male has orange head and body, and orange-buff wing-bars. Female has grey crown and nape. Juvenile similar to female, but lacks grey on head. Open coniferous and mixed forest. Resident; summers 2745–3505 m, winters 1675–2135 m. HP: nr, JK: nr, UR: nr.

3 Red-headed Bullfinch *Pyrrhula erythrocephala* 17 cm

a MALE, **b** FEMALE and **c** 1ST-SUMMER MALE Male has orange crown, nape and breast, and grey mantle. Female has yellow crown and nape. First-summer male has yellow breast. Mainly broadleaved forest. Resident; breeds 2400–3300 m, winters 1500–3900 m. HP: nr, JK: nr, UR: lcr.

4 Hawfinch *Coccothraustes coccothraustes* 16–18 cm

MALE Stocky, short-tailed and huge-billed. Mainly orange-brown, with pale wing-covert band and black chin. Wild olive forest and orchards. Winter visitor. JK: nw.

5 Black-and-yellow Grosbeak *Mycerobas icterioides* 22 cm

a MALE and **b** FEMALE Male usually lacks orange cast to mantle and rump; black of plumage duller than on Collared, and has black thighs. Female has pale grey head, mantle and breast, and peachy-orange rump and belly. Coniferous forest. Breeds mainly 1800–3000 m, winters down to 1500 m. HP: lcr, JK: cr, UR: lcr.

6 Collared Grosbeak *Mycerobas affinis* 22 cm

a MALE and **b** FEMALE Male has orange cast to mantle; black of plumage strongly glossed, and thighs yellow. Female has olive-yellow underparts and rump, and greyish-olive mantle. Coniferous and coniferous/broadleaved forests. Resident; breeds from 2700 m up to the treeline, occasionally winters down to 1800 m. HP: nr, JK: nr, UR: nr.

7 Spot-winged Grosbeak *Mycerobas melanozanthos* 22 cm

a MALE and **b** FEMALE Male has black rump and white markings on wings. Female yellow, boldly streaked with black; wing pattern similar to male's. Breeds in mixed forest, winters in broadleaved forest. Resident; 1830 m (January and June) up to 3355 m (September). HP: nr, JK: nr, UR: nr.

8 White-winged Grosbeak *Mycerobas carnipes* 22 cm

a MALE and **b** FEMALE White patch in wing. Male dull black and olive-yellow, with yellowish tips to greater coverts and tertials. Female similar, but black of plumage replaced by sooty-grey. Juniper shrubberies, and forest with junipers. Resident; breeds 3000–4200 m, winters down to 2700 m. HP: nr, JK: nr, UR: nr.

9 Gold-naped Finch *Pyrrhoplectes epauletta* 15 cm

a MALE and **b** FEMALE Small, with fine bill. White 'stripe' down tertials. Male black, with orange crown and nape. Female has olive-green on head, grey mantle, and rufous-brown wing-coverts and underparts. Undergrowth in oak-rhododendron forest and rhododendron shrubberies. Resident; summers 2800–3900 m, winters 1400–3600 m. HP: nr.

1 Crested Bunting *Melophus lathami* 17 cm

a MALE, **b** FEMALE and **c** 1ST-WINTER MALE Always has crest and chestnut on wing and tail; tail lacks white. Dry rocky and grassy hillsides, terraced cultivation. Resident; summers up to 1800 m. DE: nw, GU: nr, HA: nr?, HP: ns, JK: lcr, MP: lcr, PU: nw, RA: lcr, UP: lcr, UR: lcr.

2 Pine Bunting *Emberiza leucocephalos* 17 cm

a MALE BREEDING, **b** MALE NON-BREEDING and **c** FEMALE Chestnut rump and long tail. Male has chestnut supercilium and throat, and whitish crown and ear-covert spot; pattern obscured in winter. Female has greyish supercilium and nape/neck sides, dark border to ear-coverts, usually some rufous on breast/flanks, and white belly. *See* Appendix for comparison with Yellowhammer. Upland cultivation, grassy areas with bushes. Winter visitor, usually up to 1500 m, occasionally up to 2700 m. HA: nw, HP: lcw, JK: nw, PU: nw, UR: nw.

3 Rock Bunting *Emberiza cia* 16 cm

a MALE and **b** FEMALE Male has grey head, black crown-sides and border to ear-coverts, and rufous underparts. Female duller. Open dry grassy and rocky slopes. Resident; breeds 2000–4200 m, winters in hills mainly up to 2100 m, rarely to plains. DE: v, HA: nw, HP: lcr, JK: cr, PU: v, UP: lcr.

4 Grey-necked Bunting *Emberiza buchanani* 15 cm

a MALE, **b** FEMALE and **c** 1ST-WINTER Pinkish-orange bill, plain head and whitish eye-ring. Adult has blue-grey head, buffish submoustachial stripe and throat, and rusty-pink underparts. First-winter and juvenile often with only slight greyish cast to head and buffish underparts; light streaking on breast. Dry rocky and bushy hills. DE: np, GU: cw, HA: np, JK: np, MP: nw, PU: v, RA: nw, UP: lcw.

5 Ortolan Bunting *Emberiza hortulana* 16 cm

a MALE, **b** FEMALE and **c** 1ST-WINTER Pinkish-orange bill, plain head and prominent eye-ring. Adult has olive-grey head and breast, and yellow submoustachial stripe and throat. Female streaked on crown and breast. First-winter and juvenile more heavily streaked on mantle, malar region and breast than Grey-necked; submoustachial stripe and throat are buffish, but often with a touch of yellow that helps separate them from Grey-necked. Orchards and open woodland. DE: v, GU: v, JK: v, RA: v.

6 White-capped Bunting *Emberiza stewarti* 15 cm

a MALE BREEDING, **b** MALE NON-BREEDING and **c** FEMALE Male has grey head, black supercilium and throat, and chestnut breast-band; pattern obscured in winter. Female has rather plain head with pale supercilium; crown and mantle uniformly and diffusely streaked, and underparts finely streaked and washed with buff. Dry grassy and rocky slopes; also fallow fields in winter. Breeds in Himalayas 1200–2700 m, winters in plains and hills up to 1800 m. DE: np, GU: nw, HA: np, HP: lcr, JK: lcr, MP: lcw, PU: nw, RA: nw, UP: nw, UR: nr.

7 House Bunting *Emberiza striolata* 13–14 cm

a MALE and **b** FEMALE Has black eye-stripe and moustachial stripe, and white supercilium and submoustachial stripe; throat and breast streaked, and underparts brownish-buff with variable rufous tinge. Female duller than male, with less striking head pattern. Lacks prominent white on tail (Rock has much white on outer tail feathers) and has orange lower mandible (bill all grey on Rock). Dry rocky hills; also sandy plains in winter. DE: v, GU: nw, HA: nw?, MP: v, PU: nw, RA: nr, UR: v.

8 Chestnut-eared Bunting *Emberiza fucata* 16 cm

a MALE, **b** FEMALE and **c** 1ST-WINTER Adult has chestnut ear-coverts, black breast streaking and chestnut on breast sides. Some nondescript; plain head with warm brown ear-coverts and distinctive pale eye-ring. Dry rocky and bushy hills. Resident; breeds 1800–2700 m, winters in plains and foothills up to at least 1500 m. DE: v, GU: nw, HA: nw?, HP: nr, JK: nr, MP: v, PU: nw, UP: nw, UR: nr.

1c

1a

1b

2c

2b

3a

3b

2a

4c

5a

5b

4a

4b

6a

5c

7a

6b

7b

6c

8a

8c

8b

1   Little Bunting *Emberiza pusilla*   13 cm

a ADULT and **b** 1ST-WINTER Small size. Ear-coverts (and often supercilium and crown-stripe) chestnut, and lacks dark moustachial stripe. Fallow cultivation and meadows. Below 1800 m. GU: v, HP: v, JK: v, UR: nw.

2   Yellow-breasted Bunting *Emberiza aureola*   15 cm

a MALE BREEDING, **b** MALE NON-BREEDING, **c** FEMALE and **d** JUVENILE Male has black face and chestnut breast-band, and white inner wing-coverts. Female has strikingly patterned head and mantle, and white median-covert bar. Juvenile streaked on underparts. *See* Appendix for comparison with Chestnut Bunting. Cultivation and grassland. HA: v, PU: v, UP: nw.

3   Black-headed Bunting *Emberiza melanocephala*   16–18 cm

a MALE BREEDING, **b** MALE NON-BREEDING, **c** WORN FEMALE and **d** IMMATURE Male has black on head and chestnut on mantle. Female when worn may show ghost pattern of male; fresh female almost identical to Red-headed, but indicative features include rufous fringes to mantle and/or back, slight contrast between throat and greyish ear-coverts, and more uniform yellowish underparts. Immature has buff underparts and yellow undertail-coverts. Cultivation and bushes at field edges. DE: np, GU: nw, HA: np, HP: np, MP: nw, PU: np, RA: lcp, UR: v.

4   Red-headed Bunting *Emberiza bruniceps*   16 cm

a MALE BREEDING, **b** MALE NON-BREEDING, **c** FRESH FEMALE and **d** IMMATURE Smaller than Black-headed, with shorter, more conical bill. Male has rufous on head and yellowish-green mantle. Female when worn may show rufous on head and breast, and yellowish to crown and mantle, and is distinguishable from female Black-headed. Fresh female has throat paler than breast, with suggestion of buffish breast-band; forehead and crown often virtually unstreaked (distinguishing features from Black-headed). Immature often not separable from Black-headed but may exhibit some of the features mentioned above. Cultivation. DE: np, GU: np, HA: nwp, HP: np, JK: v, MP: nw, PU: np, RA: nw, UP: lcw.

5   Reed Bunting *Emberiza schoeniclus*   14–15 cm

a MALE BREEDING and **b** FEMALE *E. s. pallidior*; **c** MALE NON-BREEDING *E. s. pyrrhuloides* Male has black head and white submoustachial stripe; obscured by fringes when fresh. Female has buff supercilium, brown ear-coverts and dark moustachial stripe. Reedbeds and irrigated crops. DE: v, HA: v, JK: np, PU: v, RA: v.

6   Corn Bunting *Miliaria calandra*   18 cm

ADULT Large size and rather stocky. Heavily streaked and rather non-descript. Cultivation. PU: v.

APPENDIX

Vagrants (very irregular visitors that have only been recorded once or on few occasions).

Mute Swan *Cygnus olor* 125–155 cm
Adult is white and has orange bill with black base and knob. Juvenile is mottled sooty-brown, and has grey bill with black base. Large rivers and lakes. JK.

Whooper Swan *Cygnus cygnus* 140–165 cm
Only recorded in 19th century. Adult is white with black and yellow bill; has yellow of bill extending as wedge towards tip. Juvenile is smoky-grey, with pinkish bill. Longer neck and more angular head shape than Tundra. Lakes and large rivers. JK, PU, RA.

Tundra Swan *Cygnus columbianus* 115–140 cm
Adult is white with black and yellow bill; has yellow of bill typically as oval-shaped patch. Juvenile is smoky-grey, with pinkish bill. Smaller in size, and with shorter neck and more rounded head, compared with Whooper. Lakes and large rivers. GU.

Greater White-fronted Goose *Anser albifrons* 66–86 cm
Adult has white band at front of head, black barring on belly, orange-pink bill, and orange legs and feet. Upperwing more uniform than in Greylag. Juvenile lacks frontal band and belly barring. Large rivers and lakes. DE, GU, HA, PU, RA, UP.

Lesser White-fronted Goose *Anser erythropus* 53–66 cm
Smaller and more compact, with squarer head and stouter bill, compared with Greater White-fronted (like that species has orange-pink bill, and orange legs and feet). White frontal band of adult extends onto forehead. Both adult and juvenile have yellow eye-ring, and darker head and neck than Greater. Wet grassland and lakes. HA, JK, RA, UP.

Snow Goose *Anser caerulescens* 65–84 cm
All white, with black wing-tips and pink bill and legs. Also occurs as 'blue' morph with white head and neck and dark grey body. Grass by reservoirs. GU.

Red-breasted Goose *Branta ruficollis* 53–55 cm
Reddish-chestnut cheek-patch and fore-neck/breast, and black-and-white patterning to head, hind-neck, and body. Juvenile is similar to adult but duller and not so clearly marked. Habitat in subcontinent unknown. MP?

Mandarin Duck *Aix galericulata* 41–49 cm
Male is spectacular. Most striking features are reddish bill, orange 'mane' and 'sails', white stripe behind eye, and black-and-white stripes on sides of breast. Female and eclipse male are mainly greyish with white 'spectacles' and white spotting on breast and flanks. In flight, shows dark upperwing and underwing, with white trailing edge, and white belly. Large rivers. UP.

Baikal Teal *Anas formosa* 39–43 cm
Grey forewing and broad white trailing edge to wing in flight in both sexes (recalling Northern Pintail). Male has striking head pattern of black, yellow, bottle-green and white; also black-spotted pinkish breast, black undertail-coverts and chestnut-edged scapulars. Female superficially resembles female Common Teal; has dark-bordered white loral spot and buff supercilium that is broken above eye by dark crown; some females have white half-crescent on cheeks. Lakes and large rivers. GU, HA, MP, RA, UP.

Marbled Duck *Marmaronetta angustirostris* 39–42 cm
Pale brown with shaggy hood, dark mask and diffuse white spotting to body. Upperwing rather uniform and underwing very pale. Shallow freshwater lakes and ponds. DE, GU, HA, HP, JK, MP, PU, RA, UP.

Baer's Pochard *Aythya baeri* 41–46 cm
Resembles Ferruginous Pochard, but has greenish cast to dark head and neck, which contrast with chestnut-brown breast. White patch on fore-flanks visible above water. Female and immature male have duller head and breast than adult male. Female has dark iris, and pale and diffuse chestnut-brown loral spot. Large rivers and lakes. DE, HA, RA, UP.

Long-tailed Duck *Clangula hyemalis* 36–47 cm
Small, stocky duck with stubby bill and pointed tail. Swims low in water and partly opens wings before diving. Both sexes show dark upperwing and underwing in flight. Winter male is mainly white; has dark cheek-patch and breast, and long tail. Female and immature male variable; usually with dark crown, and pale face with dark cheek-patch. Lakes and large rivers. JK, PU, UP.

Common Goldeneye *Bucephala clangula* 42–50 cm
Stocky, with bulbous head. Male has dark green head, large white patch on lores, and black-and-

white body. Female and immature male have brown head, indistinct whitish collar and grey body, with white wing-patch usually visible at rest. Lakes and large rivers. DE, JK, UP.

Smew *Mergellus albellus* 38–44 cm
Small size. Male is mainly white, with black markings. Immature male and female are mainly grey; have chestnut cap, with white throat and lower ear-coverts. Lakes and large rivers. DE, GU, HA, RA, UP.

Sind Woodpecker *Dendrocopos assimilis* 20–22 cm
Recalls Himalayan Woodpecker. Distinguishing features are black moustachial stripe joining hind-neck, lack of black border to rear of ear-coverts, larger white shoulder-patch and forehead, whiter underparts, broader white barring on wing and paler pink vent. Dry forest and plantations. RA.

Oriental Dwarf Kingfisher *Ceyx erithacus* 14 cm
Tiny size. Orange head with violet iridescence, black upperparts with variable blue streaking, and orange underparts. Juvenile duller, with whitish underparts (with orange breast-band) and orange-yellow bill. Shady streams in moist broadleaved forest. RA.

Plaintive Cuckoo *Cacomantis merulinus* 23 cm
Similar in appearance to Grey-bellied Cuckoo. Adult best distinguished by orange underparts. On hepatic female, base colour of underparts is pale rufous (whiter in Grey-bellied), and upperparts and tail are strongly barred. Juvenile similar to hepatic female but has bold streaking on rufous-orange head and breast. Call is a mournful *tay...ta...tee*. Forest and wooded country. MP.

Asian Emerald Cuckoo *Chrysococcyx maculatus* 18 cm
Male has emerald-green head and upperparts, and greenish barring to white underparts. Female is similar in appearance but has rufous-orange crown and nape, and underparts are entirely barred. Juvenile is similar to female but has rufous-orange barring on mantle and wing-coverts, and rufous-orange wash to throat and breast. Call is a loud descending *kee-kee-kee-kee*. Evergreen forest. UP.

Pallid Swift *Apus pallidus* 17 cm
Very similar in appearance to Common Swift, but with paler grey-brown upperparts and underparts, darker eye-patch and more extensive pale throat. Shows slight contrast between dark outer primaries and inner wing-coverts and paler rest of wing, and has dark-saddled, pale-headed appearance (not apparent in Common). Underparts more distinctly scaled than in Common. Coastal areas. GU.

Eurasian Scops Owl *Otus scops* 19 cm
Occurs as grey and brown morphs. Not safely distinguishable in the field from Oriental Scops, although has different call and longer primary projection (usually shows six or seven primaries extending beyond tertials when the wing is closed; four to five in Oriental). Browner or darker grey in coloration compared with Pallid Scops. Compared with that species has pronounced darkening around eyes, more prominent white spots on scapulars, pale horizontal bars across streaked under-parts, and narrower and more numerous pale barring on tail (five to seven bars compared to two to four in Pallid) Call is plaintive bell-like whistle, *tyuu...tyuu...*, repeated without interruption for many minutes. Scrub in dry rocky hills and valleys. GU.

Ashy Wood Pigeon *Columba pulchricollis* 36 cm
Distinguished from Speckled Wood by buff collar, slate-grey breast, buff belly and undertail-coverts, and uniform slate-grey upperparts. In flight, from below, buff undertail-coverts contrast with dark underside to tail. Uniformly dark upper- and underwing, and darker grey upperparts, are best features distinguishing it from Common Wood Pigeon. Dense broadleaved forest. HP.

European Turtle Dove *Streptopelia turtur* 33 cm
Has white sides and tip to tail. Told from *meena* race of Oriental Turtle by smaller size and slim-mer build; broader, paler rufous-buff fringes to scapulars and wing-coverts; more buffish- or brownish-grey rump and uppertail-coverts; and greyish-pink breast, becoming whitish on belly and undertail-coverts. Cultivation in drier mountains and valleys. JK.

Little Bustard *Tetrax tetrax* 40–45 cm
Small, stocky bustard with white panel across secondaries and inner primaries. Both non-breeding male and female are buffish in coloration with variable streaking and barring (non-breeding male is less heavily marked on upperparts and whiter on underparts compared with female, and shows more white on wing). Breeding male has grey face, and black-and-white pattern on neck and breast. When flushed has rapid 'winnowing' flight action on stiff, bowed wings. Grassland and short crops. HA, JK, PU, UP.

Corn Crake *Crex crex* 27–30 cm
A stocky crake with stout pinkish bill and legs. Adult has rufous-chestnut on wings (especially prominent in flight), greyish fore-neck and breast, and rufous-brown and white barring on flanks. Juvenile has buffish, rather than grey, neck and breast. Grassland and crops. JK.

Little Crake *Porzana parva* 20–23 cm

Very similar in size and appearance to Baillon's Crake. Longer wings than Baillon's (primaries extending noticeably beyond tertials at rest), with less extensive barring on flanks, and pronounced pale edges to scapulars and tertials (features for all plumages). Adult also with red at base of bill. Male has grey underparts. Female has buff underparts. Juvenile is similar to female but has more extensive barring on flanks (but less than on Baillon's). Marshes. RA, UP.

Pallas's Sandgrouse *Syrrhaptes paradoxus* 30–41 cm

Pin-tailed and elongated outer primaries. Superficially similar to Tibetan Sandgrouse but has black patch on white belly, largely white underwing, and pale upperside to primaries. Male has narrow black gorget across breast (lacking in female) and unbarred wing-coverts (heavily marked in female). Arid plains and uplands. RA.

Asian Dowitcher *Limnodromus semipalmatus* 34–36 cm

Superficially similar in appearance to Bar-tailed Godwit. Has broad-based, straighter, all-black bill with swollen tip, and squarer-shaped head. Shows diffuse pale bar across secondaries and grey tail in flight. Underparts brick-red in breeding plumage, as in Bar-tailed Godwit. Greyish upperparts and whitish underparts, both heavily streaked, in non-breeding plumage. Juvenile has buff fringes to dark upperparts, and buff wash to breast. Intertidal mudflats and mudbanks. HA, MP, PU.

Long-billed Dowitcher *Limnodromus scolopaceus* 27–30 cm

Rather snipe-like in shape and feeding action. Superficially resembles Bar-tailed Godwit or Asian Dowitcher, but is smaller, and has shorter legs (which are greyish, yellowish or greenish rather than black). In flight, shows a clear white trailing edge to the wing, barred rump and tail, and a striking white back. In all plumages has pronounced white supercilium. In breeding plumage has rufous underparts, with some barring and spotting, and dark upperparts have narrow rufous fringes. In non-breeding plumage, has grey upperparts and breast, and white belly. Juvenile recalls non-breeding adult, but has rufous fringes to mantle and scapulars, and buff wash to underparts. Call is a high, thin *keek*. RA.

Great Knot *Calidris tenuirostris* 26–28 cm

Larger than Red Knot, and often with slightly down-curved bill. Adult breeding heavily marked with black on breast and flanks, and with chestnut patterning to scapulars. Adult non-breeding typically more heavily streaked on upperparts and breast than Red Knot, and juvenile more strongly patterned than that species, with blackish centres to mantle and scapulars, and more heavily marked breast and flanks. Intertidal flats and tidal creeks. GU.

Red Knot *Calidris canutus* 23–25 cm

Stocky, with short, straight bill, and rather short legs. Plumages are similar to Curlew Sandpiper, although has barred rump and uppertail-coverts. Adult breeding is brick-red on underparts, with upperparts patterned with rufous and black. Adult non-breeding whitish on underparts and uniform grey on upperparts; stocky shape, short bill and barred rump are best features from other calidrids. Juvenile has buff fringes and dark subterminal crescents to upperparts. Mainly intertidal mudflats. GU, UP.

Red-necked Stint *Calidris ruficollis* 13–16 cm

Very similar to Little Stint. Adult breeding typically has unstreaked rufous-orange throat, fore-neck and breast, white sides of lower breast with dark streaking, and greyish-centred tertials and wing-coverts (with greyish-white fringes); lacks prominent mantle V. Juvenile lacks prominent mantle V; has different coloration and patterning to lower scapulars (grey with dark subterminal marks with whitish or buffish fringes; typically blackish with rufous fringes in Little), and grey-centred, whitish- or buffish-edged tertials (usually blackish with rufous edges in Little); supercilium does not usually split in front of eye. In adult non-breeding plumage, is almost identical to Little, but is a shade cleaner and greyer above. Call much as Little. Mainly coastal. JK.

Long-toed Stint *Calidris subminuta* 13–15 cm

Long and yellowish legs, longish neck and upright stance result in a distinctive shape. In all plumages, has prominent supercilium and heavily streaked fore-neck and breast. Adult breeding and juvenile have prominent rufous fringes to upperparts; juvenile has very striking mantle V. In winter, upperparts more heavily marked than Little's. Call is a soft *prit* or *chirrup*. Marshes and river banks. PU.

Sharp-tailed Sandpiper *Calidris acuminata* 17–21 cm

Recalls Wood Sandpiper in shape, or a very large Long-toed Stint in both shape and plumage. Has rufous crown (indistinct in winter) and prominent white supercilium. Adult non-breeding is greyish above with breast-band of fine streaking. Adult breeding has dark markings over entire underparts, with arrowhead markings on flanks, and bright rufous fringes to feathers of mantle and scapulars. Juvenile is similar to adult breeding but has buff wash to lightly streaked breast. Freshwater and coastal wetlands. JK.

Buff-breasted Sandpiper *Tryngites subruficollis* 18–20 cm

Recalls a tiny Ruff, with shorter and straighter bill, large eyes and bright yellow legs. Upperwing lacks wing-bar, and shows no white on rump or tail. White underwing has dark crescent on primary coverts (underwing entirely white in Ruff). In all plumages, face and underparts are buff, and dark upperparts are neatly fringed with buff. Short grass, mud and seashore. PU.

European Golden Plover *Pluvialis apricaria* 26–29 cm

Very similar in plumage to Pacific Golden Plover. Is stockier with shorter and stouter bill and shorter legs. Underwing-coverts and axillaries largely white. At rest, primaries do not extend beyond tail as in Pacific. In flight, toes do not project beyond tail (noticeable projection on Pacific). Breeding plumage is similar to Pacific, although shows more white on sides of breast and flanks. In non-breeding plumage, supercilium is usually less distinct and is rather plain-faced, compared with Pacific. Grassland and mud on lakeshores and in estuaries. UP.

Caspian Plover *Charadrius asiaticus* 18–20 cm

Superficially similar to Greater Sand Plover, but slimmer, longer-legged and with finer bill. Broad white supercilium in all plumages. In breeding plumage male has chestnut breast-band with black lower border. Female in breeding plumage is similar to non-breeding plumage, but shows some chestnut on breast. In non-breeding plumage has brownish upperparts, and mottled grey-brown breast. Juvenile as adult non-breeding, but with rufous and buff fringes to upperparts. White underwing-coverts and greenish or brownish legs best distinctions from Oriental Plover (not recorded from Northern India). Mudflats and coast. GU, HA.

Collared Pratincole *Glareola pratincola* 16–19 cm

Very similar to Oriental Pratincole, and best told from this species in all plumages by white trailing edge to secondaries (although this can be difficult to see). Adult has more pronounced fork to tail, with tail-tip reaching tips of closed wings at rest. Dry bare ground around wetlands. GU, PU, UP.

Mew Gull *Larus canus* 43 cm

Smaller and daintier than Caspian, with shorter and finer bill. Adult has darker grey mantle than Caspian, with more black on wing-tips; bill yellowish-green, with dark subterminal band in non-breeding plumage, and dark iris. Head and hind-neck heavily marked in non-breeding (unlike adult non-breeding Caspian). First-winter/first-summer have uniform grey mantle. Distinctions from second-year Caspian (which also has grey mantle) include unbarred greyish greater coverts forming mid-wing panel, narrow black subterminal tail-band, and well-defined dark tip to greyish/pinkish bill. Lakes and large rivers. DE, PU, UP.

Little Gull *Larus minutus* 27 cm

Small gull, with short legs, blackish bill and buoyant flight. Adult has dark grey underwing and entirely white upperwing (lacking any black markings). Blackish head in breeding plumage; blackish rear crown and spot behind eye in adult non-breeding and immature plumages. Has distinctive black M-mark across upperwing when immature. Coastal and inland waters. DE, GU, JK, PU, UR.

Arctic Tern *Sterna paradisaea* 33–35 cm

Very similar to Common Tern. Uniform translucent primaries, with well-defined dark trailing edge, lack of dark secondary bar, shorter bill and shorter legs are good features separating it from Common in all plumages. In breeding plumage, has dark red bill normally lacking black tip. Juvenile shows white trailing edge to wing. Recorded inland in region, but usually found on coasts. JK.

Black Tern *Chlidonias niger* 22–24 cm

Superficially similar to White-winged Tern. In breeding plumage, best told from White-winged by grey rather than black mantle, uniform grey underwing, and grey (rather than white) rump and tail. Non-breeding and juvenile have dark patch on side of breast (lacking in White-winged), and grey rump and tail. Juvenile shows less contrast between mantle and upperwing-coverts (juvenile White-winged shows distinctly darker saddle). Marshes, pools and lakes. GU, PU, RA.

Red Kite *Milvus milvus* 60–66 cm

Similar to Black Kite, but has more deeply forked rufous-orange tail, rufous underparts and underwing-coverts, and whitish head. Also more pronounced pale band across upperwing-coverts, and more pronounced whitish patches at base of primaries on underwing. Lightly wooded semi-desert. GU, JK, RA.

Amur Falcon *Falco amurensis* 28–31 cm

In all plumages, has red to pale orange cere, eye-ring, legs and feet. Frequently hovers. Male dark grey, with rufous undertail-coverts and white underwing-coverts. Female has dark grey upperparts, short moustachial stripe, whitish underparts with some dark barring and spotting, and orange-buff thighs and undertail-coverts; uppertail barred; underwing white with strong dark barring.

Juvenile similar to female but with rufous-buff fringes to upperparts, rufous-buff streaking on crown, and boldly streaked underparts. Open country. GU, HP, JK, UP.

Red-necked Grebe *Podiceps grisegena* 40–50 cm

Slightly smaller than Great Crested, with stouter neck, squarer head and stockier body that is often puffed up at rear end. Black-tipped yellow bill. Black crown extends to eye, and has dusky cheeks and fore-neck in non-breeding plumage. White cheeks and reddish fore-neck in breeding plumage. Lakes. GU, HP, RA, UP, UR.

Horned Grebe *Podiceps auritus* 31–38 cm

Bill is stouter and does not appear upturned as it does in Black-necked. Head shape is different: triangular-shaped, with crown peaking at rear. Has two white patches on upperwing, with white patch on wing-coverts (usually lacking on Black-necked). White cheeks contrast with black crown and white fore-neck in non-breeding plumage (cheeks and fore-neck dusky in Black-necked). Yellow ear-tufts and rufous neck and breast in breeding plumage. Lakes and coastal waters. HP, UP, UR.

Brown Booby *Sula leucogaster* 64–74 cm

Dark brown, with sharply demarcated white underbody and underwing-coverts. Bill is yellow. Juvenile has dusky brown underbody, with pale panel across underwing-coverts, but overall appearance is similar to adult. Pelagic. GU.

Black-throated Loon *Gavia arctica* 58–73 cm

Straight bill and square-shaped head help distinguish it from Red-throated in all plumages (not recorded from Northern India). Blackish upperparts and white underparts in non-breeding plumage (more grey and white in Red-throated), and typically shows white flank-patch (more striking than in Red-throated). Unmistakable in breeding plumage, with black throat and black-and-white chequered upperparts. Flooded land, lakes and coastal waters. HA.

Asian Fairy Bluebird *Irena puella* 25 cm

Male has glistening violet-blue upperparts, and black underparts, wings and tail. Female and first-year male entirely dull blue-green. Calls include a loud, liquid *tu-lip*. Moist broadleaved forest. HP.

Lesser Grey Shrike *Lanius minor* 20 cm

Smaller than Southern Grey Shrike, with long extension of primaries beyond tertials. Adult has more extensive black forehead compared with Southern Grey, different patterning of white in wing (broad white patch at base of primaries, and all-black secondaries except for white at tips), and shorter and squarer tail with less white at sides. First-winter is similar to adult but lacks black forehead. Open dry country with bushes. JK.

Black-naped Oriole *Oriolus chinensis* 27 cm

Similar in appearance to Eurasian Golden Oriole. Best told by stouter bill, black nape-band (poorly defined in immature) and yellowish wing-coverts. Very similar to Slender-billed (not recorded from Northern India); compared with that species has stouter bill and nasal call (Slender-billed has woodpecker-like *kick* call). Male Black-naped has yellow mantle and wing-coverts (brighter than in Slender-billed). Female and immature probably not safely separable from Slender-billed by plumage. Broadleaved forest and well-wooded areas. MP.

Ashy Minivet *Pericrocotus divaricatus* 20 cm

Grey and white, lacking any yellow or red in plumage. Male has black cap (with white forehead) and black nape. Light forest. HP.

Bohemian Waxwing *Bombycilla garrulus* 18 cm

Vagrant. Mainly fawn-brown in coloration. Prominent crest, black throat, and waxy red and yellow markings on wings and tail. Open country with fruiting trees and bushes. JK.

Rufous-tailed Rock Thrush *Monticola saxatilis* 20 cm

Distinguished from other species of rock thrush by orange-red uppertail-coverts and tail (in all plumages). Male has bluish head/mantle, white back and orange underparts, which are obscured by pale fringes in non-breeding and first-winter plumages. Female has scaling on upperparts, and orange wash to scaled underparts. Open rocky hillsides. JK.

Eyebrowed Thrush *Turdus obscurus* 23 cm

In all plumages has white supercilium and white crescent below eye, and peachy-orange flanks contrasting with white belly. Male has blue-grey head. Female and first-winter have browner crown and ear-coverts, and dark malar stripe. Open forest. GU, RA.

Dusky Thrush *Turdus naumanni* 24 cm

Prominent supercilium contrasting with dark crown and ear-coverts; spotting across breast, forming breast-band and continuing down flanks (and contrasting with white belly), and chestnut panel in wings. First-winter birds can be very dull, with chestnut in wings sometimes not apparent; in this plumage, broader supercilium and spotting on flanks are best features separating it from Dark-throated. Pastures with scattered trees and cultivation. JK.

Fieldfare *Turdus pilaris* 25 cm
Large size. Blue-grey head and rump/uppertail-coverts, chestnut-brown mantle and orange-buff wash to spotted breast. Fields and orchards. HP, JK, UP.

Song Thrush *Turdus philomelos* 23 cm
Small size (much smaller than Mistle Thrush), olive-brown upperparts and orange-buff wash to spotted breast. Head rather plain, lacking supercilium. Thorn scrub. JK, PU.

Brown-breasted Flycatcher *Muscicapa muttui* 14 cm
Compared with Asian Brown has larger bill with entirely pale lower mandible, pale legs and feet, rufous-buff edges to greater coverts and tertials, and slightly rufescent tone to rump and tail. Dense undergrowth in broadleaved forest. MP.

Common Nightingale *Luscinia megarhynchos* 16 cm
Much as Bluethroat in shape and behaviour, but with longer tail. Rather nondescript with grey-ish olive-brown upperparts and greyish-white underparts, and with whitish throat. Has rufous uppertail-coverts and long rufous tail, indistinct head markings, and pale fringes to wing-coverts and remiges. Bushes. UP.

Common Redstart *Phoenicurus phoenicurus* 15 cm
Male is similar in appearance to male Black Redstart but has grey upperparts, and black of throat does not extend onto breast. Plumage of male is heavily obscured by pale fringes in non-breeding and first-winter plumages (when it is very different in appearance compared with male Black and Hodgson's). Female has buff-brown upperparts and buffish underparts (and is paler and more warmly coloured than female Black and Hodgson's). Arid areas. JK.

Hodgson's Redstart *Phoenicurus hodgsoni* 15 cm
Male is very similar in appearance to Common Redstart, but has narrow white stripe in wing (formed by white outer edge to largest tertial), and black of throat extends onto upper breast (although not as far as in Black Redstart). Female has dusky brown upperparts, and grey underparts with white on belly (lacking rufous-orange wash to lower flanks and belly of female Black). First-winter male is similar in plumage to female. Open forests, grassy areas and cultivation with bushes. UP.

Azure Tit *Parus cyanus* 13.5 cm
White crown, ear-coverts and underparts, dark stripe through eye and band across nape, grey man-tle, and broad white wing-bar and tips to tertials. Similar in appearance to Yellow-breasted Tit *Parus flavipectus* (not recorded from North India), but lacking yellow on breast of that species. JK.

Rock Martin *Hirundo fuligula* 13 cm
Smaller than Eurasian Crag Martin, with paler sandy-grey upperparts (especially rump), buffish-white throat and paler undertail-coverts and underwing-coverts. Rocky gorges and cliffs. GU.

Rusty-rumped Warbler *Locustella certhiola* 13.5 cm
Similar to Grasshopper Warbler. Is larger, with more prominent supercilium contrasting with greyish crown, more heavily streaked mantle with rufous tinge, rufous rump and uppertail-coverts, and rather dark tail with white tips. Underparts unstreaked. Juvenile has yellowish wash to underparts and light spotting on breast. Reedbeds. GU, MP.

Sedge Warbler *Acrocephalus schoenobaenus* 13 cm
Similar in appearance to Moustached Warbler, with broad white supercilium and streaked man-tle. Head pattern less striking than Moustached's; also has buffish olive-brown coloration to upper-parts, well-defined buffy fringes to tertials and greater coverts, and longer primary projection. Tall vegetation at wetland edges. JK.

Black-browed Reed Warbler *Acrocephalus bistrigiceps* 13 cm
Similar to Paddyfield Warbler, and like that species has broad supercilium. Features separating it from Paddyfield are blackish lateral crown-stripes (much more pronounced than on Paddyfield), shorter tail, long primary projection and dark grey legs. Tall grass and reedbeds. *See* Table 8 on p.296. JK.

Great Reed Warbler *Acrocephalus arundinaceus* 19 cm
Differs from Clamorous Reed in shorter, stouter bill, longer primary projection, and shorter-looking tail. Primary projection is roughly equal to length of tertials, with eight or nine exposed primary tips visible beyond the tertials (primary projection in Clamorous is two-thirds of tertial length with six or seven exposed visible beyond the tertials). Reedbeds. JK.

Radde's Warbler *Phylloscopus schwarzi* 12 cm
Similar to Dusky, with long buffish-white supercilium contrasting with dark eye-stripe. Has stout bill, and orangish legs and feet; call different from Dusky's, a nervous *prit-prit*. In fresh plumage,

can show greenish-olive cast to upperparts and buffish-yellow cast to supercilium and underparts, which are distinctive features from Dusky. Undergrowth and bushes. *See* Table 2 on p.292. RA.

Yellow-browed Warbler *Phylloscopus inornatus* 10–11 cm
Similar to Hume's. Has yellowish wing-bars and supercilium (although these become whiter in worn plumage). Bill has orange at base. Call is a piercing *chewest*. Groves and open forest. *See* Table 5 on p.294. PU, RA, UR.

Garden Warbler *Sylvia borin* 14 cm
Stout-billed, stocky appearance. Has olive-brown to grey-brown upperparts and buffish-white underparts, with white throat. Rather featureless, but with dark eye, a whitish eye-ring and just a faint suggestion of a greyish supercilium. Plain-faced appearance aids separation from *Hippolais* and *Acrocephalus* warblers. Forest undergrowth and bushes. JK.

Barred Warbler *Sylvia nisoria* 15 cm
Large size, stout bill, and pale edges and tips to tertials and wing-coverts in all plumages. Plain-faced appearance recalls Garden Warbler. Adult has greyish upperparts, yellow iris and variable dark barring on whitish underparts. First-winter has greyish olive-brown upperparts and buffish underparts, with barring on undertail-coverts and occasionally on flanks. Bushes. JK.

Lesser Short-toed Lark *Calandrella rufescens* 13 cm
Very similar in appearance to Greater Short-toed lark. Primaries extend beyond tertials (tertials reach or almost reach tip of primaries in Greater). Bill short and stout compared with Greater. Has broad gorget of fine streaking on breast, fine but clear streaking on upperparts, streaked ear-coverts, and whitish supercilia that appear to join across bill – these are indicative features that help separate it from Greater. Stony foothills. JK.

Asian Short-toed Lark *Calandrella cheleensis* 13 cm
Very similar to Lesser and Greater Short-toed Larks. Primaries extend beyond tertials (as in Lesser) and bill is small, short and stout. Broad gorget of streaking on breast. Paler and more sandy in coloration than Lesser, and streaking on upperparts and breast more diffuse. Open stony grassland, fallow cultivation, semi-desert. HA, JK.

White-rumped Snowfinch *Montifringilla taczanowskii* 17 cm
Separated from other snowfinches by white rump (very conspicuous in flight) and pale greyish upperparts (with streaked mantle and scapulars). Additional features are black lores, white throat and supercilia (which join across forehead and extend onto nape), white at sides of tail and diffuse white panel at base of secondaries. JK.

Small Snowfinch *Pyrgilauda davidiana* 15 cm
One published record, now considered doubtful. Small size, black forehead and throat, sandy-brown nape, white patch on primary coverts and streaked mantle. High-altitude semi-desert JK: v?.

Yellowhammer *Emberiza citrinella* 16.5 cm
Chestnut rump and long tail. Male has mainly yellow head and underparts, with blackish sides to crown and surround to ear-coverts, and rufous streaking on breast that may form ill-defined band. Female/first-winter has less yellow on head and underparts. Distinguished from female/first-winter Pine Bunting by yellow on throat, supercilium and belly. Some (mainly first-winter) females lack yellow and are then very difficult to separate from female Pine: however, belly is not pure white as on Pine, usually has more evenly streaked crown and narrower supercilium (on Pine, streaks are more restricted to lateral crown, and thus it tends to show more pronounced pale crown-stripe), malar stripe and breast tend to be more prominently streaked, and has yellowish (rather than whitish or whitish-buff) edges to primaries and to base of outer tail feathers. Regularly hybridises with Pine Bunting and can show a variety of intermediate characters. Upland cultivation, 1100–2750 m. JK.

Chestnut Bunting *Emberiza rutila* 14 cm
Small size. Yellow on underparts in all plumages. Male has chestnut head and breast, which may be obscured due to pale fringes in first-winter plumage. Female and first-winter have yellowish underparts, and are most likely to be confused with female/first-winter Yellow-breasted Bunting. Chestnut is smaller and slighter, with finer bill; also has less striking head pattern (with indistinct buffish supercilium, and lacking prominent dark border to ear-coverts), more finely streaked mantle, bright and unstreaked chestnut rump, and little or no white on tail. Separated from female Black-faced by buff throat and brighter yellow underparts (lacking bold dark flank-streaking of that species), chestnut rump, and little or no white on tail. Bushes in cultivation, forest clearings.JK.

Black-faced Bunting *Emberiza spodocephala* 15 cm
Male has greenish-grey head with blackish lores, and yellow underparts; non-breeding with yellow submoustachial stripe and throat. Female similar to female Chestnut Bunting, but has yellowish supercilium, yellow throat, olive rump and white on tail. Long grass, paddy-fields, marshes. UP.

TABLES

Table 1. Nightjars

Species	Size/structure	General Coloration	Crown/nape	Scapulars/coverts	Primaries	Tail	White throat patch
Grey Nightjar I = *C. i. indicus* (south of Himalayan range) H = *C. i. hazarae* (Himalayan range)	Medium. Well-proportioned, longish wings and tail, and large head	I – Uniform cold grey to grey-brown heavily marked with black. H – Dark grey-brown heavily marked with black	Variable. Heavily to very heavily marked with black drop-shaped streaks. Some with irregular patches of rufous on nape. Streaking less regular and more extensive than Large-tailed	Scapulars heavily but irregularly marked with black, usually lacking well-defined buff or white edges (although pronounced pale edges to these feathers may be prominent in some). Coverts with variable greyish-white to buffish spotting; usually poorly defined (I), more rufous in (H)	Male has small white spots on three or four primaries. On female, spots either lacking or small and rufous	I – Male variable, usually with white at tips of all but central tail feathers, with diffuse greyish margin at end. H – Male has more distinct blackish margin to white tips. Female of both races lacks white in tail	Large, central white spot in male, or buff in female
Eurasian Nightjar	Medium. Long wings and tail, and small head	Grey, neat lanceolate streaking	Regular, bold, black lanceolate streaking	Bold lanceolate streaking to scapulars, with buff outer edge. Well-defined, regular pale buff spots on coverts	Male has large white spots on three primaries and female has no spots	Outermost two tail feathers have broad white tips in male. No white tips in female	Indistinct, but generally complete, white throat-crescent
Sykes' Nightjar	Small. Shortish wings and tail, and large head	Grey with buff mottling and restricted dark vermiculations. Some are sandy coloured	Variable, small dark arrowhead markings. Irregular buff spotting on nape gives suggestion of collar	Scapulars relatively unmarked, with a few black inverted 'anchor-shaped' marks. Coverts with irregular and small buff markings	Male has large white spots on three or four primaries. Female primary spots are buffish	In male, two outermost pairs have broad white tips. In female, tail is unmarked or has buffish tip to outertail	Broken, large white patches on sides. Some have complete crescent
Indian Nightjar	Small. Short wings and tail, and small head	Grey, with bold buff black and some rufous markings	Bold, broad, black streaking to crown. Nape marked with rufous-buff forming distinct collar	Bold, triangular black centres and broad rufous-buff fringes to scapulars. Coverts with bold buff or rufous-buff spotting	Both sexes have small white or buffish spots on four primaries	Both sexes have broad white tips to outer two tail feathers	Generally broken. Large white patches on sides. Lacking in some
Large-tailed Nightjar	Large. Long-winged and long, broad tail.	Large head. More warmly coloured than Grey with buff-brown tones, heavily marked with black and buff	Brownish grey with bold black streaks down centre. Diffuse pale rufous-brown band across nape	Scapulars have well-defined buff edges with bold, wedge-shaped, black centres. Coverts boldly tipped buff	Male has white spots on four primaries; female lacks these or has smaller buff spots	Male has extensive white tips to two outermost feathers. Female has less extensive buff tips to outer two feathers	Large central white throat patch in both sexes
Savanna Nightjar	Medium. Shortish wings and tail, and large head	Dark brownish grey, intricately patterned (without bold, dark streaking) but with variable rufous-buff markings	Variable. Some only finely vermiculated, others with black, 'arrowhead' markings and others with irregular-shaped, black markings	Scapulars variably marked but most show rufous-buff outer web. Coverts variably marked with rufous-buff showing as distinct spotting in some	Male has large white spots on four primaries. Female has buff to rufous-buff wash	Outer two tail feathers are mainly white in male, but not in female	Large white patches on sides

Table 2. Small to medium-sized Phylloscopus warblers, lacking wing-bars and crown-stripe
(+ = vagrant)

Species	Head pattern	Upperparts including wings	Underparts	Call	Additional features
Common Chiffchaff	Whitish or buffish supercilium, and prominent crescent below eye	Greyish to brownish with olive-green cast to rump and edges of remiges and rectrices	Whitish with variable buffish or greyish cast to breast-sides and flanks	Plaintive *peu*, more disyllabic *sie-u*	Blackish bill and legs (compare with Greenish and Dusky)
Mountain Chiffchaff	Whitish or buffish supercilium. Warm buff coloration to ear-coverts in fresh plumage	Brownish to greyish-brown, lacking olive-green cast to rump. Edges of wing coverts, remiges and rectrices are buffish. Bend of wing is usually whitish (usually brighter yellow in Common Chiffchaff)	Whitish, with warm buffish coloration to breast-sides and flanks in fresh plumage (usually more pronounced than in Common Chiffchaff)	Distinctly disyllabic *swe-eet* or *tiss-yip*; sometimes three syllables *tiss-yuitt*	Blackish bill and legs
Plain Leaf Warbler	Whitish supercilium	Greyish brown. Lacks greenish to upperparts; edges of remiges buffish	Whitish; buff on ear-coverts, breast-sides and flanks usually less apparent than in Mountain Chiffchaff	A hard *tak tak*, low-pitched *churr* or *chiip*, and a *twissa-twissa*	Very small; short-looking tail
Dusky Warbler	Broad, buffish-white supercilium with strong dark eye-stripe	Dark brown to paler greyish brown; never shows any greenish in plumage	White with buff on sides of breast and flanks	Hard *chack chack*	Pale brown legs, and orangish base to lower mandible. Typically skulking
Smoky Warbler	Comparatively short and indistinct yellowish supercilium with prominent white eye-crescent	Dark sooty-olive, with greenish tinge in fresh plumage	Mainly dusky-olive, almost concolorous with upperparts, with oily yellow centre to throat, breast and belly	Throaty *thrup thrup*	Skulking
Tickell's Leaf Warbler	Prominent yellow supercilium concolorous with throat, well-defined eye-stripe	Dark greenish to greenish-brown upperparts, and with greenish edges to remiges	Bright lemon-yellow underparts, lacking strong buff tones	A *chit*, or *sit*; not as hard as Dusky	
Sulphur-bellied Warbler	Prominent, bright sulphur-yellow supercilium, distinctly brighter than throat	Cold brown to brownish-grey, lacking greenish tones, and with greyish edges to remiges	Yellowish buff with strong buff tones to breast and flanks and sulphur-yellow belly	Soft *quip* or *dip*	Climbs about rocks, or nuthatch-like on tree trunks
Radde's Warbler +	Long buffish-white supercilium, contrasting with dark eye-stripe. In fresh plumage, supercilium is buffish-yellow	Olive-brown. In fresh plumage can have pronounced greenish-olive cast	Whitish with buff wash on breast-sides and flanks. In fresh plumage, can have buffish-yellow wash to entire underparts	A nervous *twit-twit*, and sharp *chuck chuck*	Long tail, sometimes cocked; stout and rather pale bill; thin and strong-looking orangish legs and feet
Tytler's Leaf Warbler	Prominent, fine white to yellowish-white supercilium, with broad dark olive eye-stripe	Greenish, becoming greyer when worn	Whitish, with variable yellowish wash when fresh	A double *y-it*	Long, slender, mainly dark bill; shortish tail

Table 3. Yellow Wagtails (breeding males only)

Subspecies	Head pattern
M. f. beema	Pale bluish-grey head, complete and distinct white supercilium, white chin, and usually a white submoustachial stripe contrasting with yellow throat; ear-coverts are grey or brown, usually with some white feathers
M. f. leucocephala	Whole head to nape white, with a variable blue-grey cast on the ear-coverts and rear crown; chin is white, and throat yellow as rest of underparts
M. f. melanogrisea	Black head, lacking any supercilium, and white chin and poorly defined submoustachial stripe contrasting with yellow throat
M. f. taivana	Differs from all other races in having olive-green crown, concolorous with mantle, and broad yellow supercilium contrasting with blackish lores and ear-coverts
M. f. plexa	Dark blue-grey crown and nape (darker than *beema*), and narrow white supercilium contrasting with blackish lores and dark grey ear-coverts; chin is white
M. f. thunbergi	Dark slate-grey crown with darker ear-coverts, lacking supercilium (although may show faint trace behind eye)
M. f. lutea	Mainly yellow head, with variable amounts of yellowish green on crown and nape and ear-coverts (concolorous with mantle)
M. f. zaissanensis	Head slate-grey, with narrow white supercilium
M. f. superciliaris	Probably a hybrid between *beema* and *melanogrisea* and looks like the latter, but with a white supercilium

Table 4. Medium-sized to large Phylloscopus warblers, with narrow wing-bars, and lacking crown-stripe Note: Wing-bars may be missing when plumage is worn (when confusion is then possible with species in Table 2 opposite)

Species	Head pattern	Upperparts including wings	Underparts	Bill	Call	Other features
Greenish Warbler *T. t. viridanus*	Prominent yellowish-white supercilium	Olive-green, becoming duller and greyer when worn; generally lacking darker crown. Single narrow but well-defined white wing-bar	Whitish with faint yellowish suffusion	Lower mandible orangish, usually lacking prominent dark tip	Loud, slurred *chit-wee*	
Greenish Warbler *T. t. nitidus*	Prominent yellowish supercilium, and yellow wash to cheeks	Upperparts brighter and purer green than *viridanus*, with one or two slightly broader and yellower wing-bars	Strongly suffused with yellow, which can still be apparent in worn plumage	As *viridanus*	More trisyllabic than *viridanus*, a *chis-ru-weet*	
Greenish Warbler *T. t. trochiloides*	Prominent whitish or yellowish-white supercilium, broad, dark eye-stripe and dusky mottling to cheeks	Dark oily-green upperparts, with darker olive crown; one or two whitish or yellowish-white wing-bar	Greyish cast to underparts. Often with diffuse oily-yellow wash on breast, belly and undertail coverts	Dark bill, with orange at base, or basal two-thirds, of lower mandible	*Chis-weet*	Very similar to Large-billed; best distinguished by call
Large-billed Leaf Warbler	Striking yellowish-white supercilium contrasting with broad, dark eye-stripe, with greyish mottling on ear-coverts	Dark oily-green with noticeably darker crown; one or two yellowish-white wing-bars	Dirty, often with diffuse streaking on breast and flanks and oily-yellow wash on breast and belly; however, can appear whitish	Large and mainly dark, with orange at base of lower mandible; often with pronounced hooked tip	Loud, clear, upward-inflected *der-tee*	Large size

Table 5. Small Phylloscopus *warblers with broad, generally double, wing-bars, most having pale crown-stripe* (+ = vagrant)

Species	Head pattern	Wing-bars	Rump and tail	Underparts	Call	Other features
Buff-barred Warbler	Poorly defined dull yellowish crown-stripe; yellowish supercilium	Double buffish-orange wing-bars, although median covert wing-bar often not apparent	White on tail; small yellowish rump-patch	Sullied with grey and can be washed with yellow	Short, sharp *swit*	
Ashy-throated Warbler	Greyish-white crown-stripe, contrasting with dark grey sides of crown; greyish-white supercilium	Double yellowish wing-bars	White on tail; prominent yellow rump	Greyish throat and breast, and yellow belly-flanks and undertail coverts	Short *swit*	
Lemon-rumped Warbler	Yellowish crown-stripe contrasting with dark olive sides of crown; yellowish-white supercilium	Double yellowish-white wing-bars	No white on tail; well-defined yellowish (sometimes almost whitish) rump	Uniform whitish or yellowish-white	High-pitched *uist*	
Brooks's Leaf Warbler	Narrow, usually poorly defined yellowish crown-stripe; sides to crown barely darker than mantle; yellowish supercilium and wash to ear-coverts	Double yellowish wing-bars; bases of median and greater coverts do not form dark panel across wing as they do in Lemon-rumped	No white on tail. Ill-defined yellowish rump, often barely apparent	Yellowish throat; entire underparts washed with buffish yellow in fresh plumage	Monosyllabic loud and piercing *chwee*, or *pseo* or *psee*	Brighter yellowish-olive upperparts compared with similar species. Yellowish-horn basal half of lower mandible (bill mainly dark in Hume's)
Yellow-browed Warbler +	Lacks well-defined crown-stripe, although can show diffuse paler line; broad yellowish-white supercilium and cheeks	Broad, yellowish or whitish wing-bars; median-covert wing-bar is prominent	Lacks pale rump-patch and does not have white in tail	White with variable amounts of yellow	A loud *cheeweest*, with distinct rising inflection	Brighter greenish-olive upperparts (in fresh plumage) compared with Hume's. Bill has extensive pale (usually orangish) base to lower mandible, and legs are paler (compared with Hume's)
Hume's Warbler	Lacks well-defined crown-stripe, although can show diffuse paler line; broad, buffish-white supercilium and cheeks	Broad, buffish or whitish median- and greater-covert wing-bar; median-covert wing-bar tends to be poorly defined, but can be prominent	Lacks pale rump-patch and does not have white in tail	White, often sullied with grey	A rolling, disyllabic *whit-hoo* or *visu-visu*, and a flat *chwee*	Greyish-olive upperparts, with variable yellowish-green suffusion, and browner crown. Bill appears all dark and legs are normally blackish brown

Table 6. Large Phylloscopus *warblers with crown-stripe, prominent wing-bars, and large bill with orange lower mandible*

Species	Head pattern	Upperparts including wings	Underparts	Call	Additional features
Western Crowned Warbler	Greyish-white to pale yellow crown-stripe, contrasting with dusky olive sides of crown, which may be darker towards nape; prominent dull yellow supercilium	Generally duller greyish-green compared with Blyth's, with stronger grey cast to nape; wing-bars narrower and less prominent than Blyth's, because bases not so dark	Whitish, strongly suffused with grey, especially on throat and breast; can show traces of yellow on breast and belly	A repeated *chit-weei*	Larger and more elongated than Blyth's, with larger and longer bill
Blyth's Leaf Warbler	Tends to be more striking than Western Crowned, with yellow supercilium and crown-stripe contrasting with darker sides of crown	Usually darker and purer green than Western Crowned, although may be similar. Wing-bars are more prominent than Western Crowned, being broader and often divided by dark panel across greater coverts	Generally has distinct yellowish wash, especially on cheeks and breast	*Kee-kew-i* repeated constantly	

Table 7. Cetia *bush warblers Note: See* text for description of song

Species	Head pattern	Upperparts	Underparts	Additional features
Pale-footed Bush Warbler	Pale buff supercilium and dark brown eye-stripe; more prominent than Brownish-flanked	Rufescent brown	White throat, centre of breast and belly, strongly contrasting with brownish-olive breast-sides and flanks	Shorter, square-ended tail compared with Brownish-flanked. Pale pinkish legs and feet
Brownish-flanked Bush Warbler	Greyish-white supercilium, less prominent than Pale-footed	Olive-brown	Pale buffish grey with brownish-olive flanks with only a small area of off-white on belly	Longer, rounded tail compared to Pale-footed. Brownish legs and feet
Chestnut-crowned Bush Warbler	Chestnut on forehead and crown; supercilium indistinct and rufous-buff in front of eye and buffish-white behind	Dark brown	Whitish with greyish-olive sides of breast and brownish-olive flanks; whiter, particularly on throat and centre of breast, than Grey-sided	Larger than Grey-sided
Aberrant Bush Warbler	Yellowish supercilium	Yellowish-green cast to olive upperparts	Buffish yellow to olive-yellow, becoming darker olive on sides of breast and flanks. Some (worn?) birds have less yellow on throat and upper breast and are duller on rest of underparts	
Yellowish-bellied Bush Warbler	Crown is rufous-brown, as is mantle; buffish-white supercilium	Pale rufous-brown with strong olive cast, especially to lower back and rump; noticeable rufous fringes to remiges (especially tertials)	Yellowish belly and flanks	Small size with small and fine bill
Grey-sided Bush Warbler	Chestnut forehead and crown; short, whitish-buff supercilium is well defined in front of eye (compared with Chestnut-crowned)	Dark brown	Greyish white with grey sides of breast and brownish-olive flanks	Smaller than Chestnut-crowned
Cetti's Bush Warbler	White supercilium, lacking bold, dark stripe through eye	Rufous-brown	White on breast with greyish breast-sides and flanks; dull white tips to greyish-brown undertail-coverts	Larger than Pale-footed with longer tail

Table 8. Unstreaked Acrocephalus warblers and Booted Warbler
(+ = vagrant)

Species	Bill/feet	Head pattern	Upperparts	Underparts	Additional features
Black-browed Reed Warbler +	Dark grey legs and feet	Square-ended buffish-white supercilium, broader and more prominent than Paddyfield; broad, black, lateral crown-stripes	Rufous-brown in fresh plumage; more olive-brown when worn	Warm buff sides of breast and flanks when fresh	Shorter-looking tail, and longer projection of primaries beyond tertials, compared with Paddyfield
Paddyfield Warbler	Shorter bill than Blyth's Reed, usually with well-defined dark tip to pale lower mandible. Yellowish-brown to pinkish-brown legs and feet	More prominent white supercilium, often broadening behind eye, becoming almost square-ended, with dark eye-stripe; supercilium can appear to be bordered above by diffuse dark line (supercilium less distinct on some)	More rufescent than Blyth's Reed. Typically shows dark centres and pale fringes to tertials. Greyer or sandier when worn but usually retains rufous cast to rump	Warm buff flanks; underparts whiter when worn. Often shows whitish sides to neck	Typically looks longer-tailed than Blyth's Reed, with tail often held cocked
Blunt-winged Warbler	Longer and stouter bill than Paddyfield, with uniformly pale lower mandible or with dark shadow at tip	Shorter and less distinct supercilium than Paddyfield, which typically extends beyond eye (occasionally on worn birds may extend as thin line behind eye); lacks dark border above supercilium and lacks prominent dark eye-stripe	As Paddyfield, but more olive-toned when fresh. Colder olive-brown when worn, but with more rufescent rump and uppertail-coverts. Shows more prominent tertial fringes than Blyth's Reed	Breast and flanks washed with buff when fresh	Longer tail, and shorter primary projection, compared with Paddyfield
Blyth's Reed Warbler	Bill longer than Paddyfield. Lower mandible entirely pale or has diffuse dark tip	Comparatively indistinct supercilium; often does not extend beyond eye, or barely does so, and never reaches rear of ear-coverts. Lacks dark upper border to supercilium and dark eye-stripe	Tertials rather uniform. Generally colder olive-grey to olive-brown than Paddyfield. Noticeable warm olive cast to upperparts when fresh (more rufescent in first-winter)	Can have light buffish wash on flanks when fresh; otherwise cold whitish	Shorter-looking, more-rounded tail than Booted, and longer upper- and undertail coverts; more skulking and lethargic than that species
Large-billed Warbler	Compared with Blyth's Reed, bill is longer, stronger and broader, and tapers less towards tip; rictal bristles are shorter and weaker. Upper mandible dark, with cutting edge and entire lower mandible pale. The tarsi, toes and claws appear pale brown; has larger feet and claws than Blyth's Reed	A pale supercilium is evident but is not strongly pronounced	Upperparts rich olive-brown, with slight rufous tinge, especially on uppertail-coverts. Coloration close to fresh-plumage Blyth's Reed, but less olive, more rufous-tinged and slightly paler	Strongly washed with olive-buff, the sides are more olive-brown, and the throat is paler creamy olive	Compared with Blyth's Reed, has more rounded wings (the primary tips are broad and rather square-ended), and longer and more graduated tail with more pointed tail feathers
Booted Warbler *H. c. rama*	Longer-billed than *caligata*. Legs and feet paler and browner than Blyth's Reed	Supercilium more distinct than Blyth's Reed and lores can appear pale	Paler and greyer than *caligata* and all *Acrocephalus* (although can be rather similar to Blyth's Reed)	Off-white	More arboreal than *caligata*; behaviour often *Phylloscopus*-like compared to *Acrocephalus*. Longer-looking square-ended tail than *Acrocephalus* with shorter undertail-coverts
H. c. caligata	Comparatively short and fine bill	Supercilium more prominent than *rama*; can appear to have dark border	Warmer brown than *rama*. Fine whitish fringes to remiges and edges of outertail feathers often apparent (also shown by *rama*)	Off-white	Rather *Phylloscopus*-like in appearance, often feeding on ground. Squarer tail and short undertail-coverts compared with *Acrocephalus*

Table 9. Rosefinches

Female Rosefinches

Species	Most likely confusion species	Size/structure	Supercilium	Wing-coverts and tertials	Underparts	Upperparts	Other features
Dark-breasted	Vinaceous	Relatively small, slim-bodied, with slender bill	Lacking	Variable, broad buffish wing-bars and tips to tertials	Unstreaked, dark greyish brown	Relatively uniform dark greyish brown, with diffuse mantle-streaking	Dark greyish olive-brown rump
Common	Beautiful	Small and compact with stout, stubby bill	Lacking	Narrow, whitish or buff tips to coverts, forming narrow double wing-bar	Whitish, with variable, bold, dark streaking	Grey-brown with some dark streaking	Beady-eyed appearance
Beautiful	Common	Small and compact	Whitish, but very poorly defined	Indistinct pale tips to median and greater coverts	Whitish, quite heavily streaked	Buffish-grey, heavily streaked darker	
Pink-browed	Spot-winged and White-browed	Relatively small and compact	Prominent buff supercilium, contrasting with dark ear-coverts	Relatively uniform, lacking wing-barred effect	Heavily streaked, with strong fulvous wash from breast to undertail-coverts	Warm brownish buff with heavy dark streaking	Fulvous coloration on rump
Vinaceous	Dark-breasted	Relatively small and compact	Lacking	Uniform wing-coverts, but conspicuous whitish tips to tertials	Warm brownish-buff, lightly streaked	Warm brown, almost concolorous with underparts, with diffuse streaking	Plain-faced appearance
Spot-winged	Pink-browed and White-browed	Medium-sized and rather stocky	Prominent, very broad, buff supercilium	Prominent pale buff tips to greater coverts and outer edge of tertials	Brownish fulvous, very heavily streaked, including on throat	Rather dark brown with heavy dark streaking	Well-defined dark ear-coverts contrasting with supercilium
White-browed	Pink-browed and Spot-winged	Medium-large	Prominent, long, white supercilium, contrasting with dark lower border and rear of ear-coverts	Whitish to buff tips to median and greater coverts, forming narrow double wing-bar	White, heavily streaked, with ginger-buff wash to throat and breast	Mid- to dark brown with heavy dark streaking	Deep olive-yellow rump, heavily streaked
Red-mantled	Streaked and Great	Large, with stout, heavy bill and long tail	Rather faint whitish supercilium, weakly offset against greyish eye-stripe	Lacks wing-bars, but has indistinct paler tips to median and greater coverts	Whitish underparts, heavily streaked	Pale grey, heavily streaked	
Streaked	Great and Red-mantled	Large, with stout bill	Lacking	Lacks prominent wing-bars but has dark centres to median and greater coverts and tertials	Whitish underparts, heavily streaked	Dark grey, rather heavily streaked	
Great	Streaked and Red-mantled	Large, with stout bill	Lacking	Relatively uniform, pale grey-brown	Whitish, heavily streaked	Sandy-brown with faint streaking	
Red-fronted	Streaked	Very large, with rather long, conical bill	Lacking	Lacks wing-bars	Greyish, very heavily streaked, with variable pale yellow wash on breast	Very dark grey with bold, heavy dark streaking	Rump and uppertail-coverts more olive than back

Table 9. Rosefinches continued

Male Rosefinches

Species	Most likely confusion species	Size/structure	General coloration	Supercilium	Wing-coverts and tertials	Underparts	Upperparts	Rump
Dark-breasted	Vinaceous	Relatively small, slim-bodied, with long, slender bill	Dark maroon-pink and brown	Quite prominent, reddish-pink, contrasting with dark maroon eye-stripe	Uniform; lacks wing-bars and contrasting tertial fringes	Maroon-brown breast-band contrasting with rosy-pink throat and belly	Maroon-brown, with indistinct darker streaks, and reddish-brown fore-crown	Maroon-brown, concolorous with rest of upperparts
Common	None	Small and compact with stout, stubby bill	Bright geranium-red	Lacking	Rather indistinct bright red fringes to wing-coverts and tertials	Bright geranium-red, especially on throat and belly	Diffusely streaked bright geranium-red	Unstreaked, bright red
Beautiful	Pink-browed	Small and compact	Cold greyish-pink	Rather indistinct, pale lilac-pink	Indistinct paler fringes to wing-coverts and tertials	Cold greyish-pink with pronounced dark streaks, especially on flanks	Cold pinkish grey, with conspicuous dark crown and mantle-streaking	Contrasting, unstreaked pale lilac-pink
Pink-browed	Beautiful	Smallish and compact	Deep, warm pink	Prominent, deep pink, contrasting with dark maroon-pink eye-stripe	Rather uniform, lacks prominent paler fringing to wing-coverts and tertials	Unstreaked, warm pink	Pinkish-brown mantle and darker streaked back; unstreaked or lightly streaked maroon-pink	Unstreaked, deep pink
Vinaceous	Dark-breasted	Relatively small and compact	Dark crimson	Prominent, pale pink	Uniform coverts, lacks wing-bars but has prominent pinkish-white tertial tips	Uniform dark crimson	Dark crimson, with diffuse dark mantle-streaking	Paler, dull crimson, contrasting rest of upperparts
Spot-winged	White-browed	Medium-sized and rather stocky	Maroon and pink	Prominent, pale pink, contrasting with crown and ear-coverts	Very prominent pink tips to median and greater coverts and tertials	Rather uniform pink, with some darker mottling	Rather uniform maroon, indistinctly streaked, with irregular pink splashes	Maroon, prominently splashed with pink
White-browed	Red-mantled and Pink-browed	Medium-large	Brownish and pale pink	Prominent, long, pinkish with splashes of white; extends across forehead	Pronounced pale tips to median and greater coverts, forming narrow wing-bars	Pink, with some white streaking	Brown with conspicuous darker streaking	Pink, well-defined, contrasting with rest of upperparts
Red-mantled	White-browed	Large, with stout, heavy bill and long tail	Pink and pale brownish grey	Prominent, pink	Very indistinct paler fringing	Pink, with some streaking	Brownish grey, with pink tinge, streaked darker	Uniform pink
Streaked	Great	Large, with stout bill	Crimson-pink	Lacking	Very indistinct paler fringing	Crimson-pink, with clearly defined white spotting	Grey-brown, washed pink, and with conspicuous darker streaking	Uniform deep pink
Great	Streaked	Large with stout bill	Rose-pink and sandy-grey	Lacking	Very indistinct paler fringing	Rose-pink, with large diffuse white-spots	Sandy-grey, washed pink, with narrow streaking	Uniform rose-pink
Red-fronted	Streaked	Very large, with rather long, conical bill	Red and dark grey-brown	Short and red, extending across forehead	Very indistinct paler fringing	Red throat and breast, contrasting with dark-streaked grey-brown remainder of underside	Grey-brown, with bold, dark streaks	Deep pink, contrasting with rest of upperparts

INDEX

* = vagrant to northern India.

English Names

Scientific Names